P9-DEF-411

TEACHING INDIVIDUALS TO READ

TEACHING
Individuals
TO READ

HOMER L. J. CARTER
DOROTHY J. McGINNIS
Western Michigan University

D. C. HEATH AND COMPANY

Boston

Cur. Lib.

372/41
C 245

LB
1573
.C323

COPYRIGHT © 1962 BY D. C. HEATH AND COMPANY

No part of the material covered by this copyright may be reproduced in any form without written permission of the publisher. (6 L 1)

Library of Congress Catalog Card number 62–9496

PRINTED IN THE UNITED STATES OF AMERICA

PREFACE

This book is designed for students enrolled in reading methods courses and for in-service teachers of reading. It stresses the development at all levels of such common reading skills as vocabulary building, reading for meaning, finding and organizing ideas, effective use of books, and the art of critical thinking. Furthermore it is the purpose of this book to help every member of the teaching staff to see clearly the total reading program and his responsibility as a teacher of reading whether in the primary, elementary, or secondary grades. The continuity of the reading process and the over-all application of basic principles are set forth. Reading is regarded as a thinking process, and the emphasis is placed upon an integration rather than upon an accumulation of isolated basic skills. Teachers are given definite, practical suggestions which they can apply in their classrooms and to their children, whose interests and reading levels vary widely. Throughout the book the development of mental content resulting from experience and background is stressed, for the reader, whether young or more mature, must contribute of himself in order to secure meaning.

A distinctive feature of this book is apparent in the guided activities which follow the text of each chapter. These activities have been planned to stimulate critical study of certain reading problems through the observation and evaluation of classroom procedures at various levels.

At the end of each chapter the student is provided with a list of pertinent questions and parallel references which direct him to current practice and research. In this manner, his knowledge becomes a composite of many points of view.

The book is unique in that it contains the stories of actual students who serve as a focal point for instruction. Since the emphasis is upon the person involved, the cases presented can be used for any theoretical discussion and at whatever depth of analysis is desired with the certainty that most of the major problems associated with the teaching of reading are portrayed. In addition, the biographies illustrate many principles of child development and the dynamics of human behavior. We believe that the short biographies included in this book can be used for teaching purposes and that the increased realism resulting from the study of the individual will make instruction more effective. Surely it is an advantage to be able to present a problem simultaneously to a whole class and to have students base their reactions and decisions upon the facts presented. Teachers in training and in the classroom can then identify, understand, and evaluate some of the factors affecting the reading performance of the individuals discussed in this book and the children in their classes. This approach, which has been used successfully in medicine, psychology, sociology, and law, can be used to bridge the gap between theory and practice in education. In a thoroughgoing developmental program in reading the teacher must first become aware of the problems and then of some of the answers to them. To this end this text is dedicated.

The authors are indebted for help with photographs furnished by Mrs. Dorothy Rothrock, Consultant in Public Relations, Board of Education, Kalamazoo, Michigan. Acknowledgment is also made to Ward C. Morgan and to Joseph Schiavone, photographers, Kalamazoo, Michigan.

HOMER L. J. CARTER
DOROTHY J. McGINNIS

CONTENTS

CONTENTS

TEACHING INDIVIDUALS TO READ

1

LET'S GET ACQUAINTED

In this book an unusual approach to the teaching of reading has been utilized. We hope you will find it both interesting and effective. Reading is a communicative skill and is closely related to speaking, writing, and listening. It is a personal activity and is carried on by intelligent people everywhere. Successful teachers of reading have been able to focus their attention upon the persons with whom they work. They have become acquainted with the interests, abilities, and needs of their students. In so doing, it has been necessary to understand the environment and background of those they instruct. In this chapter we are to introduce to you seven young people who can play an important role in helping you to learn more about the teaching of reading. As you read this book, you will realize that we are stressing basic principles and that the biographies are to be used as a focal point for discussion and application of these fundamental principles. You will also recognize that these children, like so many of the boys and girls in the public schools, possess most of the major problems associated with the teaching of reading.

Reading instruction is dependent upon the developmental level and needs of the child. It is a well-accepted fact that children mature and develop at different rates. In any given grade the teacher will find children in several stages of growth. Therefore, the aims, materials, and procedures selected for the reading program should be determined by the developmental level of the children rather than their grade placement. In other words, the competent teacher must be able to teach reading at all levels. This book emphasizes the continuity of reading instruction through grades one to twelve and assumes that instruction should begin with a knowledge and understanding of the individual. Teachers in training and those working in the public schools must be highly sensitive to the meaning of the behavior of those they teach. They should understand children in general and their students in particular. Consequently, this book emphasizes the understanding of the child, his wishes and desires, and the different mechanisms he employs to obtain these goals. With this point of view in mind, let us become acquainted with some interesting personalities.

Wendy Demonstrates Her Readiness for Reading

Wendy is a happy, energetic little girl of six years who thoroughly enjoys living. She bounces from one situation to another and yet can remain quietly in a corner as she colors, draws, or plays with paper dolls. She asks questions few people can answer and appears critical of the responses she secures. Wendy wants to go to school and has gathered together several books she wants to take with her the first day. Wendy has learned to print her name and because of this attainment has been able to obtain a library card. Each week Wendy, her brother Stephen, and her mother go to the library, where each child has an opportunity to select his own books. Wendy selects from the children's room big books with pictures which she avows she can read. Her interpretation of the pictures, however, is not appreciated by Precious Child, her much beloved cat. As we think of Wendy, our problem becomes: Is this little girl ready for beginning reading?

Debbie Begins to Read

Seven-year-old Debbie is a slim, sensitive child who is "all legs." She attacks books with enthusiasm and energetically attempts to excel in schoolwork. She is a diligent pupil and an acknowledged leader of other children. Her favorite play activity is to assume the role of teacher to the neighborhood children, and the accuracy with which she portrays and imitates her teacher is astounding. When not engaged in reading activities, Debbie appears to be nervous and high-strung, and speaks in a quiet, yet high-pitched, tense voice. She is a determined little girl with decided opinions. Recently she informed her mother that she would not help with the dishes. Debbie emphatically said, "Daddy's job is to earn money. My job is to go to school and learn to read. Doing dishes and making beds— that's your job." As you read Debbie's biography, you will become aware of some of the materials and methods which her teachers have employed in teaching this little girl to read.

Joel Memorizes Instead of Reading for Meaning

Joel is a quiet, shy boy with good manners and courteous ways. He is in the fifth grade and has the reputation for reading well orally. Joel has difficulty in reading for main ideas and relevant details. Consequently his father, an attorney, believes that his son is being poorly prepared for junior high school. In trying to follow suggestions made to him by his parents, Joel memorizes the facts and information presented to him in his textbooks. He does this well and is able to recite great chunks of subject matter but demonstrates little understanding of the material. Joel tries to please everyone, and consequently frustration and lack of confidence are becoming more apparent. This intelligent boy believes that he is a poor student and that he does not belong in the group in which he is placed. Religious discrimination and emotional conflicts having their origin in the home and school add to Joel's feeling of insecurity. In the opinion of the boy's teacher, he is a competent individual who apparently is not working up to capacity in reading or the other school subjects.

Otto Wants to Build a Better Vocabulary

The people who know Otto best describe this sixth grade boy as a perfectionist. He sets high standards for himself in music and sports and becomes angry and disgusted when he fails to achieve his goals. He daydreams and idles away his time in the classroom chiefly because of his difficulty in word attack and word comprehension skills. He has an excellent speaking vocabulary, but is unable to spell even the simplest words, and this inability is more than he can tolerate at times. When confronted with the task of using a dictionary or a telephone directory, he becomes exasperated at his lack of skill and frequently becomes so upset that he flings the book away and smashes with his fist any object within reach. He is intolerant of his younger brother and seems to delight in ridiculing him. He is critical of his teachers and projects on them the blame for his disability in reading. He asks for help, however, and is willing to follow any suggestion which he believes to be practical.

Elizabeth Needs Help in Finding and Organizing Ideas

Elizabeth is in the eighth grade and is well liked by her associates in spite of her frank and outspoken opinions. She is an attractive and intelligent girl of thirteen years who has been conditioned to stand up for her own ideas against two-to-one odds provided by her provocative father and argumentative brother. She is likely to be under-assertive, however, until actually aroused by overt actions and comments of others which she considers unjust and unfair. Her teacher explains that Elizabeth has a feeling of inadequacy for which she compensates by her frequently aggressive behavior. She loves young children and plans to become, like her father, a pediatrician.

Elizabeth likes to argue, and according to reports she can maintain her point of view with a high degree of confidence. Recently she was asked by her class to debate on a subject which is distasteful to her. Her problem is to overcome her antagonism to the subject and to find and organize information in preparation for a formal debate.

Jim Learns to Make Use of Books

Everybody likes Jim, at least that is what everybody in the seventh grade says. This plump, good-natured youth of only twelve years says he wants to become a priest in the Episcopal Church. His associates in junior high have elected him their president and say that he is a "real guy." The children in his classes enjoy hearing him read aloud, "but," says Jim, "I would have a hard time telling them what I have read." Apparently, when this lad attempts to read a textbook, he becomes lost in a maze of detail and is unable to tell what is important and what is not. Outlining is difficult for Jim and he regards it as a disagreeable and unnecessary task, even in the preparation of a talk. He likes books and he enjoys stories, but—and this is characteristic of him—he does not know how to make effective use of printed materials. Jim does not know how to use books.

Kathryn Needs Aid in Problem Solving

Kathryn is one of the prettiest and most popular girls in her senior class in high school. She is a dainty, petite brunet with sparkling brown eyes and a radiant smile. She is admired by her contemporaries for her amiable disposition and readiness to cooperate with others. Kathryn is engaged to Tom, a high school senior whose vocational goal is dentistry. Their love for each other seems to be sincere and enduring, and yet it presents them with several serious problems. For example, Tom and Kathryn would like to be married as soon as they are graduated from high school, but should they? Kathryn wants to go on to college, but should she? These are but a few of the perplexing questions which Kathryn will be trying to answer when you meet her later in this book.

Suggestions for Using This Book

In this book your attention, from Chapter 3 on, is directed to a short biography of a growing reader and to instructional suggestions which may be applied in working with groups of similar individuals. The presentations begin at the primary level and are extended to the elementary, junior high, and senior high school levels. Fundamental reading skills, however, are to be thought of as developing vertically at all ages and not on horizontal planes at certain hypothetical grade levels. Selection and order have been designed to show the overlapping of reading skills and the oneness of the teaching process. Biographical data have been presented with little interpretation or theoretical structuring so that you, under the guidance of your instructor, may identify the factors contributing to the child's performance and evaluate the possible effectiveness of instructional procedures set forth in the chapter. This approach has advantages for both the beginning and the experienced teacher. Each can see portraits of individuals in a natural environment and have an opportunity for theoretical interpretation of the development of basic reading skills. The level of these interpretations will be dependent upon the background, training, and experience of the reader.

Following each biography we have discussed the different aspects of the problem involved and have directed your attention to some instructional principles which we believe to be essential to an understanding of the teaching process. This makes it possible for you and the other members of your class to consider these suggestions in terms of the interests and needs of the individual whose history has been presented at the beginning of the chapter. This plan of action on your part motivates your reading and encourages the development of a unified and objective study of the principles involved. For example, in an appraisal of reading readiness, the whole class will have an opportunity to meet Wendy and to become aware of her developmental, social, and cultural history and to estimate her readiness for reading. We have tried to present to you a little girl in order that she may become the center of your observations just as she would if seen in an actual demonstration before a class.

As a means of stimulating thinking, guided activities have been made an integral part of each chapter. These suggested procedures have been designed to increase the reader's awareness of the many problems related to the teaching of reading which he himself can investigate. Learning is an active process of adjusting to new ideas and changing conditions. It requires participation and more than the casual reading of content materials. Consequently, we hope that in response to these guided activities you will assume the initiative to think, question, challenge, and to investigate the problems presented.

To aid you in your quest for additional information and to provide a basis for your acceptance or rejection of certain teaching practices, questions and parallel references are provided at the end of each chapter. You should be aware of differing points of view and be able not only to understand but also to evaluate them. Learning to teach reading is a growing, developing, and evolutionary process which is not to be completed at any given time. Consequently, you should acquire the habit of seeking new points of view and new facts resulting from research in related subject-matter fields. It is for this purpose that the questions and parallel references are provided.

Guided Activities

1. List, in terms of your experiences, the reading skills required in classes in mathematics, English, social studies, and the sciences.
2. Observe classes at the primary, elementary, and upper grade levels. Discuss with your classmates the following questions in terms of your observations:
    a. What reading skills are being emphasized at the primary level? the elementary level? the upper grade level?
    b. What materials are being used at each level?
    c. What reading activities did you observe?
    d. How do the reading interests of the children differ at the various grade levels?

Questions and References

Questions

1. What are the responsibilities of the whole school staff in regard to the teaching of reading?

2. What developmental changes take place during the life span of the normal human being?

3. Where can one find a discussion of problems which are related to the developmental aspects of reading instruction?

4. How are tomorrow's teachers of reading being prepared, and what are some recommendations for improving that preparation?

References

1. Strang, Ruth, and Dorothy Kendall Bracken. *Making Better Readers,* Chap. 4. Boston: D. C. Heath and Co., 1957.

2. Hurlock, Elizabeth B. *Developmental Psychology* (Second Edition). New York: McGraw-Hill Book Co., 1959.

3. Henry, Nelson B. (Ed.) *Development In and Through Reading,* The Sixtieth Yearbook of the National Society for the Study of Education, Part I. Chicago: University of Chicago Press, 1961.

4. Austin, Mary C., et al. *The Torch Lighters.* Cambridge, Mass.: Harvard University Press, 1961.

Many activities in the kindergarten can be a preparation for reading.

Effective study requires the use of many books.

2

SOME VIEWPOINTS FOR TEACHERS OF READING

If you are to deal effectively with children similar to Wendy, Debbie, Otto, and all the others, it will be necessary for you to have an understanding of the reading process and some of the factors affecting their adjustment to the world in which they live. Let us begin with the question "What is reading?"

The Meaning of Reading

The process of reading has been defined in various ways. Some leaders in the field consider it to be an act of interpreting printed symbols. Some consider it to be a creative activity closely allied to thinking. Still others consider it a tool for learning in all subject-matter areas. Common to all of these ideas is the concept that the major purpose of reading is to achieve meaning. For many, this implies that reading involves word study, sentence and paragraph comprehension, problem solving, and critical evaluation. Reading, however, is more than an accumulation of isolated skills, just as a watch is more than the sum of all its parts. It is more than word study and vocabulary building. It is more than sentence, paragraph, and chapter reading. It is more than reading to solve problems and to critically evaluate the thoughts and ideas of others expressed in writing. Like speaking, writing, and listening, it is an aspect of personality. It is an activity in which the individual seeks to *identify, interpret,* and *evaluate* the ideas and points of view expressed by a writer.

In the reading process one is concerned with meaning, which is a resultant of visual sensations and mental content. In turn, mental content is the result of experience in the world in which one lives. This mental content varies from individual to individual and is proportionate to the quantity and quality of his background. It is personal in nature and cannot be shared directly with others. One identifies, interprets, and evaluates with what he has previously seen and experienced. For example, a five-year-old boy from the Southwest, who was acquainted with the flat roofs of most of the houses in his city, came hurrying in from play while visiting in Michigan and announced that the roof of his grandfather's house was broken and that something should be done about it immediately. Apparently the child had observed the roof with a pronounced pitch and had interpreted it as cracked or broken. The meaning of the facts observed by the child is the result of his background and experience. In this situation, the child has identified the concept of roof. He has interpreted it as broken and has evaluated it as a serious situation needing immediate attention.

This interpretative process is similar to that of obtaining meaning from a printed page and is dependent upon visual sensation and the mental content of the observer. A college student may read "Sigma is less affected by sampling errors than is the quartile or the mean deviation and is a more stable measure of dispersion." He may be able to *identify* the term "sigma" and yet be unable to *interpret* its meaning or to *evaluate* its use. This is primarily due to the fact that his mental content is insufficient and that his background in statistics is limited. Effective reading both for the child and the adult is a process of securing meaning and involves thinking and critical application of one's experiences and previous knowledge.

Learning to Read Is a Developmental Process

Learning to read is a gradually developing process, every step of which is dependent upon what has gone before. Growth in reading may be roughly classified into three stages. During the first period the child develops an interest in and a readiness for books and is concerned with the various aspects of word study and vocabulary building. If sufficiently mature, he develops background and mental content through activities, experiences, and conversations. The young child generally wants to read orally in order to demonstrate his prowess and he learns to read for the purpose of answering questions. During the second period of expanding power the individual makes rapid progress in the development of the basic skills. He makes use of several means of studying words and he acquires an ever-increasing vocabulary of well-known words. He discovers how to locate and organize useful information and ideas. He develops habits of independent reading and his rate of reading begins to increase rapidly. During the third stage, reading becomes a means of personal satisfaction. He learns to read with a definite purpose and is successful in securing facts accurately. A great expansion is made in vocabulary, and the individual shows a mastery of most of the basic means of word study. He learns to use the dictionary, encyclopedia, and other sources of information. He increases his skill in using the different parts of a book to secure information. He learns to read critically and for various purposes. He learns how to select main ideas and supporting details and how to evaluate the relative importance of facts. He learns how to read a chapter with a minimal amount of effort and with the highest degree of efficiency. Reading has now become a way of life and is used both as a tool and as a means of satisfaction.

Children pass through these stages of reading development at differing times and at varying rates. In these three stages of reading development, there is much overlapping and an expanding of reading skills. This expansion varies both quantitatively and qualitatively and the whole process is developmental in nature.

Reading Is a Communicative Skill

Reading, a communicative skill, is closely related to listening, speaking, and writing. These four language arts are sequentially related to one another. The child first learns to listen, then to speak, then to read, and later to write. Experience with oral language, through listening and speaking, is a prerequisite to learning to read. An important aspect of any communicative skill is organization. The processes of speaking and writing are synthetic in nature and consist of the development of ideas. The effectiveness of this development depends upon organization. On the other hand, listening and reading are analytical in nature and consist of the interpretation of ideas. Here again the effectiveness of this process is dependent upon organization. Reading is a function of the whole person and is a series of varied experiences which are as much a part of one's everyday living as seeing, hearing, smelling, and tasting. These communicative experiences are part of problem solving, the spending of leisure time, the development of widening interests, and the cultivation of extensive and varied tastes. These experiences are essential to the formation of opinions, attitudes, and points of view. In order to live effectively and solve problems in our modern world, one must communicate with his fellows by means of symbols, words, and ideas. He must speak, write, listen, and read. Each of these is an aspect of communication, and the mastery of one can lead to the mastery of others.

Reading Is Learning

Learning is frequently described as a process of adjusting to marked and significant changes in the environment.[1] It is more than the adding or subtracting of facts from a total accumulation. Reading has been defined in this book as a process in which the individual seeks to identify, interpret, and evaluate the ideas and points of views expressed by a writer. This activity is one of adjustment to new facts, new information, and new points of view. Consequently, it is possible to assume that there

[1] Warner Brown and Howard C. Gilhousen, *College Psychology* (New York: Prentice-Hall, 1950), chaps. 2, 5; Floyd L. Ruch, *Psychology and Life* (Chicago: Scott, Foresman and Co., 1958), chap. 11.

are elements or components in both processes which are the same or similar. Reading is not an act in and by itself but is a part of growing, adjusting, and living. A student may glibly recite a geometric theorem and yet not be able to interpret and evaluate the meaning of the expression. Something more is needed than mere identification and memorization. The reader must understand and interpret. These three processes are necessary if he is to think critically, solve problems effectively, and do leisure time reading with enjoyment and profit. The mature reader is expected to make use of his reading, and this means adjustment and modifications of his behavior as he applies what he reads. The ability to do this is final proof of good reading and efficient learning.

Reading Is a Continuous Process

Learning to read is a continuous process which is not necessarily completed at any given period of time in the life of a normal individual. Ability to learn can be shown as a rapidly developing curve which reaches its maximum height somewhere between the ages of twelve and twenty-five years. The point of highest ascent is maintained for several years. Investigations [2] show that in some cases learning after fifty may be more effective than it was before the age of twelve. This extension of ability to learn may be due to the increase in mental content which the individual has acquired by experience throughout his life. Obviously, the years twenty to forty are more productive of achievement than the years one to twenty. It is apparent that most individuals attend school during the first twenty years of their lives when learning ability is limited and leave academic pursuits when they have reached their most productive period. The fact remains, however, that the ability to learn many skills and attainments is considerably higher during adulthood than it was during childhood and adolescence. Consequently, public education from the elementary to the college level should be concerned with the effective teaching of reading and should not assume that the teaching of this important skill should be taught only incidentally in the junior and senior high schools.

A Modern Concept of Reading

The purpose of reading is to obtain meaning as one seeks to secure enjoyment and to acquire information from written language. Reading is a developmental process closely related to thinking and learning. It is an important aspect of communication and can be developed and

[2] Walter R. Miles, "Mental Health in Later Maturity," Supplement No. 168 to *Public Health Report,* Federal Security Agency, U. S. Public Health Service (Washington: U. S. Government Printing Office, 1942), pp. 34–42; David Wechsler, "Mental Health in Later Maturity," Supplement No. 168 to *Public Health Report,* Federal Security Agency, U. S. Public Health Service (Washington: U. S. Government Printing Office, 1942), pp. 43–52.

expanded throughout life. Learning to read is influenced by the individual's level of physical and psychological development and is critically influenced by one's environment. Reading is more than the accumulation of certain basic skills. It is a manifestation of the whole personality of the reader and his behavior. Learning to read is an individual as well as a social responsibility, and the teacher must be keenly aware of the factors affecting performance as she attempts to provide a comprehensive, balanced reading program for her students.

Some Physical Factors Affecting Reading

Motor coordination, vision, hearing, speech, and general health are some of the physical factors which play an important role in learning to read.

Motor Coordination

The ability of the child to control his muscular actions seems to be directly related to success in reading, which involves the holding of books, turning of pages, keeping the place, and other complex muscular coordination which some immature children lack. In order to read, the child must be able to focus his eyes on the words. He must be able to follow a line of print, and he must be able to make a return sweep to the beginning of each new line. Reading requires fine coordination of small muscles. The child who has not matured and learned to control these small muscles may have difficulty in reading.

Vision

Vision [3] also affects one's ability to learn to read. In the very young child, the eyeball is relatively flat and the child as a result is farsighted. As he grows and develops, the eyeball becomes more rounded and he becomes less farsighted. Between the ages of six and ten, the average child's eyes attain the roundness that permits reading without undue eyestrain.

Defects in the refractive mechanism of the eyes can interfere with learning. The child having a visual defect generally shows evidence of eyestrain and confuses letters of similar form such as *o, e, c* or *b, h, n.* On occasions he may confuse such words as *oar, ear,* and *car,* or *bear, hear,* and *near.* The child's inability to discriminate complex visual patterns may also be significant, for some individuals appear unable to react to a word as a whole. Occasionally they find it necessary to spell out the letters and to identify configurations by tracing them with their fingers. Visual difficulties may be indicated by the child's manner of holding a

[3] Marion Monroe, *Children Who Cannot Read* (Chicago: The University of Chicago Press, 1932), pp. 105–106; Helen M. Robinson, *Why Pupils Fail in Reading* (Chicago: The University of Chicago Press, 1946), chap. 2.

book or paper and by frequent loss of place in reading. Watering or inflamed eyes, along with reports of letters blurred or running together, can suggest to the teacher the possibility of a visual difficulty. Children who frequently hold a hand over one eye while reading or who rub their eyes should be observed for further manifestations of visual abnormalities. Frowning, scowling, and excessive blinking may indicate the need for a visual examination.

Tendencies to reverse letters, although not a visual problem, should also be considered. Frequently the child showing this difficulty confuses such letters as *b, d, p,* and *q; u, n; m, w; f, t;* and such words as *no* and *on,* or *was* and *saw.* Many theories of dominance have been set forth to explain reversal tendencies and reading disability; however, few of these are universally accepted. Dominance should be recognized only as one of several possible factors affecting reading performance. Nearly all children reverse to some extent until one cortical hemisphere becomes more completely dominant. Children generally remain somewhat ambidextrous until approximately the age of six and a half years. At this time a dominant foot, hand, and eye preference may become established. Some normal and many brain-injured children fail to develop an adequate system of right-left relationships within their own organisms. They are unable to see the difference between *b* and *d.* In differentiating these letters directionality is the chief factor which for these children is either confused or nonexistent. Lack of unilaterality can be a significant factor in reading disability.[4]

Hearing

Audition is a factor in reading achievement. The child who has developed auditory readiness has acquired the ability to listen to sounds. He hears the same sounds at the beginning of such words as *cat, can, come, care.* He soon learns to associate these initial consonant sounds with the letter *c.* He enjoys the use of rhyming words such as *can, man, fan,* and soon notices their likenesses and differences. As soon as he is able to interpret their meaning, he is ready to express these concepts in writing.

According to some investigators,[5] auditory defects are related to reading difficulties. The lack of auditory acuity due to partial deafness is to be considered. Some children may omit endings, non-stressed syllables, and sibilant sounds chiefly because they do not hear them. On occasions, vowel and consonant sounds may be confused. An individual having these difficulties may confuse such similar sounds as *land* and *lend, bed* and *bid, lash* and *latch.* Symptoms of auditory defects observable in the class-

---

[4] Carl H. Delacato, *The Treatment and Prevention of Reading Problems* (Springfield, Illinois: Charles C. Thomas, 1959), chaps. 2, 3, 4.
[5] Marion Monroe, *Children Who Cannot Read* (Chicago: The University of Chicago Press, 1932), pp. 106–107; Helen M. Robinson *Why Pupils Fail in Reading* (Chicago: The University of Chicago Press, 1946), chap. 4.

room are apparent inattention when the child is called upon and the ignoring of directions when these are clearly given. Some children with hearing difficulties favor the better ear by turning the head to one side and by listening with tense facial expressions. A history of enlarged tonsils and adenoids, earaches, and "running" ears can alert the teacher to the possibility of a hearing loss. Children are usually not aware of their auditory defects and because of this fact teachers should be careful and informed observers.

Speech

Faulty speech is often a contributing factor to reading difficulties. In learning to read, the child must associate the spoken word with the visual symbol. In order to profit from reading instruction, the child must be able to reproduce sounds in words correctly. If he does not reproduce the sounds correctly, there will be confusion between what he says, hears, and sees, and this confusion may impede his progress in learning to read. Poor patterns of speech, mispronunciations of words, foreign language difficulties, immaturity, loss of hearing, emotional disturbances, and serious physical and physiological defects are some of the possible causes of inadequate speech and deficiencies in reading.

General Health

It is usually assumed that such physical factors as general health and nutrition can affect reading efficiency. Abnormalities and deficiencies in these areas are general in nature and become apparent in the form of fatigue, weakness, sleeplessness, and inability to show interest and sustain effort. Frequent or long absences may indicate low health status. Many children who are below par physically have a negative attitude toward instructional help and are unable to attend to a given task for more than a few minutes at a time. The child who is not well or who is constantly tired is seldom able to devote himself to learning to read to the limit of his ability. Inadequate nutrition or insufficient rest frequently cause a child to be lethargic or nervous. According to some investigators,[6] glandular disturbances can be a causal factor in reading maladjustment. Individuals suffering from these disorders frequently show not only social maladjustment but also a childish attitude and unwillingness to put forth effort. Studies [7] report that synaptic transmission and neural activity seem to be influenced by endocrine functioning so that therapy at the glandular level

[6] Florence Mateer, "A First Study of Pituitary Dysfunction in Cases of Reading Difficulty," *Psychological Bulletin*, Vol. 32, 1935; Florence Mateer, *Glands and Efficient Behavior* (New York: Appleton-Century Co., 1935); Willard C. Olson, "Reading As a Function of the Total Growth of the Child," in William S. Gray (comp. and ed.), *Reading and Pupil Development* ("Supplementary Educational Monographs," No. 51. Chicago: University of Chicago, 1940), pp. 233–237.

[7] Donald E. P. Smith, and Patricia M. Carrigan, *The Nature of Reading Disability* (New York: Harcourt, Brace and Co., 1959).

may be advisable. If these theories are substantiated, reading disability then becomes in part a medical problem. If a child appears in relatively good health, a disability in reading is seldom recognized as having a physical basis. The frustration and emotional tension resulting from inability to make satisfactory progress in reading, however, can be disturbing to both parents and teacher as well as the child.

Psychological Factors and Reading Achievement

Some psychological factors affecting reading performance are mental and emotional maturity, mental content, and emotional stability. All of these contribute to the individual's concept of himself.

Mental Maturity

Mental maturity may be defined as the degree or level at which the individual can interpret what he sees, hears, and experiences. The level of an individual's development, which is probably determined by heredity and environmental factors, is measured roughly by tests of mental maturity. Investigators [8] have found that a child should be approximately six years and six months old mentally before he is mature enough to learn to read. Gates,[9] however, points out that the crucial mental age level will vary with materials, type of teaching, background, and the consideration given to the individual differences of pupils.

Emotional Maturity

Emotional maturity means growing up emotionally; that is, the individual learns to do the thing that needs to be done when it needs to be done whether he wants to do it or not. The mature individual is willing to face the consequences of his conduct and is able to make decisions well substantiated by facts. Such an individual tries to be independent and is willing to assume responsibility. When it is necessary, he can postpone immediate pleasures to attain ultimate goals which are important to him. Furthermore, he is able to put the welfare and desires of others ahead of his own self-interest. Studies [10] show that the emotionally immature child is dependent upon the mother or other adults and is unaccustomed to responsibility for any task. A study [11] of children referred to a reading clinic shows that comparatively large numbers of children who have difficulty in learning to read are infantile in manner, behavior, and interest.

[8] Lucille M. Harrison, *Reading Readiness* (Boston: Houghton Mifflin Co., 1936), p. 8. Mabel V. Morphett and Carleton Washburne, "When Should Children Begin to Read?" *Elementary School Journal*, 31:497–508.

[9] Arthur I. Gates, "The Necessary Mental Age for Beginning Reading," *Elementary School Journal*, 37:497–508.

[10] Mary J. Saunders, "The Short Auditory Span Disability," *Childhood Education*, 8:59–65.

[11] Marion Monroe, and Bertie Backus, *Remedial Reading: A Monograph in Character Education* (Boston: Houghton Mifflin Co., 1937), pp. 25–26.

Many of these boys and girls are unwilling to put forth the necessary effort to learn to read. Because many children are completely satisfied in this dependence upon parents, reading may become a disagreeable task which they hate.

Mental Content

Readers should be concerned with meaning, which is the product of certain physical and psychological factors. This concept can be expressed by the statement: Meaning is the resultant of visual sensation interpreted in terms of mental content. If either sensation or mental content is missing, there can be no meaning. One sees and interprets with what he has seen and experienced. Mental content resulting from experience determines the kind and degree of meaning. Obviously, meaning resulting from reading in any field requires background and mental content, and these in turn are built up by reading and experience. Deficiencies in mental content are frequently due to a lack of both mental and emotional maturity. Individuals learn and adjust in accordance with their intellectual maturation. There is a positive relationship between intelligence and the ability to identify, understand, and evaluate facts. Mental content results from experience, but an individual, in order to profit from this experience, must possess an adequate degree of intellectual maturity. A lack of emotional maturity can also interfere with the acquiring of mental content, for many children and even adults are unwilling to put forth effort when reading and learning situations become difficult. This attitude does not contribute to the acquiring of background, which is essential to an understanding of what is read.

Emotional Stability

The emotionally stable child has a consistent behavior pattern which shows both satisfying and satisfactory relationships with others. Such an individual is generally well adjusted and happy in the classroom. He likes other boys and girls and has few fears and worries. The emotionally stable child seeks help and information only when needed. He is not apt to laugh or cry easily without cause and his behavior is generally predictable. Failure to learn to read may lead to frustration, so that the mere sight of reading materials may cause disorganized and over-emotional responses which inhibit successful adjustment on the part of the child. Frequently this becomes apparent in a lack of concentration, of perseverance, and of motivation. The child's antagonism toward reading is generally due to failure to learn. A child in this situation is frequently scolded at home or held up to ridicule on the playground. The child is aware of his difficulty and is severely penalized because of it. Consequently, he may go on from semester to semester with scarcely any growth in reading because he never looks at a book unless he has to and then only with marked aversion. Studies [12] show that reading maladjustment can lead to frustration, inattention, and lack of motivation, confusion, and unwillingness to put forth effort to learn to read. Many children who have repeatedly failed in learning to read lose confidence in themselves and accept failure as inevitable. Frequently such boys and girls become aggressive or withdrawn and in some instances they become behavioral deviates. Psychologists have frequently pointed out that failure in reading results in emotional disturbances and that emotional conflicts have been responsible for failure to make satisfactory progress in reading.

When a child is confronted with a new situation for which he has no ready response and is not able to work out a satisfactory solution, a disorganized reaction occurs. Both physical and mental manifestations are apparent. Fears and worries are only two expressions of these reactions which are called emotions. Uncontrolled emotion can interfere with one's ability to concentrate and make a satisfactory adjustment. Personal and social adjustments, as well as ability to learn, are facilitated if parents and teachers can recognize the inadequate and partial solutions to emotional disturbances which may develop. These maladjustments may be quite normal for the individual under existing circumstances. Those responsible for his guidance, however, should not only recognize these neurotic manifestations but should be concerned with causes and adequate adjustments. Investigations [13] show that failure in reading has been attributed to emotional problems and that emotional maladjustment has been created by reading disabilities. Obviously, emotional and personality maladjustments are both cause and effect. In fact, some teachers have found that therapy directed toward the removal of emotional tensions has resulted in significant gains in reading achievement.

Classroom teachers should understand that many of their students, in attempting to protect themselves against failure or conflict, may resort to various types of defensive behavior. Some of the overlapping defense mechanisms recognized by psychologists will be explained briefly in the following pages. A detailed discussion of these is beyond the scope of the present volume. The mature reader should consult such books as those by Ruch, Kuhlen, and Lehner listed at the conclusion of this chapter.

Rationalization is an attempt to give a socially acceptable motive instead of the real one. For example, a child may say that he has failed to make satisfactory progress in reading because he has not been called upon to read aloud by his teacher. In making this statement he explains to him-

[12] Helen M. Robinson, *Why Pupils Fail in Reading,* (Chicago: The University of Chicago Press, 1946), chap. 7.

[13] Marion Monroe, *Children Who Cannot Read,* (Chicago: The University of Chicago Press, 1932), p. 105; Helen M. Robinson, *Why Pupils Fail in Reading,* (Chicago: The University of Chicago Press, 1946), pp. 225–226.

self and others what he probably believes to be the cause of his difficulty. Another child with a similar problem may say that he could learn to read if he really wanted to but that only "squares" and "sissies" become superior readers. Rationalization is a form of reasoning which gives a degree of comfort. Some individuals in using rationalization appear to deny the value of the goal they have set out to attain. This is frequently called the "sour grapes" explanation. On the other hand, an individual may build up, in an exaggerated manner, the value of a substitute or inferior goal which he may have used to replace the original one. This is called by some writers the "Pollyanna" explanation of failure. Any individual who feels called upon to explain his lack of success is using rationalization in order to make himself feel more comfortable and to remove some of the sting of his inadequacy.

Projection is another mechanism frequently used by children and immature individuals. This mechanism consists in placing the blame for failure on another person or thing. The use of this mechanism seems to have had its beginning in the very nature of mankind. The sacrificial lamb seems to have been required by man as a means of easing his conscience and bringing about a sense of peace. Even in minor traffic accidents it is generally the other person who is to blame. Frequently, the brother in the home consoles himself for losing his tennis racket by saying that his three-year-old sister left it on the front lawn. Political parties, states, and nations absolve themselves from failure and wrongdoing and unwise behavior by loudly proclaiming that the other party or foreign nation was primarily responsible for failure to bring about an adequate adjustment. In our world today we find parents blaming schools and schools blaming parents without attempting to investigate carefully the causal factors of the difficulties involved. It is not unusual to find parents who blame teachers for neglecting phonics and for not identifying "mirror vision" as a possible cause of their children's reading disabilities.

Compensation is a form of behavior by which some individuals make up or atone for a real or assumed feeling of inadequacy. Individuals using this mechanism develop a more persistent motive or drive than is necessary to accomplish a given task. A twelve-year-old girl in junior high school who believes that she is a poor student because of her inability to read well orally puts forth unusual effort in attempting to become an all A student. She feels inferior and inadequate because of her apparent lack of ability to read "with expression" and so she atones for this feeling of inadequacy by hard work and intensive study. Compensation can make the individual ridiculous unless the drive for success is directed into socially acceptable channels.

Substitution, as the term suggests, is an attempt to replace one goal which is difficult or impossible to attain with another. A young high school student who has a serious and progressive visual defect finds it increasingly difficult to complete her reading assignments. An ophthalmologist recommends that she learn to read and write Braille. After careful study and training, she has been able to substitute one system of communication for another. A feeling of satisfaction and security has resulted. The mechanism that she has used is a reasonable one and somewhat related to both rationalization and compensation, although in the latter there is generally an all-out attempt to make up for a feeling of failure. Substitution is generally practiced by a more mature individual who has made careful decisions.

Identification is the act of associating oneself with others in order to participate in their experiences, success, and popularity. Junior and senior high school boys and girls resort to identification by wearing sports sweaters bearing the name of their high school. In fact, most high school boys and girls strive to identify themselves with groups and appear unwilling to dress, act, or even think in a way unlike their own "gang." He who differs is apt to be regarded as a "square" and is promptly rejected. Good readers frequently associate themselves with the hero or heroine in a story and share with this person his fears, worries, and adventure, so much so that no attention is paid to an imperative call for dinner. The popularity of movies and television is partially due to the fact that the intent observer identifies himself with the personalities on the screen and in this way escapes the humdrum and monotony of our busy world. There is a possibility that some individuals need to make use of this mechanism more than others primarily because of the frustration inherent in their daily living.

Regression is an attempt of an individual under stress to assume the role of a younger or inexperienced individual so that he will not be expected to solve the problem with which he is confronted. This mechanism of escape is illustrated by the behavior of a five-year-old boy who, as the only child in the family, has made a very successful and happy adjustment. Upon the birth of his sister, however, he becomes enuretic and insists upon being held by his mother. This sudden change in his behavior is probably an unconscious attempt to avoid the responsibilities of growing up by resorting to behavior similar to that of his baby sister. This escape from responsibility is also characteristic of the adult who at times does not act his age. The older student who suddenly develops an interest in comic books after having experienced difficulty in reading his text in social studies may be an example. Satisfaction has been obtained by returning to a former stage of reading attainment.

Sympathism is an attempt to secure aid in the solution of a problem and to avoid the responsibility for failure. Sympathism generally results in getting someone to assist with a problem or at least provide attention in case of failure. This mechanism is related to regression and suggests emotional immaturity. Richard, the only child of reportedly indulgent parents, weeps and exclaims that he is dumb whenever he is faced with a difficult reading task in either the home or the school. Richard's parents report that they are sorry for him and that they want his life to be a happy one. After an unfortunate episode on the playground Richard insists upon going home. In explaining his desire, the boy points out that his mother is the only one who understands him.

Negativism is an attempt to protect oneself by doing nothing about a problem or by being contrary and practicing a form of behavior generally disapproved of by society. A child in the third grade has difficulty in distinguishing between *d, b,* and *g.* Some of the children in his class laugh aloud when he calls "God," "dog." The child who is apparently offended by his associates, refuses to make any further attempt at oral reading. This immature behavior can be described as negativistic.

Fantasy is an attempt to create an imaginary situation instead of facing reality. It is a form of wishful thinking and is frequently practiced by individuals of better than average intelligence. During a storytelling period in the first grade a little girl coming from an economically stricken and broken home tells an interesting story of her Christmas vacation. She realistically describes how her father had given her a riding horse for Christmas and how some children in the neighborhood are envious of her little pony. Upon investigation, the child's teacher discovers that she has received nothing for Christmas except a basket from a charity organization. In talking with the little girl, the teacher finds that the child actually believes her wishful story and exclaims piteously, "Why must you take everything from me?" Fantasy is not to be discouraged except when it becomes a substitute for real achievement. Some children with marked introvert tendencies identify themselves so thoroughly with personalities in books that they lose contact with reality in their environment and do not maintain an adequate social adjustment. This can be detrimental to their growth and development.

Egocentrism is the act of getting some kind of attention, even if unfavorable, as a symbol of success. Apparently, some people consider notoriety better than being entirely ignored. The naughty little boy whom the teacher, in self-defense, has placed at her side in the classroom may not receive recognition for being an excellent reader. In his own way, however, he may be the most successful child in the classroom in that he attracts more attention than anyone else. Children with reading difficulties have been known to win distinction because of their deficiencies and in so doing secure satisfaction which should have been obtained in a more legitimate manner.

Repression is the act of concealing or inhibiting an impulse or act. Instead of expressing an impulse, it is held in check and is diverted to thinking or emotion. For example, the impulse of a person on a diet to eat an extra piece of pie may be safely inhibited and yet give rise to inner frustration. An angry individual who inhibits an impulse to strike or to do some other unsocial act may have the approval of his friends and yet do some damage to himself. Children who are required to read materials which are too difficult for them are frequently required by group mores to repress their frustration and to tolerate assignments which can be damaging to their interest in reading. There is need for a well-adjusted balance between impulse and repression if the individual is to have satisfying and satisfactory human relations. Impulse and inhibition to the well-adjusted individual are similar to the motor and the braking system of a well-constructed car.

Dissociation is an unconscious attempt to split up a problem and deal with one or several parts separately. In the process of teaching reading, rate and comprehension should not be dissociated one from the other. Dissociation is a faulty solution to a problem in that the different aspects of the situation are not harmoniously integrated. It is an attempt to ride two horses simultaneously, each going in a different direction. Some individuals develop two or more contrasting and inconsistent roles of behavior for different situations. For example, a youth in junior high school may have one form of behavior when he is at home with his parents and quite another in the classroom. These contrasting types of conduct indicate a lack of integration and oneness of personality. Individuals showing these forms of behavior are in need of help and possibly the aid of the psychiatrist.

The relationship between reading and an individual's emotional development are influenced by such basic needs as satisfaction, security, and recognition. When these fundamental needs of the individual are threatened, he resorts to one or more mechanisms. Parents and teachers should understand what the individual is trying to accomplish and aid him in the realization of his goal. Success in reading activities at all levels leads to the individual's feeling of security and furnishes recognition among his fellows. Success brings approval from parents, teachers, and associates, and this is the goal for which the individual is striving.

Self-Concept and Reading Achievement

Some individuals develop the idea that they are "Can't Readers" and this self-concept affects their progress in learning to read. Roth,[14] in working with college freshmen, reports that those who improved and those who did not improve in reading showed wide differences in self-perception. Allport [15] shows that the self-image or self-concept has two aspects. These are the way the individual regards his abilities, status, and roles

[14] Robert M. Roth, "The Role of Self-Concept in Achievement," *Journal of Experimental Education,* 28:265–281 (June, 1959).
[15] Gordon W. Allport, *Personality* (New York: Holt and Co., 1937).

and what he would like to become. Snygg and Combs [16] believe that behavior is determined by all the experiences of which the person is aware at the instant of action. Awareness may vary between a low level and a high level, although presumably it never becomes completely unconscious. They believe that teachers must accept the idea that awareness is a cause of behavior and that what a person thinks and feels determines what he will do. Reading, like all other human behavior, is a function of the total personality. When we read, we perceive in accordance with our needs, goals, defenses, and values. The reader may inject meaning that will satisfy his needs and may reject meaning that is threatening to his self-concept. In other words, what he experiences and feels determines what he perceives in the book. Reading provides vicarious experience which is determined by the personality of the reader and may reflect his concept of himself, his relationship to others, and his view of the world.

In working with reading cases at various levels teachers will identify individuals with feelings of worthlessness and hopelessness concerning their ability to read. On the other hand, they will observe persons who have feelings of optimism and hope. These concepts of self are important in the learning process. When these self-images are recognized, it is the responsibility of the teacher to modify her instruction so as to meet more adequately the needs of the individual. The student with feelings of inadequacy may need structured or step-by-step instruction while the more optimistic individual may be encouraged to work on his own. All students should be provided with materials which they can read and in which they are interested. Praise and commendation should be given whenever it is justly deserved. The individual can be made to feel that he can read more effectively and that the responsibility for doing so is his. As Skinner [17] has pointed out, "Conditioning depends also upon the kind, amount, and immediacy of reinforcement, as well as many other factors."

Environment and Reading Success

Mental content and background for effective reading are gradually built up by experiences in our everyday world. The child's daily contact with his family, his friends, and his books, the use he makes of radio and television can facilitate or retard the development of effective reading. Mental stimulation through interesting conversations can create a desire to read and to learn. Homes and schools which provide adequate time and places for books help students discover that real satisfaction and

[16] Donald Snygg and Arthur W. Combs, *Individual Behavior* (New York: Harper & Bros., 1949).

[17] B. F. Skinner, *Science and Human Behavior* (New York: Macmillan Co., 1959), p. 67.

pleasure can be derived from reading. A quiet, well-ventilated, adequately heated room which is devoid of distractions and unnecessary equipment can aid the student in concentrating upon a reading project. If the environment is not conducive to effective reading, modifications or compensations must be made. In the life of the child, the chief centers of environmental factors are the home and the school.

Home Environment

Parents can create an environment which will stimulate a desire for reading. Favorable attitudes toward stories, poems, and books can be developed in the home. Because children want to do what they see adults doing, parents have a great opportunity to further the language development and reading readiness of their children. Boys and girls can be encouraged to tell of their daily experiences, to express their opinions, and to reveal their thoughts and feelings. Some studies [18] indicate that television can help children understand the meaning of words and aid in the development of their vocabularies. Surely, illiteracy and faulty English in the home can prevent children from understanding and enjoying the language of books found in the classroom. Children in some homes are neglected by parents who are overworked and suffering from emotional conflicts. These adults have little time for storytelling, interpretation of pictures, and for the answering of childish questions. There are indications that the language skills of these boys and girls are acquired only incidentally and as a result of their plays and their games with children in the neighborhood. Parents are unwise in insisting upon their children doing formal work in reading before they have reached a sufficient degree of maturity. Generally the teacher is the better judge as to whether or not this stage of development has occurred. Parents can help their children to develop a sense of responsibility when they have to put forth real effort in learning to read. Generally, children who make rapid progress in learning to read do so because of their interest in books and their desire to share in the experiences of others. Parents can develop in the home an educational and emotional climate which will encourage not only reading but also an ever-widening interest in our world.

If a child does not make normal progress, parents should, with the cooperation of the teacher, refer the child to a reading clinic or child guidance center. Parents of children with reading difficulties should not attempt to work with the child over long periods of time. Corrective work in reading can seldom, if ever, be done effectively by parents. In the case of the nonreader, it is unwise to report in the child's presence that a grandparent or some other member of the family had difficulty in learn-

[18] Clara Evans, "Tots and TV," *Childhood Education*, Vol. 33, March, 1957. See *The Reading Teacher*, Vol. 11, October, 1957. The theme of this issue is "Television and Reading."

ing to read and that this disability is of little or no consequence because of this individual's business success. It is unfortunate for parents to criticize the teacher in the child's presence. Instead it is more effective to discuss the child's problems with the teacher and work out at least a tentative solution.

School Environment

The school can provide adequate and hygienic buildings, rooms, and libraries which will make schools, in some cases at least, more comfortable for everyday living than home itself. Satisfactory heating, lighting, and ventilation are essential for the physical comfort of the growing child. Even more desirable is the creation of a climate for effective learning. Every child enrolled in the school should be able to get satisfaction, security, and recognition. The child should expect as a part of his school experience that his teacher will not require him to learn to read until he is sufficiently mature. He has a right to expect that his teacher will find adequate methods which will be suitable in his case, for not all boys and girls can be expected to learn to read in precisely the same way. The child in the classroom has a right to expect that he will be provided with adequate reading materials which will be selected on the basis of his reading level and interest. He has a right to expect adequate supplementary books at various grade levels which will afford him an opportunity to apply his reading skills in subject-matter fields such as science, social studies, and literature. The child has a right to expect that the reading program will be functional in nature and contribute to his daily living. This means that he will have an opportunity to speak, write, read, and listen as he learns to communicate effectively with his fellows. His environment can provide an opportunity for him to read newspapers, magazines, time tables, maps, charts, and other reference materials of value in our world. As a part of his school environment, he should have an opportunity to add to his vocabulary the words which he wants to know, to read a chapter effectively, to read to solve personal problems, and to evaluate critically the thoughts and ideas expressed by others. These are but some of the reading practices which the growing child can expect to be made a part of his everyday living.

The Need for Well-Trained Teachers

Well-trained teachers can be a valuable part of the child's environment. Teachers chosen by the school administration should understand the growth and development of the child and the dynamics of human behavior. They should know how to correlate information from various subject-matter fields and should have a sympathetic understanding of all social classes. They should know how to select, administer, and score tests, and how to interpret resulting data. They should understand a scientific attitude toward the problems of modern education. These well-trained teachers should have a philosophy of education which will help them to identify and evaluate goals in daily living, and they should possess a knowledge of teaching methods which can be utilized in reaching these goals.

Summary

If children are to be guided effectively and instructed wisely, their teachers should understand the various concepts of reading and be aware of the physical, psychological, and environmental factors involved. This information is as important to teachers of developmental reading as it is to those who are chiefly concerned with clinical problems. In the next chapter we will consider the case of Wendy and her readiness for reading. However, before this is attempted, the reader may find it helpful to participate in the Guided Activities.

Guided Activities

1. Observe a class in reading at the first grade level and another at the sixth grade level. Try to find answers to the following queries:
    a. What objectives in reading is the teacher at each level trying to accomplish?
    b. How are reading materials being adjusted to the interest and reading levels of the children?
    c. How does the teacher handle the problem of providing instruction for the various needs and abilities of her pupils?
    d. How do the boys differ from the girls in these grades?
2. Give examples of how it is possible to read without words.
3. Write *your* definition of reading.
4. In this chapter two forms of maturity are introduced in the discussion of psychological factors and reading achievement. *Identify* the two forms of maturity and become aware of the differences. *Interpret* or explain each term in one sentence. *Evaluate* these terms by showing which, in your opinion, is more important.
5. Summarize briefly the history of your learning to read from the elementary grades through college.
6. List the physical, psychological, and environmental factors which have contributed most to your success in reading.
7. Discuss the psychological mechanisms which you have used to protect yourself.
8. From the standpoint of the school, list the instructional factors which could have been improved in teaching you to read.

Questions and References

Questions	References
1. What are the implications of the different stages in language development?	1. Betts, Emmett A. *Foundations of Reading Instruction*, pp. 6–10. New York: American Book Co., 1957.
2. What are the reading problems the alert teacher will face?	2. Strang, Ruth, Constance M. McCullough, and Arthur E. Traxler. *Problems in the Improvement of Reading*, Chap. 1. New York: McGraw-Hill Book Co., 1955.
3. What are some different approaches to instruction in teaching children to read?	3. Yoakam, Gerald A. *Basal Reading Instruction*, Chap. 5. New York: McGraw-Hill Book Co., 1955.
4. What are the goals of reading instruction?	4. Betts, *op. cit.*, Chap. 7.
5. How can one develop an integrated reading program?	5. Yoakam, *op. cit.*, chap. 15.
6. What is the relationship between personality development and learning to read?	6. Smith, Henry P., and Emerald V. DeChant. *Psychology in Teaching Reading*, Chap. 11. Englewood Cliffs, N. Y.: Prentice-Hall, 1961.
7. How can instruction be adjusted to individual differences?	7. Bond, Guy L., and Miles A. Tinker. *Reading Difficulties, Their Diagnosis and Correction*, Chap. 3. New York: Appleton-Century-Crofts, 1957.
8. What is effective reading instruction?	8. Durrell, Donald D. *Improving Reading Instruction*, Chap. 1. Yonkers-on-Hudson, N. Y.: World Book Co., 1956.

Questions	References
9. What are some typical reactions to frustration?	9. Lehner, George F. J., and Ella Kube. *The Dynamics of Personal Adjustment,* Chaps. 5, 6. Englewood Cliffs, N.Y.: Prentice-Hall, 1955.
	Ruch, Floyd L. *Psychology and Life* (Fifth Edition), Chap. 7. Chicago: Scott, Foresman and Co., 1958.
10. How are motivation, emotion, and adjustment related in the adolescent?	10. Kuhlen, Raymond G. *The Psychology of Adolescent Development,* Chap. 6. New York: Harper & Bros., 1952.
11. What relationships exist between the endocrine glands and reading disability?	11. Smith, Donald E. P., and Patricia Carrigan. *The Nature of Reading Disability.* New York: Harcourt, Brace and Co., 1959.
12. What are some historical turning points in the teaching of reading?	12. Smith, Nila Banton. "Historical Turning Points in the Teaching of Reading," *National Education Association Journal* (May, 1952), 41:280–283.

3

READINESS FOR READING

The child who is ready to read wants to read. He would be disappointed if the opportunity to learn was denied him. Physical, mental, emotional, and social maturation has taken place so that the child is all set for beginning reading. He is ready. Readiness is not confined to a particular period in childhood but may occur at different stages of an individual's development. It may be that of a first grade child who can profit from instruction in a basal reader. It may be that of a youth in the eighth grade who is asking for information concerning word study, or it may be that of a high school student who is all set for chapter reading and problem solving. In beginning any activity, the human organism must be ready.

In this chapter attention will be focused upon Wendy, a little girl about to enter the first grade. It is our hope that the reader will be stimulated by her story and will question why she has reacted as she did and how her environment may have affected her ideas and her behavior. We begin with the child and later will discuss theories pertaining to the development of readiness for reading. It is for the reader to determine from Wendy's brief biography whether or not she is ready for systematic instruction in reading.

Is Wendy Ready for Reading?

Wendy Archambault is a child of six years. According to her developmental history, she weighed six pounds, five ounces at birth and was described as an active baby who was "very eager for food." At three months she laughed aloud and played with her hands. Occasionally she picked up objects from the table and banged her spoon against anything within reach. At six months Wendy showed distinct likes and dislikes in regard to food. She enjoyed fruit, vegetables, and milk but refused to eat cereal. She preferred to drink from a small cup, often refusing her bottle. Wendy had three teeth when she was eight months old, and a three-year session with bronchitis and asthma started at this time. At nine months Wendy was creeping and pulling herself to a standing position. The mother reported that at this age "Wendy began to display a temper. Her first spanking, which was administered by her father, made her so angry that she refused to look at him."

The parents observed that by the time Wendy was a year old she showed a lack of fear and an avid curiosity about everything. Her mother stated, "Wendy's walking and exploration resulted in various cuts and bruises but Wendy showed little concern over them. One day while she was visiting her father, who works at an army hospital, she disappeared. We spent a frantic half hour looking for her and at last found her in the company of several nurses in the Receiving Office. She appeared unafraid and at ease with those who were bestowing upon her so much attention."

Wendy's love of investigation continued. At one and a half years she spent considerable time "poking and prying into everything available." She moved quickly, walked rapidly, and was rarely still unless asleep. At this age Wendy did not care how she was dressed as long as her clothes contained pockets which she called "pockeys." It was said, "Wendy scribbles spontaneously and tries repeatedly to put on her shoes and frequently she succeeds." At twenty-two months she appeared to be a very happy child and apparently made considerable use of language. When her mother called, she would answer, "All righty." When asked her name by a family friend, Wendy replied, "Wennie Watch-em-bault."

When Wendy was three and a half years old, she was taken to a day nursery to spend an afternoon. When Mother and Wendy arrived, they observed much consternation at the receptionist's desk because a two-year-old boy had put a small pail on his head with the handle under his chin. Several attendants were trying to remove the pail but without success. Wendy unhesitatingly reached over and firmly yanked the pail off the boy's head.

As Wendy grew older she began to show a decided interest in meal-getting. When she was not quite three, she put bread in the toaster and then called to her parents and brother, "I making toast for you guys. I a mother." At four years of age Wendy frequently awakened her parents by determinedly announcing that she intended to cook breakfast on her own.

At five years Wendy attended Play School, which she enjoyed completely. During this time she learned to recognize the letters of the alphabet and numbers and was voted "Kindergarten Queen" by her classmates. She demonstrated her ability to draw a man and a house. She could dress herself and tie a bow. At this time she began to make suggestions to her mother about how to buy and prepare food. For example, one day Wendy suggested to her mother that they should buy oranges and "just squeeze them and we won't have to buy frozen juice."

Wendy is now six years old. Recently her brother Stephen came home from school with a weird story of vampire bats and their bloodthirsty ways. It is reported that Wendy listened with interest and a degree of awe. Just as she was beginning to look worried, she tossed her head and said, "Well, vampire bats can't be so bad. After all, they use them in baseball games all the time."

In describing Wendy as she is today, her mother said, "She is primarily interested in school, clothes, and being allowed to visit other children or have them visit her. She is affectionate and thinks a great deal of her brother. She uses her hands well and has no trouble with household tasks which are assigned to her, such as washing dishes or helping me cook or clean. She even sews her own patchwork. Wendy loves to color and paint. She sings and wishes for a piano to play. She likes to have a plan of activities for the day and then follow it.

"Wendy is tall for her age of six years. She weighs 58 pounds and is 49 inches tall. She takes an interest in her hair. Her braids have been cut and she can comb and arrange her hair rather well." Her mother, in discussing a picture of Wendy, says, "Does she look like a little girl who loves to trail around in robes, who has to have her hair washed every night because it gets mysteriously full of sand or mud, who when being scolded for spilling her milk for the third time in one day says softly, 'It was just a accident, sister,' and who at any time of day is likely to come up to give you a 'smooch' or a hug because 'I love you'? Then, it looks like Wendy."

The mother reported, "Wendy is story conscious. She could hardly wait to be able to print her own name so that she could obtain her own library card. She chooses books regularly, and we have a daily read-aloud time before her afternoon nap. She is fond of Dr. Seuss. She has taken pleasure in such books as *Heidi, Skip Come A Lou,* all fairy tales, *Little Phillipe of Belgium, The Funny Thing,* and *Peter Churchmouse.* She has never been particularly impressed with Mother Goose."

Mother said, "For several months Wendy has been writing notes to her grandmother. In the beginning they consisted of scribbles and flourishes but lately she has asked for help in making letters and in writing words. I have shown her how to put letters together to make words." One of Wendy's notes is reproduced here and the reader's attention is called to the instances in which she has reversed the letter *s.* This is a normal reaction for an immature child and does not necessarily indicate reversal tendencies. It will be observed that Wendy has specialized in capital letters, and this may facilitate her progress in reading, especially if manuscript writing is taught in the first grade she attends.

DEAR GRANDMA
I WENT TO
THE - CIRC
I - HAD - 2 ME ON
COTTON - CANDY.
THERE - WERE S
BEAR2 - THAT
DID - TRICKS

Some of the relevant factors in Wendy's biography may be summarized as follows:

1. Wendy is probably a child of high average mental ability.
2. Her home background has produced an educational climate which has stimulated a readiness for reading.
3. Incidents have been related which suggest emotional maturity.
4. It may be inferred from the data presented that Wendy is emotionally stable.
5. Language skills have been developed in the home which can facilitate an adequate adjustment in reading.
6. Wendy's parents have stimulated an interest in books and the desire to express ideas in writing.
7. Contact with children has contributed to a satisfactory social adjustment.
8. Activities in the home and in the child's immediate environment have fostered the development of background and mental content essential to academic progress and especially reading.

You have now had an opportunity to read a brief account of Wendy's growth and development. Is she ready for systematic instruction in reading? This is the question which Wendy's teacher must answer. You, too, will need to determine the readiness of each child in your classroom. In doing so, what factors should be considered? How can reading readiness be determined? How can the home and the school facilitate readiness for reading? These are the questions which will be answered in the remaining pages of this chapter.

Some Factors to Be Considered in Determining Readiness

Premature exposure to reading before the child develops a sufficient degree of maturity is likely to retard to a serious degree his desire to learn. Maturity varies both as to kind and degree. For example, there are great ranges of attainment in physical, mental, and emotional maturity. In general, the child's progress in learning to read is in keeping with the development of these capacities. The physical, mental, and emotional growth curves of an individual are apt to be similar. In other words, there is a positive relationship between physical, mental, and emotional maturity. Growth that is slow in the beginning is apt to continue to be slow. Rapid growth in the beginning is predictive of accelerated development. Further growth, however, can be modified by marked and significant changes in the environment.

The child whose maturation level is adequate for reading instruction shows certain characteristics. Such a child has a mental age of approximately six years and six months. He has adequate visual and auditory acuity and is able to handle books, crayons, scissors, and paper with some dexterity. The child who is ready for reading is able to pay attention, follow directions, and resist distractions. He can recite familiar nursery rhymes and tell stories from pictures. He is able to understand stories which are told to him and he shows an interest in books and their contents. He asks questions about words and can recognize a few printed words in addition to his name. He wants to learn to read.

In addition to maturation, mental content resulting from background and experience is essential to readiness for reading. Every child sees with what he has seen and he hears with what he has heard. Each new word and idea is interpreted in terms of his past experiences. If his mental content, a by-product of this experience, is missing or limited, his understanding and appreciation are quite inadequate. Wendy's explanation that "vampire bats can't be so bad. After all, they use them in baseball games all the time" serves as an excellent example of how an individual interprets what he hears in terms of his mental content. Vampires and umpires were the same to her, especially when used in conjunction with the word "bats." The mentally and emotionally mature child adds rapidly to his mental content because he is able to profit from his background and experiences. Girls usually mature earlier and more rapidly than boys. Girls at the age of six years are physiologically more advanced than boys.[1] This generally means that a girl has developed a greater readiness for reading than a boy of the same chronological age. She has benefited from her experiences in her environment and has increased her mental content and consequently her readiness for reading.

Means of Determining Readiness

Readiness for reading can be determined by objective measures, observations, and by consideration of the life history of the child.

Use of Objective Measures

Tests can be used in determining the child's readiness for reading. Measures of mental capacity provide a means of comparing the child's performance with his ability to learn. Both individual and group measures of mental maturity are available for the alert teacher. Such tests, however, as the Stanford-Binet Intelligence Scale and the Wechsler Intelligence Scale for Children should be administered only by competent and well-trained psychometrists. Group measures of mental maturity can

[1] Paul Witty and David Kopel, *Reading and the Educative Process* (Boston: Ginn and Co., 1939), p. 220.

be given by the regular classroom teacher after she has become well acquainted with the manual of directions.

Reading readiness tests, because of their nature, are frequently more helpful than tests of mental status. These measures are of value in discovering deficiencies in visual and auditory discrimination, background, and mental content, vocabulary, and perception of relationships.

In selecting tests of mental maturity and reading readiness, instruments should be chosen which furnish data of educational significance and of real value to the teacher. For example, there is little need for administering tests of mental maturity to Wendy unless there is some question involving her intellectual status. Tests should be valid, reliable, easily administered, and scored. Norms should be stated in terms of percentiles or achievement ages and, of course, the cost should not be prohibitive. The reader may wish to refer to *The Fifth Mental Measurements Yearbook* [2] for more detailed information concerning the selection and use of objective measures in reading.

Making Use of Observations

The well-trained teacher is concerned with observed facts and their interpretation. She is desirous of seeing each child as an individual and as a member of the group. She seeks to determine whether or not the child is physically, mentally, and emotionally mature for reading experiences. The following questions are of value in helping her accomplish her purpose and are suggestive of others which she may devise:

Physical Development
1. Are there evidences of good health?
2. Are there signs of good nutrition?
3. Is the child energetic and active?
4. Is he free from physical handicaps?
5. Are his movements well coordinated?
6. Does he hold his book at the proper reading distance?
7. Does he hold his book and turn the pages well?
8. Does he apparently hear what is said to the group?
9. Does he enunciate words accurately?

Mental Maturity
1. Is the child alert?
2. Does he notice likenesses and differences?
3. Can he tell of his experiences?
4. Is he learning to pay attention for longer periods of time?

[2] Oscar K. Buros (ed.), *The Fifth Mental Measurements Yearbook* (Highland Park, N. J.: Gryphon Press, 1959).

5. Does he make use of language?
6. Does he tell and recite stories and poems?
7. Does he understand that symbols may represent pictures or things?
8. Does he memorize easily?
9. Can he generalize and make inferences?

Emotional Maturity
1. Does the child easily make home-to-school adjustments?
2. Can he accept change in routine quietly and calmly?
3. Can he accept opposition and defeat without being emotionally upset?
4. Does he assume responsibility?
5. Does he plan and do things on time?
6. Does he meet and talk to strangers without shyness or undue boldness?
7. Does he take care of his equipment and materials?
8. Can he work independently?
9. Does he want to read?

Emotional Stability
1. Is the child happy and well adjusted in school?
2. Does he have few fears and worries?
3. Does he like other children?
4. Can he talk easily?
5. Does he seek help and information when really needed?
6. Does he seldom cry?
7. Does he like school?
8. Does he react to a new learning situation with confidence?

In making observations of children, the teacher should always distinguish between facts and inferences, for one can be fairly sure of the former but never certain of the latter. It should be observed that most of the answers to the questions in this list, whether positive or negative, are inferences and may not be valid.

Understanding the Child's History

Knowledge of the child's preschool history can be of value to the teacher. If, for example, the child has been slow in learning to sit up alone, to walk, and to talk, these facts may be predictive of his maturation rate. Furthermore, slowness in dentition and retardation in developing a hand preference can be significant factors in determining readiness for reading. As previously indicated, studies [3] show that the curves of

[3] Willard C. Olson, "Reading and Child Growth and Development" in C. W. Hunnicutt and William J. Iverson, *Research in the Three R's* (New York: Harper & Bros., 1958), pp. 39–43.

growth for physical, mental, emotional, and social functions tend to be similar. Usually these developmental curves are high, average, or low in all aspects of growth. Some individuals, however, are deficient in one or more phases of their development. A seven-year-old child, for example, may have reached a high physical, mental, and social level of maturation and, at the same time, be deficient in his emotional development. It is reasonable then to expect that the child's readiness for reading and his achievement in reading will be in keeping with his total growth pattern. This can mean that a child's readiness for and progress in reading are greatly influenced by the factors that have determined the extent of his development and maturation. The presence of these determining factors can be identified by the following pertinent questions: The mature reader may wish to apply these in the case of Wendy.

1. Did the child sit up without support at nine months?
2. Could he walk alone at eighteen months?
3. Could he use simple sentences and phrases at two years?
4. At three years, could he name three objects in a picture?
5. Is the child farsighted?
6. Does he have children with whom he can play?
7. Does he have a reasonable number of toys?
8. Does he have pets?
9. Does he have books?
10. Does the child participate in family conversations and planning?
11. Is he taken on trips?
12. Do the child's parents read to him and tell him stories?
13. Do the child's parents make wise use of television?
14. Is the child permitted to help his father and mother in interesting tasks about the home?
15. Does the child pretend to read when his family are busy with their books, papers, and magazines?
16. Does he ask to be told stories concerning the pictures he finds in his books?
17. Is he encouraged to tell of his experiences?
18. Does the home climate contribute to an interest in social and educational problems?
19. Does his behavior suggest that he wants to learn to read?

Means of Developing Readiness

In order to be ready for reading, some children need supplementary experiences and more time for maturation. These can be provided by parental guidance, in the pre-school and kindergarten, and even in the first grade.

Parental Guidance

Wendy began her reading activities in the home. All sorts of reading materials are so much a part of living that most children become acquainted with books, papers, and magazines at an early age. Fathers and mothers can facilitate the mental growth of their children by creating a climate in the home which will stimulate a desire for books, stories, and information. In general, young children like to do what they see adults doing. Consequently, parents have a great responsibility for the language attainments and the reading readiness of their children. Parents should provide time for storytelling, for the interpretation of pictures, and for the answering of childish questions. They should encourage their children to talk freely and well, to tell of their daily experiences, and to express their opinions. Children should have freedom for new experiences which are commensurate with their age and desires. They should be encouraged to live in their world and not have too much done for them. They should realize that they are members of a family group and, like every other member of the household, should have their responsibilities and privileges. All of these experiences aid in the development of mental content and prepare children for reading activities in the classroom.

Preschool and Kindergarten Activities

Through careful planning and guidance, teachers of preschool and kindergarten children can introduce them to experiences and activities which, in accordance with their mental maturity and background, will not only contribute to their daily living but prepare them for reading. This is the ultimate goal.

Children should be encouraged to ask questions and carry on conversations, for in doing this they learn to use words adequately. Frequent contacts with children can give rise to conversations which can be beneficial in the sharing of experiences and the building of background which children would not otherwise acquire. Observing television and discussing what is observed furnish children with vicarious experiences which can contribute to successful reading. Visits to the park, zoo, open country, and mountains provide children with mental content which will be useful to them in understanding and appreciating what they read. These experiences can lead to animated conversations, questions and answers, and a free exchange of ideas which add to the mental content of those who participate.

Children should have an opportunity to use their hands in the construction of things of interest and value to them. This type of activity adds to their store of ideas and at the same time helps them to gain control of their large and small muscles. The child who draws pictures and has the opportunity to explain his drawings to others learns to use new words in this process of communication. The creation with tinker toys of wagons, cars, and machines helps the child, through his experiences, to add to his mental content and to demonstrate his interests and even some of his aptitudes. Coloring and painting give the child an opportunity to express himself creatively and at the same time to demonstrate his knowledge of colors, form, and understanding of that which he has produced. Group participation in cooky-making and similar activities can build up mental content in various fields and at the same time furnish the child with information which will be useful to him as he learns to read.

Children can be encouraged to participate in activities which arouse their interest and curiosity. Children, after traveling, visiting, or looking at television, can be encouraged to ask *why, what,* and *how* questions. The value of such discussion is increased by group participation. Some of the science programs for children on television can provide excellent means of increasing the background and experiences of boys and girls which will aid them in understanding what they read. Going on walks or trips with adults to a department store, depot, or airport provides a wealth of experience which will aid in vocabulary building essential to effective reading.

Children can be stimulated to want to do what others do. This is especially true of the movies and television. It is interesting to observe children as they watch a baseball, football, or hockey game being shown on TV. What they learn and comprehend is amazing. Other activities, such as dressing up in adult clothes and playing store, give little boys and girls an opportunity to act and be like their elders. In fact, children playing school demonstrate many of the idiosyncrasies and characteristics of their teachers. Frequently little boys and girls pretend to read when older children and adults in the room are studying and reading for recreation. Some children insist on looking on when mother reads a familiar story aloud and immediately point out any omission which she may have made. These experiences are of value in preparing boys and girls for reading.

Children can be aided in the development of appreciation, attitudes, and social values. Here again well-chosen books, moving pictures, and television programs have much to contribute. Opinions, judgments, and points of view expressed by the teacher, parents, and other adults have a marked impact upon the child. Listening to stories, nursery rhymes, and children's poems contributes to a child's appreciation of good literature and helps him in learning to listen for a purpose. Telling and dramatizing interesting stories build up attitudes and points of view which are not only of value in reading activities but also contribute to the child's concept of what is right and wrong. Listening to good music, like listening to good stories, is beneficial to the child. Singing and reciting in unison can contribute to appreciation and aid in the establishment of attitudes.

Children can be introduced to activities which are directly related to reading. Children who print and recognize their own names have taken the initial steps in the process of written communication. This desire to express oneself has been illustrated in Wendy's letters to her grandmother. Children who learn to associate words with pictures and objects advertised on television have already begun to read. This is true of little boys and girls who observe house numbers and street names, signs, and names of papers and magazines. Some children recognize radio programs, phonograph records, books, and magazines without being able to identify the letters of the alphabet. Telling stories observed on television is a form of communication closely related to reading. This, too, is a step in the reading process. Putting picture puzzles together demonstrates the child's ability to appraise the situation and to organize the elements into a meaningful whole. Making collections of pictures and other objects and classifying these under logical headings is a step toward the evaluation of ideas. In a similar manner, making a scrapbook containing pictures, drawings, leaves, and other objects of interest to a child shows at a primary level the child's ability to evaluate and organize related ideas. Children can develop essential reading techniques before they actually read any words. They can be taught how to turn pages, to look at the left page before the right, and to survey the page from left to right and from top to bottom. These are some of the early steps in the reading process.

Kindergarten training can do much to develop a readiness for reading. Even in the very beginning, learning to read can be a part of the child's daily living. He enjoys the dramatization of children's stories. Children should be encouraged to tell of their own experiences before a group and should have an opportunity to listen to poems and stories. Even the more reticent children enjoy telling, in response to questions, what happened next in a familiar story. In the process of telling and listening, these little boys and girls have an opportunity to learn the use of new words and to share vicariously the experiences of others. Many little boys and girls enjoy looking at picture books and telling stories suggested by the pictures. When this is done, the alert teacher has an excellent opportunity to learn much concerning the child, his interests, background, and even some of his fears and worries. Children enjoy making scrapbooks of pictures taken during a vacation and experience real satisfaction when given an opportunity to tell the group of their adventures on a trip. Boys and girls can be encouraged to bring interesting books from home to be shared with the group. When this is done, children are taught to understand that books belong to children and that they are to be used by them. Many teachers find that a library corner in the classroom encourages children to look at, to handle, and to ask questions about books. These informal ac-

Free reading can be encouraged by a wise choice of supplementary materials.

Children acquire mental content as they listen to the magic of a good story.

In these cozy nooks children learn to appreciate books.

Configuration clues are utilized in word study.

tivities can develop interests and mental content which will be utilized later in the process of learning to read. Little boys and girls who complete ten months of kindergarten and who are mentally and emotionally mature enough for systematic instruction in reading are frequently disappointed unless they are introduced immediately to the use of books and the mechanics of reading.

Grouping in the First Grade

When they enter the first grade, not all children are ready for reading. Teachers frequently find that in a group of forty first grade children not more than eight or ten are ready for systematic instruction in reading. In order to adjust to this situation a flexible grouping plan may be put into operation. One group, and, to begin with, the smaller, is made up of children who are ready for formal instruction. The other group is composed of boys and girls who need supplementary experiences and time for maturation. Instead of waiting until the child is ready for reading his teacher can aid him in developing this readiness. In meeting the needs of her boys and girls the alert teacher will be actively engaged with two groups of children instead of one. The group ready for reading experiences will become larger and larger and the group which is developing this readiness will become smaller and smaller. In the work with the latter group some of the materials and activities employed at the preschool and kindergarten levels are suggestive of those which can be selected for use in the first grade.

Summary

The teacher, in determining a child's readiness for reading, must consider physical, psychological, and environmental factors. The process is facilitated by use of objective measures, careful observations, and by an understanding of the child's history. This chapter has suggested means which the home and school can utilize in developing a readiness for reading. However, many of these suggestions may be applied at all levels.

Guided Activities

1. List facts which indicate Wendy's physical growth and development.
2. List psychological mechanisms employed by Wendy.
3. Indicate incidents in Wendy's history which suggest that she will adjust well socially with a group of children her age.
4. Enumerate facts which may indicate that Wendy is mentally mature enough for systematic instruction in reading.
5. List evidences of Wendy's language development.
6. Outline the advantages and disadvantages of kindergarten training for Wendy.
7. Locate facts which may indicate Wendy's emotional maturity.
8. Fold a sheet of 8½″ × 11″ paper the long way. Write the word *Facts* on

one side and the word *Inferences* on the other. List the significant facts in Wendy's biography and the inferences which can be supported by them.

9. Prepare a brief outline indicating what you would tell Wendy's mother concerning Wendy's readiness for reading.

10. Observe a child of five or six years so as to determine readiness for reading. In considering physical development, mental maturity, emotional maturity, and emotional stability, make use of the information presented in this chapter.

Questions and References

Questions	References
1. How does reading begin?	1. Monroe, Marion. *Growing Into Reading,* Chap. 1. Chicago: Scott, Foresman and Co., 1951.
2. What are the characteristics of the child who is ready for reading?	2. Dawson, Mildred A., and Henry A. Bamman. *Fundamentals of Basic Reading Instruction,* Chap. 3. New York: Longmans, Green and Co., 1959.
3. What are some tests of mental maturity, reading readiness, and means of appraising visual and auditory discrimination?	3. Betts, Emmett A. *Foundations of Reading Instruction,* pp. 735–739. New York: American Book Co., 1957.
4. What makes for success in beginning reading?	4. McKim, Margaret G. *Guiding Growth in Reading,* Chap. 3. New York: Macmillan Co., 1955.
5. How can the teacher provide pre-reading experiences?	5. *Ibid.,* Chap. 4.
6. What are the first steps in learning to read?	6. *Ibid.,* Chap. 5. Yoakam, Gerald A. *Basal Reading Instruction,* Chaps. 8, 9. New York: McGraw-Hill Book Co., 1955.
7. How can readiness for learning be developed?	7. DeBoer, John J., and Martha Dallmann. *The Teaching of Reading,* Chaps. 5A, 5B. New York: Holt, Rinehart and Winston, 1960. Yoakam. *op. cit.,* Chap. 7.

4

BEGINNING READING

The period of readiness for beginning reading is generally observed in the first and second grades. For some children, however, it may begin earlier and for others much later. Systematic instruction may start as soon as a child shows evidence of readiness for learning to read. This readiness, as shown by Wendy in Chapter 3, is essential to satisfactory progress in reading. For an individual child the period of beginning reading may be of short or long duration. Generally the child with an adequate background of experience and effective instruction will make normal progress in the fundamental reading skills as he proceeds through pre-primers, primer, and finally the first reader. The average child will probably use first readers in the second grade, while slow learners may need books at the first reader level as late as the third, fourth, and even fifth grade. In such instances, the interest level of the material must be more mature than that generally found in the usual first reader.

In this chapter, the biography of Debbie, a little girl in the second grade, is presented to illustrate some of the aims, materials, and procedures which her teachers have utilized during a part of this period of beginning reading.

How Debbie Began to Read

Debbie is a demure little girl of seven years who thoroughly enjoys her work in the second grade. Her teacher reports, "Debbie is an accurate and careful child who is more mature than her age would suggest. She reads and writes well and listens with interest to the contributions of the other children. She expresses her ideas quietly and with confidence. She works and plays well with others and is both courteous and cooperative. Debbie completes her work promptly, follows directions, and makes good use of her time after assigned tasks are completed. She takes excellent care of her property and is at times impatient with other children who are poor housekeepers. Debbie is a determined little girl who knows exactly what she wants to do. She appears to have sufficient rest, follows safety practices, and observes good health habits in the classroom. Debbie is seldom absent from school and is never tardy."

After Debbie had completed kindergarten, her teacher's report to the parents pointed out, "Debbie accepts responsibility unusually well and enjoys music and rhythm activities. She shares her ideas with the group and listens when others talk. She is especially fond of stories and rhymes. Debbie prints her name in manuscript, recognizes colors, and can differentiate between her left and right hands. She identifies likenesses and differences and tells her own address and phone number. She is interested in nature, especially animals, and can express well her ideas with art materials." Her teacher summed up this report by saying, "Debbie is a mature child and will be a good first grader."

During the early weeks of Debbie's stay in the first grade, effective use apparently was made of three pre-primers. Each of these books contained short and interesting stories with good plots showing humor, surprise, and unexpected outcomes. An activity book accompanied this series and provided new, interesting, and thought-provoking situations in which boys and girls might apply and practice specific reading skills. Debbie's teacher explained that the little girl's progress in reading was rapid and that she and several other children began early their use of the first primer and its accompanying activity book. These boys and girls made up the fast-moving group which chose for itself the name "The Pussywillows." A special junior primer was bypassed of which the primary purpose was to furnish the slow-learning, the immature, or frequently absent child opportunity to grow in interpretative skills and to acquire an initial sight vocabulary before beginning the first primer.

The teacher, in discussing further her adjustment of materials used by "The Pussywillows" pointed out that she had also decided to omit the use of a readiness book. "These children," she said, "have developed well their visual, auditory, and motor skills. They have shown rapid growth in oral language and have demonstrated superior interpretative abilities. The readiness book designed to accomplish these objectives is generally introduced before the three pre-primers and is of value in meeting the needs of average and slow-learning children."

An examination of the anecdotal records and the lesson plans of Debbie's first grade teacher reveals that the underlying aims of the reading program were to promote enthusiasm and anticipation for learning to read and to foster in each child the belief that he could succeed. In addition, it was her purpose to provide opportunities for the children to become acquainted with and to enjoy many stories, books, and poems as well as to help the children develop skill in word perception and in understanding, organizing, and effectively using ideas gained from reading.

The teacher's daily procedure, although varied in detail, followed a general pattern throughout the school year. The first step was to prepare the children for the day's lesson by relating the story to their personal experience and by using orally words which would be met for the first time in the reading situation. A background of necessary concepts for the stories was developed. New words were introduced in meaningful context, and an attempt was made to develop interest in the actual reading of the story.

The second step centered around the interpretation of the story. The children, under the guidance of the teacher, discussed the pictures accompanying the stories and were encouraged to give their impressions of the motives and feelings of the characters and to draw conclusions about the setting of the story and the characters depicted. This was followed by silent reading of the story for specific purposes; for example, to find out more about the action, to discover exactly what was being said, and to confirm their opinions concerning the character's motives and feelings. Pertinent questions were asked by the teacher to determine if there had been proper comprehension of the ideas presented and to stimulate interpretation of the material. Oral reading was encouraged as a means of proving a point or to confirm opinions expressed earlier. Often children were asked to assume the roles of story characters and to read aloud the parts spoken by these characters.

The third step in the reading lesson was usually presented from the board or through the use of phrase cards, pictures, and other materials. It was designed to develop and extend skill in interpreting main ideas, making inferences and judgments, noting details, and anticipating outcomes. Emphasis was placed on contextual, picture, and configuration clues as well as the development of a basic sight vocabulary. Particular attention was paid to identifying words in capitalized and uncapitalized initial-letter forms, auditory perception of rhymes, and visual-auditory perception of initial consonants. The children were introduced to structural analysis through recognition of words formed by adding s to known words and recognition of compound words made up of two known root words. The use of the activity book followed step three and provided the children with practice and application of the skills presented in the lesson.

The final step in the procedure included dramatizations, discussions of stories and poems, art works and games, all of which were designed to extend the children's interest in reading.

Early in March Debbie was ready for the first reader and the activity book which accompanied it. In response to a number of questions concerning this workbook, Debbie said, "We work with it only when our teacher thinks we are ready. She tells us what to do and then we do it. We mark only one page at a time. We all talk about the first question and when everyone knows what to do we mark by ourselves. Some of the pages are easy and some are hard to do. If we get done early, we can read new books until the other children catch up. When we are all done, the teacher tells us the right answers. If we make mistakes, we make changes with a crayon of a different color. We all talk about our mistakes and the teacher tells us why we are wrong. I like the activity books. Our teacher says they tell her about each one of us and what we need to learn. When we are all done with our book, we can take it home and show it to our parents. My father says I am a good reader and Mother says she is proud of me. Even Jennie, my little sister, thinks it's nice for me to read to her. She likes comic books and so do I."

In addition to following a basal reading program, Debbie's first grade teacher explained, "We generally had two and sometimes three groups of children operating in the morning, and then in the afternoon we made use of informal reading, generally in the nature of experience charts. Frequently the children composed a letter to their parents. These were worked out on the board and later copied. The children were also encouraged to select books from their school library and to engage in free reading. We tried to relate reading to other language arts by having the children copy the words of the reading lessons, make their own picture dictionaries, write stories, letters, and riddles, and cooperatively prepare an occasional newspaper."

Debbie's parents, in discussing her progress in the first grade, made it clear that they were enthusiastic supporters of not only her first grade teacher but her kindergarten teacher as well. Her mother explained, "Both of Debbie's teachers have helped her to grow and develop. Her activities in the kindergarten have prepared her for reading in the first grade. It was there that she learned to adjust to other children and it was her first teacher who helped her to gain confidence in herself. In the first grade she learned to enjoy books, many books, and she has made excellent progress. At home she plays teacher with children in the neighborhood serving as her pupils. From these activities I have learned much concerning her teacher in the first grade. Debbie wants to be like her and I hope she will succeed.

"Perhaps you'd be interested in how Debbie plays school," the mother continued. "She has prepared a list of the children in her class and begins by taking the roll. If any child is absent, she carefully places a mark opposite the name of the child who is missing. Then she begins to teach. She points out to the children the mistakes which they make and her most frequent remark is, 'We learn by our mistakes.' It's interesting to observe her efforts to teach the children because I'm sure she is repeating the same procedures her teacher has followed that day in school. Of course, we don't want to give you the impression that we think Debbie is perfect. She isn't. She is wiggly, very active, and seems to have an excess of nervous energy except while she is reading. Then she is very quiet and completely unaware of everything around her. She doesn't hear me call her when she's reading and at times this can be quite annoying. I think she ought to help with some of the housework but occasionally when I ask her, she replies, 'That's your job. Daddy has his work and I have mine.' I realize that she is absorbed with books, but I try to be consistent in following through on reasonable requests."

Debbie's father announced later, when Debbie was playing with her sister, that the school principal had reported Debbie was reading as well as a child two months in the third grade. "I hope she continues to make as much progress as she has made during the last two years," he added hopefully. "During the time Debbie has been growing up," he continued, "we have read to her, told her stories, and recited all the Mother Goose rhymes we have known. When we have taken trips, we have prepared her for what she would see and have tried to stimulate her interest in lakes, boats, animals, planes, and motels."

"I wish Debbie were less interested in comic books," exclaimed her mother as the interview was about to end. "She reads every one she can find and trades the ones she has completed for others in the possession of her friends. She figures out for herself the new words and reads aloud to her sister. Both girls enjoy them. I am doubtful, however, as to the value of even the best." When Debbie was asked about this matter, she said quietly, "I like them," and that was all she would say.

Debbie has been a second grader for more than six months. Her present teacher reported, "Debbie is a quiet, thoughtful, but independent little girl who is loved by her friends. She is an excellent reader and a happy child who thoroughly enjoys all her school activities. Six children in my second grade serve as group leaders, and Debbie is one of them. She enjoys reading aloud to the other children and can be depended upon to assist others in their activities. She is one of my best helpers. Just recently I introduced the dictionary skill, alphabetizing by a single letter, and Debbie learned how to do this more quickly than any of the other children. I'm pleased with her progress in reading."

Pertinent factors in Debbie's history may be summarized as follows:

1. The facts presented suggest that Debbie is mentally, emotionally, and socially mature for a child of her age.
2. She demonstrates many characteristics of the child who is ready for systematic instruction in reading.
3. Her teacher has utilized the basal reader approach to the teaching of reading.
4. Informal reading activities have been used to supplement the materials and procedures outlined in the basal readers.
5. Children in Debbie's class have been grouped according to their readiness for reading and according to their attainment of fundamental skills.

6. In the process of providing instruction her teacher has been concerned with reading objectives to be obtained, materials to be used, and with adequate procedures to be followed.
7. Debbie has shown evidence of leadership and has made progress in reading. As a result, her parents have become enthusiastic supporters of the school and of Debbie's teachers in particular.

Debbie's teachers have employed a variety of materials and procedures in helping her learn to read. As a prospective teacher, you are probably ready to learn how you can be of most service to children like Debbie. We believe that sound instruction in reading is based not only upon an understanding of the individual but upon a knowledge of the reading process itself.

Initial Objectives and Related Activities

Reading is a function of the whole personality of the individual. It is more than an accumulation of worthwhile skills such as word recognition, word study, vocabulary building, use of phonics, structural analysis, sentence and paragraph reading. Instead, reading is an integration of language skills which are manifest in everyday living. Reading is a complicated process that involves the perception of words, it is true, but reading also includes thorough comprehension of meanings and feelings, thoughtful reaction to ideas and information, and the integration of all these into the reader's experience, causing him to decide on courses of action, to change his attitudes, and to modify his behavior in the light of newly acquired evidence. One of the major purposes of reading is to aid us in thinking.

Reading is an aspect of life, and every child should have an opportunity to learn to read as soon as he is sufficiently mature. Ours is a reading culture, and every child is entitled to the very best instruction possible if he is to achieve the goals of education and become a happy, successful individual and a competent, effective citizen. Any successful reading program is concerned with the development of understandings, skills, abilities, habits, and attitudes that ensure acquisition of the power to read. A good reading program also builds personal satisfaction through enabling children to enrich and extend their experiences in the pursuit of personal desires and interests.

The teacher who recognizes these objectives can provide guidance and well-planned systematic instruction to help children achieve their reading goals. She can introduce them to experiences and activities which are in keeping with their mental maturity and which will contribute to their daily living. The emphasis should not be upon the activities alone but *upon what is to be accomplished by these experiences.* The teacher provides guidance and well-planned instruction and serves children in a much higher capacity than that of the baby sitter who is chiefly concerned in keeping children busy, contented, and happy.

The teacher of beginning reading can help children develop a readiness for books by showing them how to use and adequately care for them. She can show them how to open a book carefully to avoid breaking the binding, how to turn pages without tearing them, and how to keep books clean. The teacher can show children how to hold a book properly. She can call attention to the parts of the book, the table of contents at the front, the separate stories, and the page numbers. She can show them where the title of the story is placed and how to look at a series of pictures and words in a left-to-right direction. These skills contribute to the fundamental mechanics of reading, assist in the development of correct visual practices, and help to prevent the formation of poor reading habits.

The teacher of beginning reading can help children develop background and mental content through activities, experiences, and discussions so that they learn how to interpret ideas from pictures in verbal statements and improvised stories. In the early stages of instruction children can learn that words have useful meanings and that they should learn to see each word as a unit or whole. It is desirable for children to acquire a working knowledge of certain basic sight words before systematic instruction in reading is attempted. During this period it is important for the teacher to stress meaning and its association with the general pattern of the word. Likenesses and differences in word forms may be pointed out but word analysis can be delayed until the child is more mature.

As these skills are being developed, interpretation can be stressed. Boys and girls can be shown how to read both sentences and short paragraphs and how to read silently to answer questions asked by the teacher or by children in the group. They can be shown how to follow printed or written directions in order to color, draw, or play a game. At this level, initial forms of word-attack skills and work-study habits can be developed, and children can be expected to read for meaning so as to appreciate a story as a whole. They can find ideas and facts in printed materials, and some may be initiated into reading for detail. Quick-learning children, like Debbie, can be shown how to identify the central idea in a paragraph and will be able to read for pleasure and entertainment. The more mature children in the group will want, and should be permitted, to read to their associates for the satisfaction of both listener and reader.

Generally boys and girls completing the third grade, if they have been taught effectively and are sufficiently mature, have some proficiency in the reading skills suggested in this recital of reading objectives. The child at the end of this stage should be encouraged to consolidate his gains and acquire new, yet related skills. His progress can be continuous as he further develops these basic skills and utilizes them in the learning process from elementary grades through high school and beyond.

Approaches to Beginning Reading

In general, there are three approaches to beginning reading which are being employed by teachers today. One is an informal method which makes use of the children's everyday experiences; another, frequently called the basal reader approach, involves the direct introduction of books; and the third is a combination of the two.

Informal Reading

Informal methods of teaching reading, such as the experience approach and the picture method, are generally based upon materials prepared by the teacher and frequently dictated by the children. The use of the term "informal" does not imply that this method is incidental or unplanned. Quite the opposite is true, in fact, for the informal methods of teaching reading require expert execution of carefully formulated plans.

The *experience approach* to informal reading utilizes reading charts based on any experience of the children which serves the interests and needs of the group. The teacher engages the children in discussion of the experience and encourages them to suggest ideas for the chart. She accepts one sentence at a time, revises it with the help of the other students, and finally prints it on the chalkboard. When the story is complete, the children are permitted to read it aloud for their enjoyment. Later the story can be copied on chart paper or for individual use on 8½" x 11" sheets of paper. An example follows.

> *A Happy Time*
> Stephen went to Lake Michigan.
> He saw the water.
> He saw the trees.
> Stephen had a happy time.

Children's stories recording the experiences of one or more in their group are frequently called experience charts. In preparing these materials the teacher selects an interesting event which the children have shared, such as a trip to a farm, dairy, or fire station. Then, serving as a guide, she helps the children to compose a story which relates the important details of their experience. As the children dictate, she records their ideas. Experience charts are usually written at the chalkboard, where corrections and changes can be made easily. If the children wish to have a permanent record of their experience, the story can be transferred from the chalkboard to a large sheet of paper. Ordinary newsprint, size 24" by 36", is recommended. If the chart is to be read from all parts of the room, the letters should be approximately three inches in height. If it is to be read by one individual at his desk, the letters should be about one-half inch in height. Manuscript writing can be used with large crayons, felt pens, or rubber letter stamps which can be purchased commercially. Some teachers like to make word, phrase, or sentence cards to accompany the experience charts. These can be made on heavy paper, such as tagboard. To add interest to this type of informal reading, children can be encouraged to prepare illustrations to accompany the stories which they have written. Illustrations are best placed at the top or bottom of the story or, as in dictionary charts, to the right side.

Special care must be taken in the preparation of experience charts. In the beginning they should be simple. Only a few sentences should be chosen for each story, and manuscript writing should be used. The teacher should understand that in her use of informal reading, she has little control of vocabulary which may be needed in preparation for the use of basal readers. She must be careful in selecting the vocabulary so that an adequate number of words, yet not too many, is introduced and repeated sufficiently so that mastery results. Wise control should be exercised over the introduction of new words, and use should be made of as many familiar words as possible. Basic words should be repeated frequently and a record should be kept of words taught.

Experience charts serve a valuable purpose in that they can be the result of social participation on the part of every child. They are based on the experiences of the group and provide children with an opportunity to summarize these common happenings and to make use of oral language. As a result, mental content is built up and each child has an opportunity to add many words to his speaking and reading vocabularies. The charts arouse interest and make the use of words in sentences meaningful because they have been based upon the children's own experiences. Reading is demonstrated as a left-to-right process and one which requires the reader to step down from the top, one line at a time. Surely, this is an important beginning. Debbie's teacher, as you will recall, made considerable use of informal reading as a means of developing many basic skills.

In addition to recording a shared trip, as suggested earlier in this chapter, the experience story can be used to describe any activity which is commonly carried on at school, at home, or in the community. An experience chart does not have to be in the form of a story. It can be a set of directions or even a list of words. It can report news items of interest to the children. It can contain a set of directions or a list of materials needed for carrying on an activity. It can list rules for playing or working together, for getting information, for crossing streets, or for keeping healthy. In other words, any experience of the children may serve as a basis for an experience chart.

Eventually a transition from experience stories to books will be necessary. Adequate preparation for this change is essential. Some teachers carefully examine the books to be introduced and determine the content, vocabulary, and background necessary for reading them. Once this has been accomplished, they control the making of experience stories so that concepts, background, and vocabulary directly related to the selected books are developed. Another procedure utilized by teachers is to make booklets by assembling a series of charts that tell an extended story. The children are assured of success as they read their first "books" because of their familiarity with the experience stories making up the booklets.

There are other procedures which can be effective in making this important transition. For example, some teachers prepare charts which are actually based on the content of the first book to be read. Still others read aloud from books and encourage the children to look at picture-story books about places and things with which they are familiar. Others tell stories to the children and permit them to listen to recordings of favorite stories in order to build mental content, enrich language, and arouse interest in books. All of these activities can help the teacher to make certain that the child's first attempts to read books will be enjoyable and successful. The achievement of this objective will do much to prevent failure which could handicap the child in his future adjustment to reading.

The *picture approach* is another means of informal approach to beginning reading. It gives the children an opportunity to associate a word with an object in a picture projected upon a chalkboard. In other words, a symbol or visual image is associated with another visual image. To be more specific, a picture of special interest to a group of children is projected upon the board. Free discussion is encouraged. Objects in the picture are identified and labeled in manuscript writing. The children are then asked to identify the words which the teacher uses in sentences. After this has been done, the current to the projector is switched off and the children are again asked to identify the words on the board. If difficulty is experienced, the current is turned on and the picture is restored. The children are then encouraged to tell a story concerning the picture. This story is written on the board and the pupils have an opportunity to read it. At this point, the teacher may emphasize phrase reading and the use of the words on the board in other sentences. Each sentence of the story can be reproduced on a separate strip of tagboard and, as a means of increasing visual discrimination, the pupils can match each sentence of the strip of paper with the corresponding sentence on the board. Later this same procedure can be used with phrases and with words.

This technique, modified and supplemented by filmstrips of interest to children at the first, second, and third grade levels, has been utilized in the New Castle plan of teaching beginning reading which is described later in Chapter 6. Pictures of local interest add greatly to the child's enthusiasm and understanding. Such a program provides a common background of experiences and mental content which is essential for the reading process. It aids the visually immature child by placing all required reading at chalkboard distance. Furthermore, the young child is able to avoid some of the complex muscular coordination involved in holding a book, turning pages, and keeping his place while reading. Teachers report that attention is increased because of a common center of interest for the entire group. This procedure can facilitate work with books by building the child's experiential background and vocabulary.

The Basal Reader Approach

In most school systems where the use of a series of basal readers is prescribed, a readiness book, several pre-primers, a primer, and several readers of increasing difficulty are employed in the elementary grades. The content of the books consists of experience stories, literary selections, informational articles, and recreational materials. In general, the stories in pre-primers and primers revolve around the home and community. Gradually the content of each successive book becomes broader and more complex, although there is continuity from book to book. Most basal readers make adequate use of beautiful illustrations, are written in an appealing and interesting style, and conform to acceptable standards. Criticism of basal readers has been directed chiefly toward the content of experience stories in the beginning books, on the ground that the stories do not depict life as it is actually lived in the child's community. Some criticisms directed against basal readers, however, are not justified and should be redirected toward the manner in which the basal reader is misused by uninformed and careless teachers who have not made adequate use of accompanying guidebooks.

There are many ways in which basal readers may be employed. Some teachers use one basal reader at a time, presenting the selections in the order in which they appear in the book, and giving practice in reading skills as suggested in the accompanying guidebook. Other teachers center their instruction around the interests of the children, around projects or units of work, and utilize several basal readers for developmental instruction and free reading. In general, the basal reader approach consists of (1) the development of readiness for reading by building appropriate concepts, introducing new words in meaningful context, and stimulating interest in the story to be read; (2) guided reading, which includes both oral and silent reading; (3) the practice of basic skills of word recognition and comprehension; and (4) activities to enrich and extend reading.

One of the advantages of the basal reader approach is that it introduces children directly to books. Many children, like Debbie, look forward to the time when they can read from a book. It is an important occasion and one which they do not wish to delay. In order to maintain this enthusiasm it is essential that the teacher plan well for the introduction and use of the beginning book in reading. In planning any class presentation, the teacher should know what she intends to accomplish, what material she intends to use, and how she plans to utilize materials in order to achieve her goals. Each story deserves a well-planned introduction which will create a desire on the part of the children to read it. The teacher can stimulate their interest by having them look at pictures, by encouraging discussion, and by anticipating the action and plot of the story. The teacher may permit her boys and girls to experience a feeling of leisure and to express their ideas as to what is about to happen. Background can be built up by discussion and by an interpretation of pictures. New words necessary to an understanding of the story can be presented. Only after an adequate introduction should pupils be encouraged to read. When the pupils are ready, they can read one sentence at a time and for the purpose of discovering answers to questions asked by the teacher. At the pre-primer level questions can be phrased so as to suggest the correct wording of the response. It is also advisable to permit children to read silently before they read aloud. If possible, the story should be completed during the class period and the teacher should make sure that each child experiences a degree of success and enjoys the satisfaction of real achievement. In all instances, the use of books should be a pleasurable adventure which will be eagerly anticipated again and again by the children.

The basal reader approach to beginning reading offers many advantages to the inexperienced teacher. The content of the books making up the series of the modern reader generally contains meanings that are familiar to the child and are based upon experiences and subjects which are of interest to young children. The careful control of vocabulary is another aspect of these books. The number of words, the methods by which they are introduced, and the number of repetitions are in accordance with generally accepted standards of initial instruction. Attempts are made to select words in the child's listening vocabulary and those which will be useful to him later in reading other books. The introduction of new words in the story and on each page has been carefully considered. In order to provide sufficient practice for word identification, each important word is repeated at spaced intervals throughout the text. In many series the vocabularies include words which are suitable for phonetic study at an elementary level.

Use of the basal reader should be carefully supervised. It is a tool with which the child learns to read, and it should not be used by him except under the direction of the teacher. Teachers and especially parents should understand the difference in function between the basic text and the supplementary text; that is, books for free and independent reading. Frequently a mother will insist that a basal reader be sent home so that she can "work" with her child and help him in his reading. Such a request, after a sympathetic explanation, should be refused. Books for free and independent reading, however, can be made available for use at home.

The methods and procedures proposed for the use of basic texts in reading should not overshadow the child's enjoyment of the interesting stories and poems making up the content of the books. The teacher's guidebook for any series of basal readers gives definite and specific guidance for classroom procedures with which every teacher of reading should be familiar. It cannot meet, however, all the contingencies nor can it provide satisfactory solutions for all of the problems encountered in the classroom. The teacher must recognize its limitations and adapt suggestions and procedures to the specific background, needs, and interests of the individuals in her group. Nevertheless it will provide excellent suggestions for the inexperienced teacher and can aid her in planning and carrying out a sound program of instruction. One use of teaching guides which should not be overlooked is in extending interests and experiences for children. Most guidebooks contain extensive bibliographies of appropriate materials. Use of these suggestions, along with careful observation and frequent consultation with each pupil, helps to promote wide reading and enables the individual to pursue his own special interest at his own ability level. As we have implied earlier in our discussion, guidebooks should be used wisely and discreetly. The teacher should be capable of creative planning and should not become solely dependent upon any technique or guide no matter how good it may be.

In an attempt to facilitate word study and provide an opportunity for children to make use of ideas gained through reading, some series of basal readers provide accompanying workbooks. When these are to be used, the teacher should carefully direct and supervise the activities of her pupils. This is necessary for, in some instances, the exercises may be so unfamiliar and complicated that immature children become uncertain and frustrated. In this state of mind they frequently learn and practice errors which should be avoided. The workbooks have been designed to serve a purpose and are not to be employed merely as a means of keeping children busy. Debbie's mature statement in regard to workbooks suggests that her teacher used them wisely. Debbie said, "I like the activity books. Our teacher says they tell her about each one of us and what we need to learn." Workbooks can provide the teacher with information which can be valuable to her as she plans her instructional procedures.

In general, there are two major types of workbooks being used by classroom teachers. Some accompany the basal reader series and provide supplementary training in vocabulary, comprehension, rate of reading, and work-study skills. Usually the drills are divided into work-type activities which are directly related to particular lessons in the reader. Other workbooks are published independently of any basal reading series. Some of these are general in nature while others concentrate on certain aspects of the reading program such as word recognition, phonetic analysis, comprehension, using the dictionary, and outlining. Both types of workbooks have been designed to measure achievement, to discover specific needs, and to provide practice in essential reading skills. Workbooks also provide children with an opportunity to study independently and to assume responsibility for their own achievement. Workbooks should never be used as a disciplinary measure or as a procedure for keeping children busy. It is inadvisable for a child to "go through" a workbook routinely. Instead it is suggested that the teacher have available several copies of a number of workbooks so that those activities which are appropriate to the needs of each child may be selected. In this way, the teacher can individualize her instruction. She should prepare the children for the proper use of the materials in the workbook by explaining the purposes and procedures in such a way that all pupils know what they are doing and why they are doing it. She should evaluate each child's performance promptly so that he can correct errors before they become habitual. Workbooks provide children with supplementary experiences and furnish the teacher with tangible evidence of the child's progress in certain aspects of reading.

Every teacher of reading should be able to evaluate basal readers. The following suggestions may serve as helpful criteria in judging the various series of readers which are available:

1. The content should be well balanced and organized around the interests and experiences of children. The stories should be carefully developed and expanded, beginning with experience stories and gradually leading to informational and recreational materials.
2. The style should be pleasing and natural and should contribute to the children's development of other language skills. The basal reader should be logically and psychologically developmental in nature and should contribute to the creativity of the teacher.
3. Beginning stories should be interesting in terms of plot, characterization, action, humor, and surprise.
4. The increase in difficulty level should be gradual. In the beginning, sentences and paragraphs should be short, simple, and direct. The vocabulary should be carefully controlled so that only a limited number of new words are introduced on each page and in each book. Adequate repetition of words in meaningful context is essential.
5. Mechanical aspects of the book, such as the size of type, width of mar-

gins, color and quality of paper, as well as the size and binding of the book, should conform to accepted standards.

6. The book should be attractive to the child. The cover design should be meaningful, and illustrations should be appropriate and correctly placed with reference to the related context. In beginning books, the illustrations should be simple and large and should provide picture clues for identifying words.

Teachers should have standards such as the following by which to evaluate workbooks:

1. Workbooks should be useful. They should provide numerous exercises for practice of specific reading and thinking skills. The exercises should be challenging and should become increasingly difficult from book to book.
2. Simple and clear directions and illustrations should be provided so that all children may understand what they are to do.
3. The vocabulary should correspond to that of the reader with which the workbook is to be used.
4. The content should lend itself to diagnosis and evaluation of the child's performance.
5. The workbook should be attractive and appealing to children and should meet accepted standards in terms of size of type, spacing, quality of paper and binding, space for pupil responses, and quality of printing.

Careful consideration should be paid to the teacher's guidebooks which accompany basal readers and workbooks.

1. The aims, materials, and procedures suggested should be clear and understandable and should conform to worthwhile standards of teaching. The steps in the teaching process should not be too rigid and should contribute to creativity on the part of the teacher.
2. The guidebooks should be easy to use with adequate headings and few cross references to other pages. They should contain a usable table of contents and index.
3. These books should simplify the work of the teacher and should not be verbose or too detailed.
4. They should provide flexibility in methods so that the teacher can take care of individual differences and needs.

The Combination Approach to Beginning Reading

According to some authorities, the trend in reading instruction is toward a combined experience-book approach in which simultaneous use is made of experience charts, basal readers, story books, and children's weekly and monthly publications. Most of the reading material selected for the primary grades is of narrative type and is utilized for both recreational and study-type reading. The teacher does not necessarily differentiate between the basal reader and supplementary materials. Many books are used and are selected because they help to develop needed skills and techniques. One of the advantages of the combined approach is that it lends itself to flexibility. Different books can be used with different individuals and different groups. For example, a simple book can be selected for children who are having difficulty in reading. At the same time a higher level book can be assigned to the better readers. Children are given ample opportunity to read many books and are permitted to progress from book to book as rapidly as their ability permits. If this approach is to be adopted by a school system, it is advisable for the primary grades to purchase several copies of each of the leading series of basal readers as well as many well-chosen, interesting story books which cover a wide range of subject matter and are representative of various levels of difficulty. These should be lodged in a central place in the school where each teacher can select books on the basis of the needs, abilities, and interests of her pupils. The combined approach also makes use of experience charts as a means of building vocabulary, developing concepts, and relating reading to other language arts.

In general, the first step in the combined experience-book approach is to develop background for reading. This can be accomplished in many ways, by engaging the children in purposeful discussion, by encouraging the writing of experience stories, and by introducing activities directly related to the content of the story to be read. The second step is to help the children develop concepts necessary for an understanding of the new words in the story. Here again the teacher can make use of experience charts in showing the students how to identify and understand the meanings of words. The third step is to develop interest in the story and a purpose for reading it. This can be done by encouraging the children to read the title, to look at the pictures, and to discuss what they think the story will tell. The fourth step consists in permitting each child to read the story silently and to follow this silent reading by discussion and oral reading.

The combination method requires an understanding of children, skillful teaching techniques, and a broad acquaintance with children's literature. To use this method successfully, the teacher must be able to select and utilize the right materials at the right time and be able to provide systematic instruction in basic reading techniques. Above all, she must be constantly aware and cognizant of the readiness, interests, abilities, and skills of her children.

Meeting Individual Differences

The teacher of beginning reading must know how to deal with the individual differences of her pupils no matter which approach she uses. In order to accomplish this objective it will be necessary for the teacher to utilize all sources of information which are available to her. Many teachers believe that they are well acquainted with their pupils and yet when asked for specific information concerning a child in their class, they are unable to provide valid and reliable data. Facts must be gathered first so that inferences may be established later. Careful observations are necessary if the teacher is to determine the reading needs of her children, select materials in accordance with their interests and reading levels, and help pupils adjust to the world in which they live.

In Chapter 2 the reader has been shown some of the physical, psychological, and environmental factors which may affect the reading performance of the individual. The reader has had an opportunity to become acquainted with some of the conditions she should look for in the study of the child. As the teacher lives day after day with children in the classroom, incidents will occur which may indicate and suggest interests, needs, and problems of the pupils which should not be neglected. The capable teacher will have the human concern of the parent for his child and at the same time the objective attitude of the laboratory technician. She will not only sense the significance of her observations but will appreciate the value of recording them in a more or less permanent form. Much reliable information can be summarized in cumulative records and later utilized by other teachers. In each instance, however, the teacher should make her own observations and arrive at her own conclusions without being affected by the opinions of others.

Use of Anecdotal Records

The anecdotal record can be used by the teacher as a means of gathering specific information regarding each child in her classroom. It is a short report of a single incident of behavior which suggests an inference of value in studying a child. It generally consists of a brief statement of fact, an interpretation of this fact, and a summary of action taken in dealing with the situation.

In order to make effective use of anecdotal records in the observation and study of children, teachers should differentiate between facts and inferences. Facts can be verified by observations; an inference, however, is a logical conclusion based upon supporting facts. The following illustration may make this differentiation clear.

January 27, 1961

Debbie   2A

Observation of Fact
Debbie has a grade score of 3.2 on an objective measure of reading achievement. Her mother reports that Debbie frequently plays school and that her daughter helps children to read as she plays teacher.

Inference
Debbie may be able to serve as a group leader.

Summary of Action
Debbie has been asked to serve as a group leader. She has been successful and is well liked by her associates.

From a study of this anecdotal record, it is apparent that observations were made, inferences were established, and action was taken. This account of an incident in Debbie's history may be of value to other teachers who will be concerned with her instructional problems and guidance.

Using Objective Measures

Evidences of growth and the reading levels of children can be determined by standardized tests. Measures of both oral and silent reading can be used to advantage in evaluating the achievement of elementary pupils. Oral reading tests can be employed not only to measure oral reading ability, but, in individual cases, to identify reading errors and to appraise word attack skills. Furthermore, in the case of older students, these tests may be used in determining the highest reading level at which the individual can read with full understanding and with freedom from mechanical difficulties. This level is frequently spoken of as the individual's independent reading level.[1] Oral reading tests may also be utilized in securing the student's level of frustration. This is the level at which he is thwarted or baffled by the vocabulary and the sentence structure of the reading material. After the teacher has determined the independent reading level and the frustration level of the pupil, it is possible to anticipate his instructional level, for this should fall below his level

[1] Emmett A. Betts, *Foundations of Reading Instruction* (New York: American Book Co., 1957), chap. 21.

of frustration. For example, when Debbie was eight months in the first grade her independent reading level was that of a first grader and her frustration level was that of a third grader. Obviously then, her instructional level would be that of a little girl in the second grade even though her performance on a silent reading test was that of a child two months in the third grade. In support of these inferences, reading clinicians have observed that scores on standardized measures of reading ability closely approximate the frustration level of the child tested. *The Gilmore Oral Reading Test* and the *Gray Standardized Oral Reading Paragraphs Test* are satisfactory instruments for the teacher who can work with the individual for the purpose of identifying his disabilities and levels of attainment. These tests, like most tests, can be employed as tools to accomplish a specific purpose. They are not intended as adequate measures of all aspects of reading.

Standardized tests in reading can be justified for purposes of survey and research. Some teachers use them to identify pupils above and below an arbitrarily chosen point of reference who may be in need of guidance or corrective treatment. Other teachers use data resulting from tests to determine the grade levels of their students so as to select and adjust materials to the requirements of the individual. The use of objective measures in some teaching situations can be questioned, for there is a tendency to emphasize average group performance and to neglect the differences of achievement that exist within a class. Some teachers are proud of the fact that the average of their class is up to standard and ignore the needs of their pupils at both extremes. Test scores are wisely interpreted when they are considered along with data resulting from observations and histories of individual children.

If tests are to be administered, scored, and interpreted by the teacher, careful preparation on her part is required. Manuals accompanying the tests should be studied thoroughly and directions followed precisely, for if modifications are made in administrative procedures, existing norms cannot be used correctly in the interpretation of results. At the end of this chapter, questions and parallel references refer to standard professional texts dealing with the selection, administration, scoring, and interpretation of tests which may be utilized by teachers of beginning reading.

In order to provide for the individual differences of children, the use of observations, school histories in the form of anecdotal records, and test scores have been discussed. Through these procedures the teacher can become aware of the great diversity of needs, interests, and aptitudes on the part of her boys and girls. The conscientious teacher will then want to adjust aims, materials, and procedures so as to provide adequate instruction for each child. The problem is, how can this be accomplished?

Grouping of Children

As the first grade teacher becomes acquainted with her children, she will discover that many are not ready for reading experiences even though they have spent one year in the kindergarten and have met the age requirement for the grade. Some children need help in developing a readiness for reading. Some are ready for informal reading activities and a few, perhaps not more than five or six, are mature enough for experiences with a basal reader and even supplementary materials. It is the teacher's problem to meet these needs with a minimal expenditure of time and effort. In some school systems an attempt is made to reduce extent and range of reading needs by grouping children according to mental maturity. Such groups are often labeled X, Y, and Z. According to this multiple-track plan, group X is composed of the most intelligent children; group Y, the average; and group Z, the less intelligent. Still another attempt to reduce reading needs is accomplished by grouping children according to reading levels as indicated by tests. Both of these attempts to secure homogeneity of needs of children have their advantages and disadvantages. After each plan has been placed in operation, however, there still remains a wide range of ability and diversity of individual reading needs. There is also the possibility of a stigma accompanying both forms of segregation. Many authorities object to what they label the undemocratic practice of grouping children in reading because of the caste system it seems to create. Frequently pupils in the slow-moving group are labeled "dumb" by their associates in the average and in the more elite and fast-moving groups.

It is possible, however, to use a *flexible grouping plan* to adjust aims, materials, and procedures to the needs of children and at the same time avoid most of the disadvantages of ability and achievement grouping. In using flexible grouping, teachers assign pupils temporarily to groups on the basis of their reading needs, the objectives to be accomplished, and the interests of the children themselves. Small groups of boys and girls working together make it possible for materials and activities to be selected so as to meet the needs of the individual pupil. Individual participation is encouraged in small groups, and there is greater opportunity for the child to grow and develop at his own rate. Grouping enables the child and teacher to become better acquainted. Small groups provide a social climate in which children are stimulated to greater effort and yet are not discouraged by the reading performance of others. As the interests and needs of the children change, new groups are formed to accomplish new objectives. Some groups may maintain their identity for only a few days while others may function for several weeks. Flexible grouping is one way of taking care of the instructional needs of students. It has many advantages and some disadvantages. Various forms of grouping will be discussed in Chapter 6, and the teacher should become acquainted with the merits of the different plans.

An adequate amount of time should be planned for group activities in reading. At least 45 minutes are generally required for the activities of two or three groups. Work time within each group is dependent upon the interest and attention displayed by the children. If two or three groups are working simultaneously, it may be necessary to make use of group leaders who can give help to those needing assistance. This aids in the development of leadership. Furthermore, the help of these more mature children will be greatly appreciated by the teacher who is operating this group plan.

Some teachers may experience difficulty in managing several groups simultaneously. This may be due to the teacher's inadequate control of the children, their faulty work habits, or to a lack of careful planning by both teacher and pupils. Occasionally the teacher will find a child who cannot work well in a group. This may be due to mental or emotional immaturity or to personality deviations requiring psychological and in some cases medical aid. Such cases should be discussed with the school nurse and principal. Anecdotal records may be of value in these conferences.

Some teachers are able to *individualize* their reading instruction by a modification of the flexible grouping plan. For example, in a class of thirty-two children, twelve boys and girls may be doing free reading using books of their own selection. In another group six pupils may be listening quietly to the seventh child, who is reading orally to them. A group of eight may be planning an illustration for an experience story previously dictated by the group during an informal reading period. The teacher, meanwhile, is focusing her attention upon the activities of five children who are seated near her in a corner of the room. These boys and girls have been selected because three need individual help in word recognition and because two require aid in sentence reading. Each child confers with his teacher alone while the remaining four read silently or engage in other directed activities. This plan of individualized teaching makes it possible for each of the thirty-two children to meet at least once each week with his teacher. Careful planning in cooperation with the children makes this combination group and individualized procedure quite effective.

Word Study During Beginning Reading

Vocabulary growth is dependent upon the child's background and experience. There are four types of vocabulary: listening, speaking, reading, and writing. When children enter school, they generally have two vocabularies. Their listening vocabulary, which is the result of their home environment, is quite large, whereas their speaking vocabulary is usually much smaller. It is the responsibility of the teacher to help develop a reading vocabulary and to expand the meaning of words in daily use. As children come in contact with new words on objects in the classroom, on the chalkboard, on the bulletin board, and in books, they are confronted with the problem of their *identification* and their *interpretation*. These processes should not be separated in the instructional program. In discussing these aspects of word study, some writers use the terms "word-attack skills" and "word-comprehension skills." Both of these forms of word study will be discussed in Chapter 5.

In the meantime, a more general program of word study will be considered which will make use of both word-attack skills and word-comprehension skills during this period of beginning reading. Children at this level can be introduced to color, number, and action words. They can have the experience of matching objects and pictures with words. Boys and girls enjoy word games and like to identify likenesses and differences in sounds as well as in printed forms. They can be taught to observe plural forms of words and later they can be shown how to use children's dictionaries and how to follow written directions on how to cut, color, draw, and construct. As pupils establish more mental content, picture and contextual clues can be introduced.

Picture clues are used to emphasize the relationship between a word and the object represented by the word. It has already been suggested in this chapter that pictures of interest to children can be projected upon the chalkboard, discussed by the group, and used to associate word symbols with actual objects. In this manner picture clues can be used with older students and, in the process of group discussion, mental content can be developed. Pictures have a stimulating effect upon the child and aid him in recognizing and interpreting words, phrases, and sentences. The construction of picture dictionaries by the children has been found to be beneficial in vocabulary development. During the period of beginning reading children depend largely on pictures to secure meaning but in later stages rely less upon them and begin to use contextual clues.

Contextual clues are suggestions of meaning provided by the use of words in their natural setting. Observe, for example, this sentence in which the final word may be difficult for a child to identify.

Mother put the car in the garage.

From the child's mental content, which has resulted from his previous experiences and from his familiarity with the other words in the sentence, he is able to make use of the suggested clue and properly recognize the unfamiliar word. On the other hand, if the child lives in the southwestern part of the United States he may erroneously identify the underlined word as *carport*. This illustration shows that young children cannot be expected to make effective use of contextual clues as the only means of recognizing unfamiliar words. In general, this method of word attack is used most effectively by the more mature reader and in combination with other word-attack skills.

Language-rhythm clues can be utilized by young children in their identification of new words. Not only are unfamiliar words recognized but meaning may be established as well. This is accomplished through a feeling for the rhythm of language in such associated words as *high* and *low, up* and *down, far* and *near,* or in a series of numbers in their proper sequence. Dramatizations and expressive movements can be helpful in the use of language-rhythm clues. Poems which appeal to children can be utilized to develop the meaning of words and to establish new meanings through imagery. Meaning is developed by an integration of visual-auditory-kinesthetic impressions. Ideas can become more meaningful to young children because of the association of these images. Finger plays such as the following combine all three modalities and express movement and rhythm.

> This little pig went to market.
> This little pig stayed home.
> This little pig had roast beef.
> This little pig had none.
> This little pig cried wee, wee, wee all the way home.

Configuration clues may be helpful to children in the identification of words during the period of beginning reading. This type of aid gives the reader a visual attack on the word form itself. The child is primarily concerned with the general pattern of the word and not with a phonetic analysis of its parts. Visual discrimination between high and low letters and their placement in the word pattern is an essential factor in the recognition of these clues. For example, in observing the differences between the names Wendy and Debbie, one notes that two of the letters in "Wendy" are above the line with one below, whereas in the word "Debbie" three letters are above the line. This emphasis upon likenesses and differences is important in both word discrimination and pronounciation. Configuration clues, however, should be used along with other means of word identification.

It is obvious then that children who are beginning to read may be taught four aids, or clues, to word recognition: picture, contextual, language-rhythm, and configuration clues. Use of these aids can continue until the child is sufficiently mature and ready for phonetic and structural analysis of words in later reading activities.

In the development of an adequate initial sight vocabulary both the informal and basal reader approaches have been suggested for use during the period of beginning reading. A well-planned and balanced reading program will make use of these approaches simultaneously as children progress from the primer stage through first readers, to second readers, and into third readers. Sight vocabularies should grow continuously so that boys and girls will not become frustrated by a mass of unfamiliar symbols. Many repetitions of the basic words should be provided so that the child may attain a mastery of them. This reteaching must be challenging, purposeful, and interesting both to the instructor and to her pupils. Surely, words most frequently met in context will be those most rapidly and easily mastered. Words repeatedly used in sentences, on the chalkboard, in workbooks, and in carefully selected basic readers give the child more and more meaningful associations and consequently further clues for immediate recall. Other clues may be established by careful observation of the visual details of a word. Children can be taught to discriminate, to compare, and to contrast word forms and especially words that begin or end in a similar manner. They can also observe the visual details of word patterns in a left to right sequence. Furthermore, children can be taught to associate both sound and meaning with the word form. This can be accomplished if the printed word is shown to the child as the spoken word is used in a meaningful situation. These fundamental concepts essential to the teaching of reading are an integral part of most basic reading programs. As the inexperienced teacher follows these programs, step by step, she soon learns to appreciate the aid which they provide and the psychological principles upon which they are based. In brief, she grows professionally as her children grow in their ability to read.

Developing Ability to Interpret

Children like Debbie want to know what books have to say. They want to understand "the talk that is written down." Effectiveness of interpretation is dependent upon the child's ability to make use of mental content resulting from his previous experiences. Teachers can provide children with the opportunity to acquire the background necessary for the interpretation of new words and ideas before these are actually encountered in reading situations. Sometimes this can be accomplished by well-planned trips and activities which can furnish adequate background for reading. Audio-visual materials, such as films, slides, and filmstrips can provide vicarious experiences essential to the understanding of some reading materials. A display of pictures, interesting objects, and small animals can be used in preparing the group for the introduction of a new book or story. A question, the answer to which may be found in the reading of the story, provides purpose and stimulates interest. Unusual or difficult words may be written on the board and explained. In doing this, the teacher should emphasize meaning rather than form of words.

In the beginning, and certainly for some pupils, it may be necessary for the teacher to ask factual and interpretative questions as the child reads sentences, paragraphs, parts of the story, and later the whole story. *What* and *why* questions are of marked value, for some children have difficulty in attaching meanings to thought units of increasing length. This is frequently due to the fact that these boys and girls are merely reading words without a well-defined purpose. Good questions clarify the reading goals, and as the children become more mature they can be taught to ask their own questions and to read for the answers. This activity can be encouraged at all levels.

Class discussion of the story can contribute to its understanding. Special attention can be given to the *why* and *how* questions asked by children. Frequently a child may be referred to his book in order to verify his facts or for the purpose of seeking more information. When these data are available, he should have an opportunity to present them to the group. Meanings of words can be discussed along with situations in the story which, for some, were not clearly understood. Class discussions can lead to further activity, such as the oral reading of certain interesting and dramatic parts of the story, actual dramatization during another class period, illustration of announcements, word study, and other productive activities.

In general, teachers can develop the interpretative skills of their pupils by preparing carefully for the introduction of every new story. They can aid in the interpretation of the story by guiding the reading of their boys and girls by questions and, when necessary, by rereading to verify facts and to secure new information. They can extend the skills and abilities of their children by further development of word-attack skills, meeting individual needs, and by the systematic use of well-chosen supplementary books. Furthermore, teachers can extend the interest of growing readers by introducing new materials requiring the application of skills previously developed. Literary elements can be discussed so as to expand and deepen an appreciation of literature. Creative art activities can result in additional interest and genuine satisfaction.

The activities of the classroom and school can stimulate an interest in reading. In utilizing these activities the bulletin board can be made a focal center for directions for work, games, and classroom activities. Interesting announcements can be posted along with letters to and from friends. Announcements of selected television programs of special interest to children can be displayed. Some teachers have made use of directions of how to make toys and how to feed and care for small animals and fish. Diaries of actual experiences not only furnish interesting reading but also provide recognition for those children who were willing to write of their trips and unusual adventures. Original stories can be posted and the attention of the group can be directed to their merit. School schedules, special events, and holidays can be listed so as to be of interest to young readers. Excursions for the class can be announced and later these trips can be described in detail. In these ways the bulletin board can become immediately a focal point of attention for each child. It is but one of the many ways of stimulating interest and, of course, it can contribute to interpretative reading.

The Primary School Curriculum

In the primary grades, the total program of daily activities furnishes a meaningful background for learning to read, to write, to speak, and to listen. Little, if any, differentiation is made between the various aspects of communication. Each is utilized to enhance the development of the others. For the beginning pupil, storytelling and reading aloud are prominent activities and are of special value because they encourage thoughtful listening, build background, acquaint children with good literature, and provide examples of acceptable language. Reporting of experiences, answering of questions, and dramatizations of stories are examples of activities in which beginners may participate. During the first year the teacher stimulates interest in writing by showing the children how to copy their names and by encouraging them to write their names on their papers and drawings. In time the children learn to label pictures and to write simple stories of their own. By means of experience charts they learn about sentences, when to use capital letters, periods, and question marks. Experience in reading, writing, and spelling can also be provided by having the children prepare simple picture dictionaries of their own. Trips to local places of interest and projects in which the children assume the roles of community workers are other examples of activities which contribute to background and provide opportunities to speak, to listen, and to write. Sharing with the class stories they have read and reading parts of a favorite story aloud are other procedures which form a major part of the first year's program. The use of signs and labels in the room and the posting of simple messages on the bulletin board are ways in which first grade teachers attempt to make reading a functional tool in the classroom.

In the second and third grades the language arts program can be centered around a theme such as Pets, Health, Weather, or Our Friends. Children can be encouraged to do "research in these areas" by writing for information, reading many books, and answering specific questions. They can learn to use the resources of the library, to give short oral reports, and to listen to the findings of others in the class. Work-type reading can be developed through the use of story books, subject texts, and juvenile periodicals. The children's reading can be guided by directed study assignments, by questions on the board, or by prepared lesson outlines. The children can discuss with others in the group the information which they have obtained from reading. These are but a few of the ways by which the alert teacher can determine how well the children are using reading as a tool in thinking.

In the primary grades the teacher should encourage the children to discuss stories both before and after reading them. Vocabulary, mental content, and interest are thus developed, and the children are encouraged to read for a purpose and to think as they read. For example, one teacher, whose children were reading a story about pets, stimulated interest by having the children tell about their own pets, why they liked them, and how they cared for them. The bulletin board was used to display pictures and names of animal pets. The children talked about the animals in their picture-story book and volunteered their opinions as to what the story would tell. After the story was read, a lively discussion followed when the teacher asked such questions as "Why do you think Tom took the kitten home?" "What do you think might have happened if Tom had not seen the kitten?" Later the teacher and pupils summarized their ideas on the board and the children had an additional reading experience.

Another teacher encouraged her students to read for the purpose of finding a suitable story for dramatization. When a child found one which he believed would be satisfactory, he told the story to the class. This was followed by a discussion as to whether or not the children would like to dramatize it. Another teacher encouraged her children to write letters to the pupils who were absent because of illness. The children discussed ideas for their letters and the teacher listed them on the board. Then each child wrote his letter and later read it to the class before mailing it. In this way, the children learned to spell words and learned about sentences, paragraphs, the use of capital letters, and punctuation marks.

Another teacher planned a daily story period during which time she read folk tales, fairy stories, and poetry aloud. This provided the children with a demonstration of oral reading at its best and with an opportunity to listen and to enlarge their oral vocabularies.

By now, it should be obvious that there are many ways in which reading can be related to speaking, writing, and listening. Clever primary teachers will create opportunities to utilize these and other procedures as they attempt to promote growth in all phases of the language arts. These activities make up the primary school curriculum.

Sequence of Steps in Beginning Reading

Some authorities in the field of education recommend the following sequential order of instructional procedures which may be employed by teachers of beginning reading but which are equally applicable at later grade levels.

1. Aid the child in building concepts and mental content for the materials to be read.
2. Arouse anticipatory response, suggesting what may be found. If materials are to be presented informally, encourage children to tell of a common experience. Transcribe ideas of children into short sentences in manuscript writing on a chalkboard.
3. Encourage children to identify sentences and phrases, having them say the words as they look at them.
4. Encourage children to read silently to discover facts, to locate information, and to find answers to questions. Have children prove statements by reading orally.
5. Develop independence for word attack and word comprehension by means of configuration clues, contextual clues, and structural and phonetic analysis.
6. Encourage children to read for pleasure by helping them develop an interest in books. Audience reading begins here.
7. Aid children in developing initial work-study skills such as reading for information and making use of dictionaries.
8. Start the development of critical reading by having the children give their reactions to the materials they have read.

Anticipated Achievement

Teachers cannot expect uniformity in reading performance. Some children, like Debbie, learn rapidly while others progress slowly. A slow learner may spend most of the first year in developing a readiness for reading while a few boys and girls may require two years to achieve what typical learners accomplish in one year. Studies [2] show that these children seldom profit by retention in the same grade for another year. Instead it is common practice to send them on to the next grade and expect the teacher to meet their instructional needs. This plan of automatic or social promotion places added responsibility upon the teacher because of the extended range of reading levels within her group. For example, a teacher of the second grade may find it necessary to aid some of her pupils in developing a readiness for reading. Some of her children may be reading at the first grade level while others will need instruction at the second grade level. Some will be reading third grade materials while a few may be reading from books generally used in the fourth and fifth grades. This wide range of reading achievement within a group is found in elementary schools, high schools, and colleges and necessitates readiness on the part

[2] Grace Arthur, "A Study of the Achievement of Sixty Grade I Repeaters as Compared with That of Non-Repeaters of the Same Mental Age," *Journal of Experimental Education*, 5:203–205.

of the teacher to meet the instructional needs of all her pupils, not merely those whose achievement is that of the grade she is teaching.

Even though each child is expected to progress according to his own abilities and background, the reading skills of typical children in the second year of their training can be evaluated and described. In fact, these boys and girls, like Debbie, show most of the following achievements:

1. They can read and understand simple stories and can answer questions concerning details.
2. They can locate these stories when given page and title.
3. They use activity books effectively and without detailed supervision.
4. These children enjoy reading in audience situations and are proud of their ability to hold the attention of their associates.
5. They can identify and interpret approximately 200–400 of the most common words.
6. They are aware of the differences and similarities in words and demonstrate initial forms of word analysis.
7. They make use of contextual clues.
8. They enjoy reading books and materials other than those found in the classroom.
9. The more mature children actually make use of their reading skills in gathering information for group projects and for purposes of their own.

Making Use of Supplementary Readers

Well-prepared supplementary readers can be used effectively by teachers at all levels notwithstanding their commitments to either the informal or the basic reader approach. In any grade the teacher can expect to find a wide range of achievement. For example, in the sixth grade the reading levels of the children may vary from the second to the ninth grade and obviously no one book can be adequate for all. The instructional level of each individual can be determined by standardized tests or evaluated by informal inventories. Then, with the interest level of the child in mind, supplementary readers can be selected and utilized to marked advantage.

Many reader series have been misused by teachers who have made them the whole reading program instead of employing them as a part of it. Both supplementary and basic readers have been misapplied by teachers to children who, because of their interest and reading levels, were unable to make effective use of them. This malpractice in the public schools will not continue when teachers become better informed as to the reading needs of their children. Supplementary readers are efficient tools which are planned to meet these needs. They are an essential part of the reading program. The reader series provides those teachers who know the books well a view of their responsibilities for reading growth and a storehouse of materials designed to extend the reading interests and to whet the child's appetite for further reading.

Teachers who emphasize the development of specific reading skills can make use of supplementary readers as they work with children in flexible groups and in *individualized* reading programs. There need not be "high" groups and "low" groups but instead groups of boys and girls reading various materials with differing purposes and interests. There can be regular preparation of new vocabularies and systematic development of techniques for the determination of meaning with a gradual increase in the difficulty of materials presented to the children. There can be a common pool of essential words which can become the basis of word analysis. As adequate skills are acquired, children can be encouraged to apply them to the materials of their own choosing. In this manner the supplementary reader can be a means of bridging the gap between the systematized instruction of the classroom and independent reading.

Well-prepared supplementary readers can contribute to the creativity [3] of the teacher. If both the teacher and the student are to be creative, adequate tools and materials are essential. These minimal requirements are provided by the supplementary reader, which can be used as a means of differentiating instruction by teachers at various levels of professional competence. The ability to read critically and evaluate information can be stressed. Furthermore, supplementary readers can be employed as a means of developing background and mental content and not merely as a classroom exercise. They can be a part of a well-planned reading program and their effectiveness as such is dependent upon the teacher. The reading series can provide procedures for teaching the student new skills and helping him to apply previously acquired skills as he reads new and interesting material. The child's horizons are extended. If the teacher in any educational environment is dominated by supervisory influences or restricted to the use of a single text, there can be little originality. Creativity can be fostered by the teacher who possesses understanding of the sequential development of basic reading skills and freedom to improvise and to use supplementary reading materials.

Guided Activities

1. Show how Debbie's experiences in the kindergarten prepared her for reading.
2. Choose one of the following topics to discuss in a ten-minute talk:
    a. Kindergarten experiences that contribute to reading readiness.
    b. Criteria by which a teacher can determine a child's ability to read printed symbols.

[3] Harold H. Anderson (ed.), *Creativity and Its Cultivation* (New York: Harper & Bros., 1959).

Children can learn to work alone and in groups.

In order to group effectively, furniture must be movable.

Learning is an active process requiring freedom of movement.

    c. Procedures for developing a background of concepts.

    d. Establishment of real and worthy purposes for reading.

    e. The place of comic books in reading.

3. Secure the teacher's guidebooks for a basic reading series. Outline the basic word perception and interpretation skills developed in them.

4. Visit a children's library. Make a list of children's books appropriate for the beginning reading stage.

5. Write a short article on ways to meet individual differences in beginning reading.

6. Take a team of four observers to visit a first-grade classroom. Have each member of the team report the following:

    a. The teacher's objectives in the particular reading lesson observed.

    b. The activities engaged in by the children.

    c. The classroom environment and its effect on reading.

    d. Reading materials in the classroom.

7. Consult the guidebooks that accompany three series of basal readers. First determine how they are alike and then try to discover how they differ.

8. Use a file of 5" x 8" cards to make the following records:

    a. Describe some of the procedures for developing background and mental content preparatory for beginning reading.

    b. List the objectives of beginning reading.

    c. Outline the criteria which should be considered in selecting materials for recreational reading.

    d. Describe methods of teaching children how to attack words which are unfamiliar to them.

9. Observe a teacher and a group of children develop an experience chart. Evaluate the activity in terms of the principles set forth in this chapter.

Questions and References

Questions	References
1. How can teachers develop skill in teaching new words?	1. Dawson, Mildred A., and Henry A. Bamman. *Fundamentals of Basic Reading Instruction,* Chap. 6. New York: Longmans, Green and Co., 1959. Hester, Kathleen B. *Teaching Every Child to Read,* Chap. 11. New York: Harper & Bros., 1955. Russell, David H. *Children Learn to Read,* Chap. 9. Boston: Ginn and Co., 1961.
2. How can teachers provide direct reading instruction for primary children?	2. McKim, Margaret G. *Guiding Growth in Reading,* Chap. VII. New York: Macmillan Co., 1955.

Questions	References
3. What are some characteristics of an effective reading program?	3. Durrell, Donald D. *Improving Reading Instruction,* Chap. 2. New York: World Book Co., 1956.
4. What are the fundamentals of reading in the first, second, and third grades?	4. McKee, Paul. *The Teaching of Reading in the Elementary School,* Chaps. 8, 9, 10. Boston: Houghton Mifflin Co., 1948.
5. How can teachers develop basic reading abilities?	5. Betts, Emmett A. *Foundations of Reading Instruction,* Chap. XXIII. New York: American Book Co., 1957.
6. What are the goals of reading instruction?	6. *Ibid.,* Chap. VII.
	Burton, William H. *Reading in Child Development,* Chap. 5. Indianapolis: Bobbs-Merrill Co., 1956.
7. How can teachers direct the reading activities of their children?	7. Betts. *op. cit.,* Chap. XXII.
8. How can word comprehension skills be developed?	8. Dawson and Bamman. *op. cit.,* Chap. 7.
9. What is the function of oral reading?	9. *Ibid.,* Chap. 9.
	Durrell. *op. cit.,* Chap. 8.
10. What are the first steps in learning to read?	10. McKim. *op. cit.,* Chap. V.
11. How can the teacher prepare the child for beginning reading?	11. McKee. *op. cit.,* Chap. 7.

12. Why is interpretation so important in the reading process?

12. Monroe, Marion. *Growing Into Reading*, Chap. 7. Chicago: Scott, Foresman and Co., 1951.

13. How does the art of reading develop?

13. Strang, Ruth, and Dorothy K. Bracken. *Making Better Readers*, Chap. 1. Boston: D. C. Heath and Co., 1957.

14. What part does reading play in the primary grades?

14. Hildreth, Gertrude. *Teaching Reading*, Chaps. 10, 11, 12, 14. New York: Holt & Co., 1958.

15. What tests will the teacher of beginning reading find of value in measuring the achievement of her boys and girls?

15. Dawson and Bamman. *op. cit.*, pp. 263–265 and Appendix B.

16. What is the New Castle approach to reading?

16. McCracken, Glenn. "The New Castle Reading Experiment—A Terminal Report," *Elementary English* (January, 1953), 30:13–21.

McCracken, Glenn. "The New Castle Reading Experiment," *Elementary School Journal*, March, 1954.

McCracken, Glenn. "We Must Modernize Reading Instruction," *The Reading Teacher* (December, 1954), 8:100–106.

McCracken, Glenn. "The New Castle Reading Experiment, A Progress Report," *The Reading Teacher* (April, 1956), 9:241–244.

5

VOCABULARY BUILDING

A useful, functional vocabulary is essential to the development of reading proficiency. In the beginning stages of reading, the child builds up a basic sight vocabulary which provides a foundation for other aspects of vocabulary development. During the period of expanding power, the child needs to develop and extend his skills in attacking words independently. He must grow into a versatile and independent reader so as to become proficient in different subject fields. Versatility and independence in reading are to a large degree dependent upon the quantity and quality of one's storehouse of words. Hildreth [1] has shown that by the end of the second grade more than half of the words in the typical child's vocabulary have been permanently mastered. By the end of the third grade, 80 per cent of the words have been permanently learned, and by the end of the fourth grade 95 per cent or more of the words are entirely familiar. Hildreth further shows that the average learner has a "bank" of 200–400 words by the end of the first grade, 800–1200 words by the end of the second grade, 1500–2000 words by the end of the third grade, and 2800–3000 by the end of the fourth grade. The typical student's vocabulary continues to enlarge until by the end of the high school period it reaches some 10,000 words. Surely, the child's knowledge of words contributes to his ability to think and to communicate. The development of an adequate vocabulary is an important aspect of the teaching of reading and is far more difficult to achieve than many teachers assume.

It is the purpose of this chapter to show how word-attack and word-comprehension skills may be developed and further extended as the child proceeds in school. As a beginning, the reader may be interested in Otto and his adventures with words.

Otto Learns How to Study Words

"I always have trouble with words," exclaimed Otto as he began a conference with his sixth grade teacher. "Reading and spelling have always

[1] Gertrude Hildreth, *Teaching Reading* (New York: Holt and Co., 1959), pp. 98–99.

been my poorest subjects. I guess it is because I have heard so much German both at home and when we were overseas," he continued, and then he added, "Dad says this is nonsense."

"I've been talking to some of your former teachers and studying your school records. They indicate that you have difficulty in reading but that you seem to enjoy books," his teacher commented.

"I do like to read comics and easy stories but even the words in these books bother me. I try to use a dictionary, but I guess I don't know how. It takes me so long to find the word. When I tried to use the telephone directory the other day, I hunted and hunted for the Mead Bicycle Shop. Finally I got sore and called Information," Otto told his teacher, apparently in disgust.

In an interview with the teacher, it was learned that Otto and his family had recently returned home from a three-year stay in Germany where his father had been assigned for military duty. Otto's father is an officer in the American Army who is reported to be a strict disciplinarian both with his men and with his children. The parents are of German stock and speak German in the home when visitors are not present. There are two children in the family: Otto, who is twelve years of age, and his brother, who is seven. Records indicate that when things go wrong at school "Otto ridicules his younger brother and is very rough with him." Another teacher who is well acquainted with the boy adds, "When Otto does work in handicraft, he wants every project to be perfect. If there are minor defects, he becomes discouraged and dissatisfied with himself."

Otto entered kindergarten at the age of five years. It is reported that he was a leader of his class and adjusted well to the ways of the school. Before the end of the year the family was transferred to another community where, because of conflicting standards of promotion, he was required to remain in the kindergarten another semester. Here, it is reported, he showed a quarrelsome and defiant attitude. Formal work in reading was introduced in the first grade and apparently an emphasis was placed upon oral reading. The school records indicate that Otto had difficulty in keeping his place and that he could read his book upside down as well as he could in its proper position. At the end of Otto's stay in the second grade, the family moved to Germany, where they remained for three years. Otto's progress in the third grade was described as fair, and his teacher reported to his parents, "Otto is capable of accomplishing more in the classroom. He dreams and idles away his time. He becomes impatient when he meets difficult words in his reading. He is a poor reader and performs as well as a child just entering the first grade (1.0)."

Otto's teacher in the fourth grade described him as a poor student whose chief interest was sports. She said, "Otto gets along best with teachers who are strong disciplinarians. He has great respect for authority and likes subject matter and teachers that may be described as definite and positive." Otto's performance in the fifth grade was characterized as adequate in all subjects except reading and spelling. The teacher's records indicate that the boy told his teacher confidentially, "I don't like school. It's only for sissies. I want to join the Navy as soon as I'm old enough."

In the sixth grade Otto had two major interests, sports and band. The boy's early training on the piano resulted in his ability to read music, and the possession of this skill, so it is reported, has helped him to make rapid progress with the trumpet. The band leader affirmed the fact that Otto spent six hours each week in uninterrupted practice on his instrument without protest. "Otto," he said, "sets high standards for himself and becomes impatient with those who are content with average performance." Otto's interest in sports was centered chiefly in baseball. He was familiar with the records of many outstanding players in both the American and the National leagues. He was especially interested in the fortunes of the White Sox and knew well the achievements of each player."

Records in the possession of the sixth grade teacher indicate that when Otto was one month in the sixth grade, his chronological age was twelve years and two months. His IQ's resulting from the administration of the Wechsler Intelligence Scale for Children are verbal scale 114, performance scale 108, and full scale 112. His grade scores as determined by measures in reading, arithmetic, and spelling are 2.6, 7.4, and 2.4, respectively. In a written summary of these data are found these statements, "Frustration in the home and school may be a result of the higher standards set up by his parents in contrast to those maintained by other parents in the neighborhood. Sibling jealousy may be a significant factor in this case. Otto has had throughout his school career inadequate word-attack skills and becomes irritated when he meets new and difficult words. At times he shows an inability to recognize words which he apparently knows when these words are placed in new locations on a page. He still has some difficulty with such words as: *then, when, where, what, who,* and *how.* He makes little or no use of contextual clues, phonics, or structural analysis. His main method of word attack seems to be guessing. He also has a marked tendency to look only at the beginnings of words. For example, he will look at the words *playmate* or *place* and call them *play.* He never seems to look at the whole word, only the beginning. The school psychologist has reported that Otto is a mixed sinistral. This means, of course, that he is left-handed and right-eyed. His spelling is poor. I have tried to help him, but there is little opportunity to teach reading as it should be taught in the sixth grade. So many of my children need help just as much as Otto does."

In an interview with Otto, he described his early experiences in reading by saying, "My first and second grade teachers asked the kids to read aloud and when we did not know the hard words, they told us. I did not like to read because my face got red when the teacher helped me with the words. I don't remember much about reading in the third grade because we had so many activities. My fourth grade teacher went all out with sounds of words, and I really learned to say the rules and pronounce most of the words. Even then I couldn't remember them. I guess because we didn't learn their meanings. We spent our time learning how to say the words. Sometimes I turn letters like *b* and *d* around. Even parts of words get mixed up and then I really have trouble. In the fourth grade we had to look up the meaning of words in our dictionaries, but I had trouble in finding them. I quit trying and, well, my parents bawled me out. Our sixth grade teacher has a new way to study words which we all like. She explains to us the meaning of prefixes, suffixes, and roots. We have studied such words as *unable, prehistoric,* and *flexible.* I like to use these words and other difficult ones in sentences when talking with the folks at home. Sometimes Dad looks up as if a firecracker had gone off under his chair. Don't worry. I can tell him their meanings. In our sixth grade room we learn to study the words which we need to know to do our daily work. We learn to pronounce these words, to know their meanings, and to use them in sentences. Our teacher has shown us a new way to study words. We look at the word, its beginning and its ending. We say it quietly to ourselves. Next we spell it to ourselves. Then we trace it with our finger. After this, we write it and then compare the word we have written with the one on the chalkboard. If we have made a mistake, we do the whole thing over again. Our teacher writes the most difficult words on cards. She then asks a question and omits the word we have studied. When she comes to its place in the question, she shows us the word and we are expected to answer the question. All of us fellows like this way of studying words. It is so practical."

In a final conference with Otto's sixth grade teacher which was held at the end of the school year, she confirmed his interest in word study and added, "Otto is now developing a well-balanced procedure of word-attack and word-comprehension skills. He has learned to apply both phonic and structural analysis in the study of words. Contextual clues are being used effectively, and finally location skills have been mastered so that he can make efficient use of his dictionary. Really, in working with Otto, I have discovered some of the reading needs of the other children in my group and how to meet them more adequately. I wish I had more time for the teaching of reading."

At this point it may be well to summarize some of the pertinent factors in Otto's history:

1. Otto is a boy of high average intelligence whose achievement in the language arts, especially reading, is far below the expected level.

2. Otto has difficulty in identifying and interpreting unfamiliar words. Furthermore, he has trouble in locating words in the dictionary. He has no method of word attack, frequently resorts to guessing, and has a tendency to make reversals.
3. Otto resorts to projection as he ascribes his difficulty in word recognition to persons and conditions rather than to himself.
4. In this bilingual home the father, a strict disciplinarian, imposes standards which are difficult for Otto to attain.
5. Facts in Otto's history suggest that he is a perfectionist when working in fields of his major interest.
6. As a result of conflicting educational policies and frequent transfer from one school system to another, it is reported that Otto has developed a sense of frustration and inadequacy in regard to his achievement in reading.
7. Frustration, a hazard in any learning situation, frequently manifests itself by daydreaming and by defiant and quarrelsome attitudes toward a younger brother.
8. His interests are chiefly in sports and music. Here sustained effort has resulted in success and real achievement.
9. Structural analysis and a systematic procedure for word study were enthusiastically accepted by Otto.
10. Ability to make effective use of contextual clues and skill in using the dictionary were finally developed.

In perusing the academic history of Otto, you have become acquainted with an intelligent boy who has had difficulty in expanding his reading powers because of his inadequate knowledge of words. If such a situation can develop with a boy in the sixth grade who has an IQ of 114, surely it is more apt to occur with children of lesser ability. This chapter suggests means of preventing and overcoming some of these difficulties with words. It will show you how to help your students study words and build more adequate vocabularies.

A Basic Sight Vocabulary Is Essential

A basic sight vocabulary, which Otto apparently did not possess, can serve as the foundation upon which other methods of vocabulary development are dependent. Such a vocabulary of easily recognized, common, and everyday words facilitates reading for meaning and makes it possible for the child to understand and enjoy simple stories. These words are basic tools which are essential in beginning reading. The initial sight vocabulary consists of words which are learned as wholes without the aid of phonics, breaking the word into syllables, or spelling the word aloud.

Continual repetition of words in meaningful sentences in experience charts, on the chalkboard, and on the bulletin board usually results in the addition of many words to the child's sight vocabulary. In teaching children to recognize and recall words, it is advisable for the teacher to develop a readiness for learning the new words through oral language activities based on real or vicarious experiences of the children. The new words should not be taught in isolation but should be presented in meaningful context. The children should have an opportunity to identify the words again and again in different contexts until they can recognize them instantly in any setting.

A well-developed stock of sight words is necessary before analysis procedures and use of the dictionary are attempted. The Dolch Basic Sight Vocabulary of 220 Service Words makes up over 50 per cent of the content of textbooks in reading and social science. Consequently, if a child is familiar with these basic words, he can read with greater ease and direct his attention to the realization of his immediate goal. In teaching these tool words along with the sight words required in the reading activities of the children, configuration, contextual, picture, and language-rhythm clues can be utilized. These basic words can be taught incidentally when needed in a natural setting without emphasis upon formal procedures. Later phonic and structural analysis as well as the use of the dictionary can be introduced. Let us turn now to a discussion of several methods of word study.

Methods of Word Study

In teaching children like Otto to *identify* and *interpret* words, certain clues and means of analysis are available. Of these ways of studying words, three facilitate pronunciation and five contribute to meaning.

Pronunciation	*Meaning*
Configuration Clues	Contextual Clues
Dictionary	Dictionary
Phonetic Analysis	Language-rhythm Clues
	Picture Clues
	Structural Analysis

Duplication is apparent and, as the reader will later observe in the chapter, one type of contextual clue, familiar expression, aids in pronunciation. In fact, any classification of these skills can be misleading and faulty. For example, contextual clues and structural analysis appear to contribute more to an interpretation of unfamiliar words than to their identification. In some situations, however, and with some individuals, this may not be true. On the other hand, configuration clues and phonetic analysis are apparently more closely related to word identification and pronunciation than to word interpretation.

In the process of learning to read the child must develop an independence in word identification and word interpretation. To facilitate this growth, several ways to aid children in their recognition and understanding of written words are discussed in some detail.

Configuration Clues

In making use of configuration clues in the reading process, the reader is concerned with the pattern of the word as a whole. Length, shape, form, and profile are the elements generally considered as making up the word pattern or configuration. The shape or form of a word is probably the most significant clue in the visual perception of a word. Such words as *am,* and *an, ran* and *run* are more difficult to distinguish than words containing more strikingly different letters such as the words *squirrel* and *Christmas.* For both children and adults the foreparts of words furnish the dominant clues probably because, as a result of conditioning, the eyes move from left to right in perceiving the configuration of the word. This may account for the omission of word endings on the part of children and even by more mature individuals.

Readiness for the use of configuration clues has to be developed by the teacher. Children can be taught to observe and discuss likenesses and differences in objects and symbols before they begin to identify words. The guidebooks of most basal readers provide materials and suggested procedures for developing on the part of children skills in observing significant differences in a series of objects before words are introduced. Such exercises are provided for the purpose of developing a readiness for differentiating one word form from another. Later in the reading process, the child must learn to distinguish the configurations of words, as, for example, the word form *mother* from the configuration *father.* Well-directed questions by the teacher can help boys and girls to identify significant differences and likenesses in the word forms under consideration. Special attention can be directed to form and shape of the word, unusual features, height of individual letters, and letter groups. Questions as to what children see in a word will bring a variety of responses. For example, one child reported that he could always remember the written word *look* because it reminded him of mother and dad swinging a rope so that the twins could jump it. Another child was able to identify the word *look* because it reminded him of an owl with two eyes. In working with young children, it may be wiser to determine what they see than to tell them what to see.

In addition to the suggestions already made, children can be aided in making use of configuration clues in many other ways. For example, matching exercises can be utilized. The children can be asked to find words in their story books which match the same words printed in larger type on the board. Or they may be told to draw a line under the two words which are alike in a row of words.

saw	say	saw	was
boy	toy	joy	boy

Children may be asked to choose and underline the correct word in a sentence. For example:

You   may / way   play with my doll.

The   hand / band   is playing.

In another activity the children may match words and pictures.

This is a mouse.
This is a house.
This is a ball.

Still another activity is to write on the chalkboard lists of words which are somewhat alike in appearance. The teacher pronounces one of the words and a pupil points to it and says it.

ran	book	boy
run	look	toy

The teacher will observe that both visual and auditory imagery are utilized in teaching configuration clues. Visual and auditory imagery will not become functional in a language situation until the child has spoken the word, felt and heard himself say it, associated the object with the word, and used it in a meaningful sentence. This procedure is essential in helping children to become good readers.

In doing independent reading, a pupil will discover that these clues are insufficient when relied upon exclusively. In fact, specialization in any one approach to word identification should be discouraged. Versatility in the use of other clues and techniques of word analysis is recommended.

Language-Rhythm Clues

Meaning is expressed by an integration of visual-auditory-kinesthetic imagery. Adults make use of imagery in their gestures and in such symbolic behavior as shaking hands, saluting the flag, acts of worship, and in their display of affection and respect. Meaning is expressed in action, and action can be productive of meaning. Rhythm suggests repeated action generally associated with pleasure and satisfaction. In dealing with words, language-rhythm clues are of value in developing a readiness to anticipate meaning through a feeling for the rhythm of language. The connotation of language-rhythm is all the ideas suggested by the combined imagery and will vary from person to person. Such words as *high* and *low*, *right* and *left* suggest rhythmic action and consequently emphasize meaning. As was suggested in Chapter 4, language-rhythm clues are of value in developing the meaning of words in work with young children. Even in the adult world such words as *ventral* and *dorsal*, *introvert* and *extrovert* take on new meaning as the dichotomy of the concepts is made clear through implied action. Rhythmic movement in prose, as well as in poetry, can accentuate meaning by balancing phrase against phrase and clause against clause.

An excellent example of rhythmic movement in prose is the following quotation from Winston Churchill:

> Do not let us speak of darker days;
> let us speak rather of sterner days.
> These are not dark days: these are great
> days—the greatest days our country has
> ever lived; and we must all thank God that
> we have been allowed, each of us according
> to our stations, to play a part in making
> these days memorable in the history of our race.

Picture Clues

Pictures aid adults as well as children in their identification and interpretation of words, phrases, sentences, and paragraphs. Picture clues are similar in nature to contextual clues and can emphasize the relationship between a word and the object represented by the word. For many children pictures represent ideas more clearly than detailed and even striking descriptions. Growth in picture interpretation is the product of mental maturity and experience. Young children of only three years can *enumerate* the objects observed in a picture. As these boys and girls become more mature, they may be able to *describe* accurately that which they see in the picture. Later these children may be able to *interpret* the picture in terms of their experience. Of course some individuals of even three and four years can make an interpretation. In the later elementary grades and in junior high school young students can use such graphic representations as diagrams, charts, and graphs to supplement the concepts expressed in their textbooks. Obviously, students at all academic levels can make use of such picture clues.

Young children who prepare their own picture dictionaries make excellent use of picture clues. Some teachers encourage their pupils to use a loose-leaf notebook so that new words may be added in alphabetical order. Children select words from their reading activities and daily experiences. The word and the picture representing the word are arranged so as to include a definition and a sentence making use of the word. Dictionaries prepared in this manner emphasize meaning rather than the mechanics of word recognition. Children are motivated by the ever-increasing pages in their dictionaries and by the usefulness of their work. As the dictionaries grow in size, children learn to locate words they themselves have selected, illustrated, and defined. Correct use of the alphabet becomes a necessity in the arrangement and location of terms. The habit of using a dictionary can be acquired by even young children.

Pictures in the form of visual aids can be used in the development of vocabulary. As suggested in Chapter 4, a picture rich in detail and of interest to a group of children can be projected upon a chalkboard. Objects in the picture can be named by the children and labeled by the teacher. In this manner, children learn to associate words with definite objects. A discussion of these objects, their purpose and function, increases the association. Meaning becomes more apparent, and interest is increased. A group of fourth grade boys and girls whose homes were far removed from a rural environment were reading a story of country life centered mainly around the use of a farm tractor. As they read, it became obvious to their teacher that these children not only had little mental content related to farm activities but that they were unfamiliar with the words essential to a discussion of farm tools. In an attempt to improve their background, she projected on the chalkboard a picture of a farm tractor being used in the process of plowing. Discussion of the picture was encouraged and many new concepts were developed and carefully explained. Such objects in the picture as *gang-plows, furrow, moldboard, landside, clevis, transmission, hitch,* and *differential* were demonstrated and labeled. The choice of these terms was determined by their use in the story and by the children themselves. After the words had been interpreted, attention was called to their pronunciation, spelling, and use in sentences. Questions were asked by some children, and interesting contributions concerning farm life were made by others. Obviously, mental content was developed and the children had an opportunity to identify and interpret eight words which in the beginning were unfamiliar to them. This procedure can be employed effectively at all academic levels and especially in the sciences and social studies. This technique could have been used profitably with Otto in aiding him not only in establishing mental content but in facilitating *perception* and *comprehension.* Furthermore, he would have had an opportunity to *react* to the new ideas expressed and to *integrate* the new concepts into his well-established background of experience.

Teachers can capitalize on pictures drawn by young children, for they draw that which they understand and can interpret. Frequently questions produce answers which tell much concerning the background of the child. Attitudes toward parents, brothers, and sisters can sometimes be inferred from the child's drawings and from his responses and explanations. The child's use of language in discussing his picture can be significant. His choice of words, verb forms, and diction provide clues indicative of his environmental and cultural background. In discussing the picture with the child, suggestions of tension, frustration, and anxieties are sometimes discovered. In drawing inferences based upon this projective technique, the teacher must take care to differentiate between observed facts and the generalizations set forth. The former may be both significant and true; the latter may be erroneous.

Contextual Clues

Contextual clues provide one of the most important aids to word identification and interpretation. They consist of suggestions of meaning provided by the use of words in their setting. Unfortunately, few children receive adequate instruction in how to use the context to construct the meaning of an unfamiliar word. Too often children, like Otto, have been encouraged to guess rather than to think. When taught as a reasoning procedure, contextual clues can facilitate word study. In beginning reading particularly, many children upon meeting a strange word sit and stare helplessly at the word, waiting for aid from the teacher. To counteract this, children can be taught to read the whole sentence in an attempt to determine the unknown word. Systematic guidance can be provided for helping children to think through the meaning of the unknown word. This can be done by discussion, illustration, and practice in the seven types of contextual clues. A brief discussion and illustration at various reading levels of each of the seven types of contextual clues follows:

1. *Definition.* The unknown word is defined in the descriptive context. For example: A house on a boat is called a *houseboat.*
2. *Synonym.* This type of contextual clue consists of a known synonym for the unfamiliar word. For example: Mother was angry and father was *irate* too.
3. *Familiar expression.* This type of clue requires a background and knowledge of common expressions and acquaintance with familiar language patterns. For example: She was as proud as a *peacock.*
4. *Experience.* Children and adults may depend upon their experience and mental content to supply the meaning of the new word. For example: The color of grass is *green.*
5. *Comparison or contrast.* The unknown word may be compared or contrasted with something known. For example: John is extravagant, but his brother isn't. John's brother is so miserly he could almost be called *penurious.*
6. *Summary.* The new or unknown word may summarize the ideas that precede it. For example: Down the street they came. First there were the girls twirling batons, then the marching band, and then the men in uniform. It was a *parade.*

7. *Reflection of situation or mood.* The general tone of the sentence or paragraph provides a clue to the new or unknown word. For example: The clouds were black and ominous. Occasionally streaks of lightning slashed the sky while low rumblings of thunder could be heard in the distance. Silhouetted against this threatening background was the dark and foreboding house where I hoped to secure refuge against the storm. Without warning, a strong feeling of *apprehension* gripped me.

Various activities can be rewarding in developing the attitude of reading for meaning and the ability to use context for identifying and interpreting unfamiliar words. The use of experience records and materials of high interest level are effective means of developing skill in anticipating meaning. Permitting children to complete sentences is helpful. For example, children can be allowed either at the board or at their seats to complete sentences such as these: The cat has a long _____. Peaches grow on _____. In a similar exercise the children may select from a group of words the correct one to complete the sentence. For example:

> Billy laughed at the _____ clown.
>
> dog   sad   funny

> Here is a train. See it _____.
>
> go   look   cry

Another worthwhile exercise is to choose the appropriate word from two or three with similar configurations. For example:

> One _____ a boy found a ball.
>
> may   day

> The boy _____ out of the house.
>
> ran   man

Some teachers find it helpful to read aloud to the children and then permit them to predict what will come next in the story.

These are just a few of the many activities which will help children to anticipate meaning as they read. It is urged that the teacher devise and utilize her own materials and exercises and that she take advantage of every opportunity to guide the children in the use of contextual clues through direct explanation and supervised reading.

Structural Analysis

During the initial reading instruction, emphasis is placed on the use of configuration, contextual, picture, and language-rhythm clues as aids to the identification and interpretation of words. Later analytical techniques can be introduced, such as structural and phonetic analysis. Frequently these approaches to word study can be utilized simultaneously. Generally, however, structural analysis should precede phonetic studies of unfamiliar words. Structural analysis is the process of studying words for the purpose of identifying prefixes, roots, and suffixes. For example, the word *incredible* is made up of the prefix *in,* the root *cred,* and the suffix *ible.* A *root* is an original word form from which words have been developed by the addition of prefixes, suffixes, and inflectional endings. It furnishes the basic meaning. A *stem,* which is the main part of a word, is derived from and is often identical with the root. A *prefix* consists of one or more syllables joined to the beginning of a word to change its meaning while a *suffix* consists of one or more syllables which are added to the stem and which provide a clue as to the word's grammatical use.

For intermediate and upper grade children as well as adults, a knowledge of the meanings of prefixes, roots, and suffixes can lead to the understanding of thousands of words. Below are listed some of the common prefixes, roots, and suffixes which are most common in the English language.

Common Prefixes

Prefix	Meaning	Examples
a– (*ab–*)	from, away	avert, abnormal, absent
ad–	to, toward	adjust, admit, annex
ante–	before	antecedent, antedate
anti–	against, opposite	antithesis, antagonist
con– (*co–, col–, com–*)	together, with	concur, collect, combine
de–	from, down from	delegate, degrade
dis– (*di–*)	apart, not	dispatch, dishonor
ex–	out of, from	exit, expel, exhume
fore–	front, in front	forefoot, foreground
	before, in advance	foretell, foresee
in– (*il–, im–, ir–*)	into, not	inconsistent, impatient
		illegible, irreverent
inter–	between	interpose, interrupt
mid–	in or near the middle of	midnight, midsummer
mis–	wrong, wrongly	mislead, mischance
	bad	misspell, misunderstand
non–	not	nonalcoholic, nonentity
post–	after, behind	postpone, post-mortem
pre–	before	precede, prelude
pro–	for, forward	propose, program
	in front of	prologue
re–	back, again	renew, reiterate, repress
sub–	under	subway, subnormal
		subject
super–	over, above	supercilious, supernatural

| trans– | beyond, across | transgress, transatlantic |
| un– | not | unkind, unnecessary |

Common Roots

Root	Meaning	Examples
cap, cip, capt, cept	take	captive, precept precipitate
dic, dict	say	dictate
duc	lead	conduct, aqueduct
fac, fic, fact, fect	make, do, cause	fact, fashion, difficult perfect
fer	bear, produce, carry	fertile, refer
graph, gram	write, describe	graphic, diagram
log	idea, word, speech study, reason, science doctrine	logic, eulogy, biology
mitt, mit, miss, mise	let go, send	dismiss, missionary
pend	to hang	pendent, depend
plic, plect, plex, pli	fold, twist	duplicate, complicate complex, pliable
pos	place, put	position
scrib, script	write	scribble, transcript
spec, spic, spect	look, examine	inspect, spectacle
sta, stat, stit, sist	stand	static, station, insist
ten, tin, tent	hold	tension, attention
ven, vent	come	venture, advent
vert, vers, vort, vors	turn	avert, vortex

Common Suffixes

Suffix	Meaning	Examples
–able, –ible	capable of being	serviceable, credible
–ace, –acy, –ancy, –ance	state of being	disturbance, intimacy
–al, –eal, –ial	relation to, that which, on account of	judicial, credentials elemental
–an, –ean, –ian	one who, relating to	American, statistician
–ant	adj.: being	resonant, vacant
	noun: one who	attendant, servant
–ary	adj.: relating to	residuary, contrary
	noun: one who	dignitary
	place where	sanctuary
–ate	adj.: having quality	fortunate, desolate
	noun: one who	prelate, advocate
	verb: to make	celebrate, agitate
–dom	the office, realm or territory of	dukedom, earldom kingdom
	the state of being	freedom, wisdom
	all who are	officialdom

Suffix	Meaning	Examples
-ee	one who is object of action	trustee, employee devotee
-en	little, made of	maiden, kitten earthen, olden
-er, -or	a person or thing that	actor, baker, defender elevator
	a person who lives in	cottager, islander
-ful	the amount that fills	cupful, handful
	full of, having much of	beautiful, fanciful
	giving, bringing or causing	healthful, painful
-hood	state, condition	motherhood, manhood
-ic	like, made of	plastic, magic
-ion	act, or state of being	coercion, fusion
-ist, -ite	one who	optimist, theist
-itis	inflammation of	appendicitis
-ity, -ty	state	unity, vicinity
-ive	relating to	legislative, decorative
-less	without	hopeless, worthless
-like	resembling that of	doglike, homelike, lifelike
-ly	in a manner or way	compactly, exactly
	that is like	cowardly, queenly
	every	daily, yearly
-ment	state of being	amendment development
-ness	the condition of being	darkness, goodness
-ose, -ous	abounding in	verbose, gracious
-ship	the state or condition of	friendship, relationship
	the office or position of	clerkship
		professorship
	the art of	workmanship
	something made up of	membership, township
-some	full of	troublesome quarrelsome
-ward	turning to in direction of	heavenward, forward
-y	like, full of, tending to	bumpy, silky, sleepy
	somewhat, rather	chilly
	the state of being	honesty, jealousy

In order to employ structural analysis adequately, the student must be skilled in syllabication. The following principles set forth by Carter and McGinnis [2] may serve as a reference guide for the teacher:

[2] Homer L. J. Carter and Dorothy J. McGinnis, *Effective Reading for College Students* (New York: Dryden Press, 1957), pp. 146–147.

1. Generally, there are as many syllables in a word as there are vowels, except when two vowels are sounded as one or when the final *e* is silent.

frog   float   take

2. If the first vowel sound in a word is followed by a single consonant, that consonant usually begins the second syllable.

la dy   ba by

3. If, however, the accent is on the first syllable, the consonant following the vowel usually is included in the first syllable.

pres i dent   Flor i da

4. If the first vowel sound in a word is followed by two consonants, the first syllable usually ends with the first of the two consonants.

lad der   fol low

5. The syllables in a word do not often break between consonant blends or special two-letter consonant symbols.

re ply   an gry   leath er

6. If the last syllable of a word ends in *le* preceded by a consonant, that consonant usually begins the last syllable.

ta ble   la dle

7. In a word of more than one syllable the letter *v* is usually included with the preceding vowel to form a syllable.

trav el   rav el

8. Prefixes and suffixes remain separate syllables.

re pro duc tion   bi month ly

In addition to a knowledge of syllabication, an understanding of stress and accent is required. *Stress* is the prominence given to a word or syllable which makes it stand out from the adjoining words or syllables. The term *accent* is used to indicate stress given to syllables. The following general suggestions regarding accent should be understood.

1. The first syllable in a two-syllable word is usually accented.

ig' loo   prov' erb

2. The root or stem of a word is usually stressed in the pronunciation.

pro duc' tion   de scrip' tive

3. In words ending in *tion* and *sion* the accent is placed on the next to the last syllable.

or gan i za' tion   dem on stra' tion

4. Words of two or three syllables usually are accented on the first syllable except when a prefix is used.

qual' i fy   pre tend'

5. A word used as a noun frequently has a different accent when it is used as a verb or an adjective.

Noun	Verb	Adjective
sub' ject	subject'	
con' duct	conduct'	
reb' el	rebel'	
ad' dress	address'	
com' pact		compact'
in' valid		inval' id
min' ute		minute'
ab' stract		abstract'

There are many ways in which teachers can aid their pupils in the development of skill in syllabication, pronunciation, and structural analysis. Such procedures as direct explanations, illustrations, games, work with compound words, and dictionary usage are a few examples.

Phonetic Analysis

One of the first objectives in beginning reading is the development of a basic sight vocabulary. Instruction in this aspect of word identification involves the use of meaning and configuration clues. The second major objective is the development of independence in word recognition by means of word analysis. One aid to independent identification of words is phonetic analysis, a process of associating appropriate sounds with printed words. Writers in the field of developmental reading seem to agree that phonics has a place in the teaching of reading but that there are certain dangers which must be avoided. One of the chief dangers is that it may be overemphasized with the result that the entire reading program is built around endless, perhaps even meaningless, drills consisting of the blending of phonograms into words. Betts [3] and others state that a desirable phonics program can be utilized by the teacher providing she realizes that (1) phonics is only one aid to word recognition and that other methods of word analysis must be taught and developed; (2) phonic instruction should be provided incidentally when the need

[3] Emmett A. Betts, *Foundations of Reading Instruction* (New York: American Book Co., 1957), pp. 614–615.

arises; (3) the phonics program should be based on analyzing words into their speech sounds rather than synthesizing sounds into words; and (4) phonetic analysis should be taught only to those pupils who can profit from its use. In general, then, phonetic analysis can be a valuable tool for analyzing words but it is not the only skill needed by children as they develop independence in word recognition.

A thorough knowledge of phonetics is essential if the teacher is to provide effective instruction in phonetic analysis. Many teachers have found that a course in phonetics, usually offered by speech departments, is of inestimable value in helping them to understand the phonetic qualities of the English language. A brief introduction to the subject, however, may be helpful to the beginning teacher.

Since there are only twenty-six letters in the English alphabet and approximately forty-three phonemes or sound units in the English language, it is obvious that the same letter or combinations of letters must have more than one sound. The consonants are used to represent a single consonant sound but can represent several sounds, as, for example, the letter g in *gingerbread* and *gate*. The vowel letters represent more than one sound each. For example, the letter a in *ale, care, add, account, arm, ask,* and *sofa* represents different vowel sounds. A study of phonetics also reveals that the same sound may be represented by different letters or combinations of letters. For example, the long a sound in *hate, day, break, weight,* and *bouquet* is represented by different letters or combinations of letters.

The three terms *digraph, diphthong,* and *blend,* should be understood by the reading teacher. A *digraph* consists of two letters representing one speech sound. Vowel digraphs include *aw* (*raw*), *ai* (*said*), *ay* (*say*), *ee* (*seek*), *ea* (*eat*), *ew* (*new*), *oa* (*oat*), *ow* (*low*), and *oo* (*book*). Consonant digraphs include *sh* (*shoe*), *ch* (*choke*), *ng* (*rang*), *wh* (*when*), *ph* (*phone*), *th* (*think*), and *gh* (*rough*).

A *diphthong* consists of two vowels pronounced in a sound sequence that gives the impression of one sound. Diphthongs include *oi* (*oil*), *oy* (*boy*), *ou* (*out*), *ow* (*cow*), and *ew* (*few*).

A consonant *blend* is composed of a combination of consonant letter symbols, each representing a blending of the separate consonant sounds without the loss of identity of any of the sounds. Examples are *bl* (*blue*), *nk* (*blink*), *sm* (*small*), *st* (*stall*), *ts* (*rats*), *str* (*strong*), *tr* (*trick*), *pl* (*please*), *spl* (*splash*), and *qu* (*quick*).

These facts, and many more, are discussed in considerable detail by Betts in his book *Foundations of Reading Instruction.*[4] It is suggested that the prospective teacher become thoroughly acquainted with this material.

[4] Emmett A. Betts, *Foundations of Reading Instruction* (New York: American Book Co., 1957), pp. 620–635.

It may also be well for the teacher of reading to consider the following general principles concerning phonetic analysis in the reading program:

1. *Phonetic analysis should not be introduced until the children are ready.* Children should have many background experiences, adequate speaking and listening vocabularies, a good sight vocabulary, and many chances to hear rhymes and other word sounds before systematic instruction in the analysis of words is presented. Since there appears to be a relationship between mental age and readiness for using phonetic analysis, it is advisable to delay work in phonics until the child has a mental age of seven years or more. Phonetic analysis should not be introduced until the child indicates by his actions and attitudes that reading is a useful and enjoyable activity and that he needs additional help in understanding and pronouncing new words. Never should the teacher lose sight of the fact that phonetic analysis is only one method of word recognition and should be used only when the pupils are mature enough to profit from the systematic and continuous work in phonics which the teacher will provide.

2. *Phonetic analysis should begin with familiar words.* Experience indicates that phonetic analysis is most effective when it is initially applied to the child's sight vocabulary. Eventually the child who is successful will be able to generalize about the sounds he meets in new words. Children should be taught to react to a word as a whole with emphasis on its phonetic elements. It is not advisable to have the children memorize "families" of words and large numbers of phonograms. An effective phonetic analysis program is not based on the memorizing of lists of similar-sounding words. Instead, children should be helped to develop skill in generalizing about the sounds of words, and to do this they must know many words which can be used to illustrate the generalization.

3. *Care must be taken to differentiate clearly between sounds and letters.* Letters are seen. Speech sounds are heard. In her work with children, the teacher must be exceedingly careful to differentiate between the two. Children should never be asked to point to sounds in words because this is an impossible task. They can point to letters but not to sounds. Sounds are heard. Letters are seen. Similarly, children should not be asked to listen for letters in words nor should they be asked to find words within words that do not sound the same. For example, having children find the word *fat* in the word *father* is ridiculous, for the word *fat* is not heard in the word *father*. Neither should the teacher confuse children by distorting the sounds in words, such as *hu-at* for *hat*. Sounds must be heard as they are normally pronounced.

4. *The teacher must have an adequate background in the principles of phonics.* A few of the more important principles are discussed here. It should be realized, however, that there are exceptions to many of them.

a. When a syllable ends in a consonant, its vowel is usually short: *man, net, sit, tot, run.*

b. When there are two vowels in words of one syllable, usually the first is long and the second is silent: *hope, date, dream, frame.*

c. A single vowel in a word or syllable not ending with a consonant is usually long: *be–gin, a–corn, i–dentical.*

d. In words or syllables containing only one vowel which is followed by *r*, the sound of the vowel is controlled by the *r*: *for, her, sir, far, fur.*

e. When the only vowel in a word or syllable is *a*, followed by *l* or *w*, the *a* usually has neither its long nor its short sound: *raw, tall, balk, ball, final.*

f. *C* is soft before *e, i,* and *y;* otherwise it is hard: *can, come, cut.*

g. *G* is usually soft before *e, i,* and *y;* otherwise it is hard: *genuine, gin, gyroscope.*

5. *Phonetic analysis is only one approach to the development of independence in word attack.* Phonics is not a method of teaching reading. It is useful only as a means of comprehending unfamiliar words which one meets in his reading. The goal of all reading instruction is to understand printed symbols. Phonetic analysis is introduced to aid in the perception of unfamiliar words. It is introduced in combination with structural analysis, contextual clues, and configurational clues. It is only a tool for unlocking unfamiliar words. It is not an end in itself. The wise teacher will not permit this method of word attack to dominate her instruction in reading.

Instructional procedures in phonics will be dictated largely by the children's needs and readiness. In general, initial sounds will be introduced first. The children can be taught how to listen for beginning sounds, how to match visual symbols and sounds, and how to tell words apart. Activities in which the children can engage include underlining like elements in words, crossing out words that do not begin alike, matching words that begin alike, and substituting initial letters to make new words. Later, emphasis can be placed on the final sounds of words. Children can be given help in listening for ending sounds and in rhyming words. They can have the experience of crossing out words that do not end alike. They can match words that rhyme and can substitute final letters to make new words.

The children's reading experiences should serve as a guide in determining the order in which sounds are stressed. It is wise to begin with sounds the child can both identify and hear. Most first-readers introduce the use of initial consonants and short and long vowels in monosyllables. The second-reader makes use of a knowledge of consonant blends, digraphs, diphthongs, and compound words. At the third level syllabication, prefixes, and suffixes are introduced. We strongly recommend that beginning teachers make use of the guidebooks accompanying basic readers. Phonics can be useful at all levels.

The Dictionary

There is no more effective, independent aid to the child than the dictionary. It is an excellent tool for determining the meaning, construction, pronunciation, and use of unfamiliar words. Like any tool, it cannot be used effectively without guidance and directed practice. Some pupils in the third grade and many in the fourth grade can profit from the use of an elementary dictionary. Previously they may have been taught incidentally to use picture dictionaries and glossaries. However, most children, when they reach the fifth grade, are ready for formal instruction in the use of the dictionary. This need was apparent in the case of Otto, for he recognized the value of such instruction. Readiness for training should be evaluated in terms of language ability and the needs of the child rather than in terms of grade placement. Effective use of the dictionary requires an integration of nearly all the language skills and can only be accomplished by careful study and persistent practice. We never outgrow the need for this tool for learning. The dictionary is a basic text and reference book for use in all fields of human endeavor.

In teaching children how to use the dictionary, it is advisable for the teacher to explain the general contents and over-all plan of the one they are to use. In the discussion of scope and format she should plan so that each child may have his own copy available for immediate use. The modern dictionary is designed to make the young student more independent in helping himself with word difficulties in reading, writing, and spelling. For most of these dictionaries there are built-in guides and manuals containing step-by-step suggestions as to how the book can be used effectively. One modern dictionary includes sixty-seven lessons providing specific instruction in nearly all the necessary dictionary skills. Each of these is developed through simple explanations, illustrations, examples, and procedures essential to the efficient use of the dictionary. The following are some of the most widely used school dictionaries:

> *Elementary Dictionary for Boys and Girls*
> American Book Company, New York, New York
> *Thorndike-Barnhart Beginning Dictionary*
> Scott, Foresman and Company, Chicago, Illinois
> *Thorndike-Barnhart Junior Dictionary*
> Scott, Foresman and Company, Chicago, Illinois
> *Thorndike-Barnhart Senior Dictionary*
> Scott, Foresman and Company, Chicago, Illinois
> *Webster Elementary Dictionary*
> G. and C. Merriam Company, Springfield, Massachusetts
> *Winston Simplified Dictionary for Schools*
> John C. Winston, Philadelphia, Pennsylvania

Children learning to use the dictionary for word meanings should be shown how to find the correct alphabetical section and to observe the page headings in order to find the first, second, third, and fourth letters of a word. Development of these location skills makes it necessary for the child to know the sequence of the letters of the alphabet. That is, they should know that *above* comes before *acorn* and that *adobe* comes before *adult*. Knowledge of the sequence of letters may to some teachers appear to be of little consequence, but it is not unusual to find in high school and even in college individuals who lack skill in alphabetizing.

After locating the correct alphabetical section and after observing the page headings in order to utilize the guide words at the top of the columns, the student should have no difficulty in locating the word itself. Meaning should probably be given first consideration. Selection of the most appropriate meaning must be made in terms of the context in which the word appears. This process is greatly facilitated if children have been taught to make use of contextual clues. Children should understand that many words have more than one meaning and that in most dictionaries these meanings are numbered. Some words with different meanings are spelled alike, and some words are used as more than one part of speech. Mature children can be shown the meaning of *n., v., adj., adv.*, and other abbreviations indicating the use of the word in a sentence. These language skills are essential to meaning and there should be direct teaching of such concepts as noun, verb, adjective, and adverb if the meaning of words is to be thoroughly understood.

After meaning, pronunciation is next in the order of importance. To say a word correctly after it is located in a dictionary requires an integration of several language skills. The young student must be familiar with vowel and consonant sounds and he must be acquainted with syllables and accent. He can be taught to use the pronunciation key which is a part of his dictionary. Most modern dictionaries furnish detailed instruction as to how this key can be helpful in the pronunciation of words. Exercises are often included, and some children can work independently on these while others will require formal instruction and continued guidance.

Dictionaries published recently provide information on how to use the dictionary which can be of value to the teacher or parent. Occasionally new practices are introduced which are effective and helpful. For example, many of the modern dictionaries have made use of the term *schwa* to indicate the soft unstressed vowel sound heard only in the unaccented syllables in such words as *canvas, problem, engine, gallop,* and *August*. The use of schwa (ə) is becoming more common in texts dealing with the language arts.

Frequently class periods should be set aside for lessons in the use of the dictionary. A flexible grouping plan will make possible the adjustment of instruction to the maturity and needs of individual students. It is advisable for each group to concentrate upon one dictionary skill at a time, utilizing words selected from their own reading. For most children, incidental teaching is not sufficient.

Activities of Children

Children in the elementary grades have listening, speaking, reading, and writing vocabularies which are growing daily as a by-product of their experiences. The good reader is a master of words and makes use of a large and meaningful vocabulary. Meaning, the resultant of physical and psychological factors, is the product of purposeful activity. Words are symbols and represent real or vicarious experiences. It is generally assumed that word study should be the result of a consciously planned program and not the product of chance. In order to make possible real learning and to avoid only verbalization, the teacher should build up background for adequate understanding by means of excursions, dramatizations, and manipulation of the objects for which the symbols stand. In brief, children should grow into the use of words through experience.

If boys and girls like Otto are to become interested in new words, their teachers must have a suitable background and a keen appreciation of their use. For example, if children are reading stories of the Southwest and of Mexico, they may find such unfamiliar words as *tortilla, enchilada,* and *tacos.* An explanation by the teacher can make plain to the children that the *tortilla,* a thin, flat corn pancake, along with ground meat, chili, and sometimes melted cheese, is used in preparing both *enchiladas* and *tacos.* These words can be written on the chalkboard and the children can be taught how to pronounce and use them correctly in sentences.

Storytelling and reading aloud by the teacher can focus attention upon new and interesting words. Such words as *sandwich, calico* and *jovial* have interesting histories which even young children can appreciate. The teacher who is acquainted with children's literature can select stories which add to and enrich ideas and concepts being discussed in the group. The reading aloud of extracts from *The Song of Hiawatha* can give new meaning to such words as *wigwam* and *tepee.* The rhythm, choice of words, and emotional tone of such selections will have a lasting effect upon boys and girls. Those who have "caught" the effect of the words and the spirit of the story may wish to construct the wigwam of Old Nokomis, for ideas can and should lead to action.

Generally, projects which children assume and work out for themselves are filled with meaning for them. For example, the third-grade boy who has built for himself a crystal radio set has become well acquainted with such terms as *antenna, circuit, coil,* and *ground.* Teachers can utilize these interests and activities by clarifying and enriching the meaning of such words and by demonstrating their appreciation and understanding of the project. New sources of information can be suggested and the child can be made to feel that he is engaged in a form of research which is, for him, worthwhile and creative.

Making Use of Imagery

Some individuals for various reasons have persistent difficulty in identifying and interpreting words in spite of long and careful instruction on the part of their teachers. In addition to this disability some students like Otto have a history of spelling disorders and marked reversal tendencies. Certain writers [5] in the field of reading have suggested the use of a procedure known as V.A.K.T. This instructional technique utilizes the association of visual, auditory, kinesthetic, and tactual imagery. The following steps are employed:

1. Look at the beginning and ending of the word. The analysis of words within words should be restricted to those roots, inflectional endings, and prefixes and suffixes which convey direct meaning.
2. Pronounce the word silently, being sure to associate each syllable with its corresponding sound and being certain that the proper sequence of syllables is maintained.
3. Spell the word silently, paying careful attention to each syllable.
4. Trace the word with the index finger.
5. Write the word.
6. Compare the word written with the word selected for study.
7. Repeat this process until the word can be spelled and written correctly.

In applying this technique, young students making up a small group should be encouraged to select from their reading words which are unfamiliar. After the meaning of these words has been developed, the teacher can use this technique step by step in demonstrating how a word may be studied. The word can then be written or printed in manuscript on a card of adequate size. The individuals making up the group can then be taught to identify and use it in its proper place in a sentence. For example, the word *family* may have been taught as indicated, and a flashcard containing the word prepared. The teacher may ask, "Does your _____ live in the city?" At the proper time in asking the question, the word *family* can be shown to the group and a member would be expected to answer, "Yes, my *family* does live in the city."

[5] Grace M. Fernald, *Remedial Techniques in Basic School Subjects* (New York: McGraw-Hill Book Co., 1943), chap. V.

In the case of Otto, use of this technique has been effective as a reteaching or corrective measure. Care must be taken to avoid emphasis on isolated words so as to prevent the development of word readers. Specialization in any technique, no matter how effective it may be, is unwise.

Guiding Principles for the Teacher

Teachers in the elementary grades and throughout the high school are responsible for the teaching of word-attack skills. In their work with boys and girls, they should emphasize many methods so that the children may learn to use any and all methods which will help them to unlock the meanings of words. Some guiding principles which will prove beneficial to teachers are summarized in the following list:

1. Before expecting the child to learn the visual forms of words, give him practice in auditory perception and in the correct pronunciation of the words.
2. During the beginning stages of reading, establish the habit of using the context for identification and recognition of words.
3. Aid the child in developing the ability to distinguish marked differences in the visual forms of the sight words which he is to learn.
4. Aid the young child in establishing a left-to-right direction in his attack on new words by helping him to see familiar beginnings, endings, and similarities as well as differences in the configuration of words.
5. Make use of games and interesting activities in seeking to make the identification of sight words automatic.
6. In the primary grades the child should be introduced to alphabetizing words according to the first, second, and third letters and he should be shown how to make use of picture dictionaries. This practice will prepare him for the use of the regular dictionary, which many teachers introduce at the fourth grade level.
7. Systematic instruction in the use of the dictionary should be emphasized in the fifth and sixth grades and should continue until the individual has developed effective use of the dictionary as an aid to pronunciation and as a means of securing the meaning of new and unfamiliar words. At the same time the students can be taught to identify words with more than one spelling and to form the plurals of new and intriguing words. Construction and word forms can also be emphasized.
8. Apply word-attack skills only to those words which are met in meaningful situations and avoid drill on isolated words which are not met in familiar context.

9. Provide sequential training in all of the word-attack skills. Use the teacher's guidebooks, for they have been carefully prepared on the basis of sound principles and can be of real value to the teacher.
10. Teach word-attack skills as the need arises and as they can be applied in the daily work of the children.
11. Refrain from beginning phonetic analysis of words until the child has reached a sufficient degree of mental maturity. This may be as late as seven or eight years.
12. Generally it is unwise to teach structural or phonetic analysis before the child has developed a sight vocabulary of from fifty to one hundred words.
13. Teach phonetics gradually and incidentally and only as a device for recognizing and pronouncing unfamiliar words.
14. Whenever it is possible, teach structural and phonetic analysis together rather than as separate devices for identifying and interpreting words.
15. Visual analysis of a word should generally precede any attempt to sound or blend parts of a word, for the individual must first identify phonetic and structural elements before he can blend them in an attempt to sound the word.
16. Generally structural analysis should precede phonetic analysis because the child must first identify familiar parts, including phonetic elements, before he can fuse them in pronouncing a new word.
17. Do not demand mastery and use of a skill at any one level. Instead continue the use of the skill until it becomes a functioning tool in the identification of new words.
18. Refrain from depending on the use of rules as a device for working out word recognition at any level.
19. As the child develops a greater degree of maturity, he should be encouraged to attack longer and more complex word forms and he should secure practice in structural analysis which will aid him in breaking new words down into prefixes, stems, and suffixes.
20. Word analysis should be continued throughout the elementary and junior high school periods.

Vocabulary Development, a Responsibility for Teachers in the Content Fields

Each teacher in the content fields is responsible for developing background and mental content in his area of concentration and for increasing the special and technical vocabulary of his subject. Three aspects of reading are essential to a mastery of subject matter in the content fields. It is necessary for the student to identify, interpret, and evaluate words and concepts. In order to achieve these skills, mental content resulting from experience is a fundamental requirement. In other words, the student must contribute from his own background as he attempts to identify, interpret, and evaluate ideas presented in his textbook. What he perceives is dependent upon what he has to contribute. The teacher can aid his students in building up mental content by demonstrations and class discussions. Terms can be illustrated and defined. Drawings and visual equipment can be utilized. In this process, mental content can be increased and vocabularies can be enlarged.

In every subject-matter field there are words and technical terms which are especially significant in that particular area of specialization. The alert teacher in any field can acquaint his students with the various forms of *contextual clues,* which, when thoroughly appreciated, can aid the student in determining meaning that can be verified later by the *use of the dictionary.* Teachers can demonstrate the usefulness of *structural analysis* to their students, for in many of the sciences, such as biology and physiology, meaning can generally be determined from a knowledge of prefixes, stems, and suffixes. Spelling vocabularies can be developed by students if their teachers are willing to explain and demonstrate a modification of the methods set forth by Fernald, Betts, and others which make use of visual, auditory, kinesthetic, and tactual imagery. The responsibility for vocabulary development is not the sole responsibility of the primary teacher but must be shared by all teachers within the school system.

Teachers from the elementary grades through high school should be familiar with the procedures for vocabulary development described in this chapter. The study of words is a continuous process and the basic principles involved are applicable at all levels and in all subject-matter fields. No teacher is exempt from the responsibility of inspiring and instructing his students in the art of word study.

Guided Activities

1. Assume the role of Otto's teacher and explain to two of your classmates, who are impersonating Otto's father and mother, why he scores so well on intelligence and arithmetic tests and yet has difficulty in word recognition and word comprehension.
2. Engage in a panel discussion, making sure that each of the following questions is discussed in detail:
    a. What evidence does Otto show of emotional tension?
    b. How would you help Otto improve his spelling?
    c. What psychological mechanism is Otto using when he ascribes his difficulty in word recognition to a foreign language spoken in the home?
    d. What are the arguments for and against the use of V.A.K.T. in Otto's case?

3. Construct examples of contextual clues suitable for use with individuals at the grade level you intend to teach.
4. Look up and practice the pronunciation of the following words and outline the procedures you would use in teaching them to a group of students.

hospitable	inexplicable	apropos
quay	*faux pas*	genuine
ennui	tragedian	maraschino

5. Suggest a plan for helping a boy like Otto improve his spelling and reading vocabularies.
6. Prepare the arguments for and against the use of phonics.
7. Outline the steps in a well-balanced program for developing identification and interpretation of words at any grade level in which you are interested.
8. List and explain the factors which may account for an individual having difficulty in using a dictionary.
9. Teach the words *doily, form, intolerable,* and *indisputable* to a child who is unfamiliar with them, making use of configuration clues. Describe to the class your experience and explain some of the advantages and disadvantages of these clues.
10. Read the book *Why Johnny Can't Read* by Rudolph Flesch (New York: Harper & Bros., 1955). This book attacks present methods of teaching reading and advocates the use of phonics. Select from the *Education Index* articles by leading educators written in refutation of Flesch's arguments. Discuss with your classmates the strength and weakness of Flesch's suggested reading program.

Questions and References

Questions

1. Where can the teacher find a list of common prefixes, roots, and suffixes?

2. How are phonics taught?

3. How can words be studied in the higher grades?

4. How can word-attack and word-comprehension skills be developed?

References

1. Carter, Homer L. J., and Dorothy J. McGinnis. *Effective Reading for College Students,* pp. 159–168. New York: Dryden Press, 1957.

2. Hildreth, Gertrude. *Teaching Reading,* Chap. 15. New York: Holt and Co., 1958.

3. *Ibid.* Chap. 20.

4. Dawson, Mildred A., and Henry A. Bamman. *Fundamentals of Basic Reading Instruction,* Chaps. 6, 7. New York: Longmans Green and Co., 1959.

Questions	References
5. How can kinesthetic methods be used for helping nonreaders?	5. Fernald, Grace M., and Helen Keller. "Kinaesthetic Methods for Helping Nonreaders," in *Research in the Three R's,* C. W. Hunnicutt and William J. Iverson, pp. 241–242. New York: Harper & Bros., 1958.
6. How can the teacher help primary children learn to work with words?	6. McKim, Margaret G. *Guiding Growth in Reading,* Chap. 9. New York: Macmillan Co., 1955.
7. What are the developmental phases of vocabulary building?	7. Russell, David H. *Children Learn to Read,* Chap. 9. Boston: Ginn and Co., 1961.
8. Should vocabulary be taught directly or incidentally?	8. Gray, William S., and Eleanor Holmes. "Should Vocabulary Be Taught Directly or Incidentally?" in *Research in the Three R's,* C. W. Hunnicutt and William J. Iverson, pp. 147–153. New York: Harper & Bros., 1958.
9. How useful are phonics in reading?	9. Agnew, Donald C. "How Useful Are Phonics in Reading?" in *Research in the Three R's,* C. W. Hunnicutt and William J. Iverson, pp. 71–81. New York: Harper & Bros., 1958.
10. What effect do workbooks, vocabulary control, and phonetic drill have on beginning reading?	10. Gates, Arthur I., and David H. Russell. "Workbooks, Vocabulary Control, Phonics, and Other Factors in Beginning Reading," in *Research in the Three R's,* C. W. Hunnicutt and William J. Iverson, pp. 81–93. New York: Harper & Bros., 1958.

Reading is an education in itself
and children need to know how to make effective use of books.

Writing, an aspect of communication, is closely related to reading.

Children are taught to use words in sentences and not merely to identify them.

Interest must be utilized in developing reading skills.

Students can justify their points of view by referring to
several sources of information.

Even in a formal typing situation reading skills can be emphasized.

11. Why are some children poor spellers?

11. Russell, David H. "Why Are Some Children Poor Spellers?" in *Research in the Three R's,* C. W. Hunnicutt and William J. Iverson, pp. 287–293. New York: Harper & Bros., 1958.

12. What methods of teaching spelling are better?

12. Zyve, Claire. "What Methods Are Better?" in *Research in the Three R's,* C. W. Hunnicutt and William J. Iverson, pp. 301–309. New York: Harper & Bros., 1958.

13. Where can one find a description of some interesting activities for developing word recognition and word comprehension skills?

13. Hester, Kathleen B. *Teaching Every Child to Read,* pp. 161–193. New York: Harper & Bros., 1955.

14. Where can one find a detailed discussion of vocabulary development?

14. Betts, Emmett A. *Foundations of Reading Instruction,* Chap. XXIV. New York: American Book Co., 1957.

15. How can children develop independence in attacking new words?

15. Gray, William S. *On Their Own in Reading.* Chicago: Scott, Foresman and Co., 1948.

16. How can students learn to use the English language effectively?

16. Foley, Louis. *How Words Fit Together.* Melrose, Mass.: Babson Institute Press, 1958.

6

READING FOR MEANING

In the discussion of vocabulary building in Chapter 5 the emphasis has been placed upon the identification and interpretation of words. Words, however, are only the foundation materials of the reading structure. We now approach the keystone, so to speak, of that structure—reading for meaning. This process should begin early in the first grade. It is not unusual, however, to find some individuals at the high school and even the college level who have difficulty in reading some materials with understanding.

The quest for comprehension is only a means to an end, for one may read for pleasure or one may read in order to carry on his work. Various writers have shown that we read for fun and enjoyment during leisure hours to get away from the stern realities of everyday life and to relive childhood experiences. We read to enjoy contrasting emotional reactions, to satisfy our curiosity concerning people and their motives, and to give pleasure to others. We read for information concerning strange people, countries, times, and everyday happenings. We read to identify ourselves with others and to enjoy vicariously experiences otherwise unattainable. In order to carry on our work, we read to understand assignments and directions, to solve complicated problems and experiments, and to know what is happening in our time. Individuals seek information in order to influence and convince others and to learn how to act in new situations. We read for facts to help us to arrive at conclusions concerning cause and effect, relative values, and guiding principles. We read for information concerning how to travel by ocean liner, train, bus, and plane. In fact, we read to live.

It is the purpose of this chapter to discuss some of the factors affecting meaning and to show how reading skills essential to meaning may be developed. Before we begin this presentation, it may be well to focus our attention upon the problems of Joel and some of his difficulties in reading.

Joel Learns How to Read for Meaning

"We want Joel to understand what he reads," exclaimed his father as he discussed his son's problem with the school principal. "Just this morning," he continued, "Joel read aloud to us several pages of his elementary science text but he was not able to answer any questions about the material. I don't understand how it is possible for a person to read well orally and yet comprehend so little. Joel will soon be entering junior high school, and his mother and I are anxious for him to get along well. Frankly, we fail to see how he can be successful without being able to read silently and to understand what he reads."

Joel's fifth grade teacher wrote the following comment: "Joel has been under my supervision in the fifth grade since September of this year. I have known of him since he was in the first grade and apparently he has a history of spotty progress in reading. He reads fairly well orally but has difficulty in comprehending what he reads silently. Joel, like many of the other children, can do exercises well, but these same boys and girls fail to combine these skills in reading a chapter. Joel is a bright boy and is not a discipline problem in the classroom or on the playground. He seems to get along well with the other children although there is some evidence of maladjustment. I like Joel very much. This shy and quiet lad is mannerly and courteous. He is interested in the activities of the group and is willing to work as well as anyone. When he talks, he does so in an unhurried way, and he reads aloud at the same rate. Yesterday he asked that I pronounce our spelling words slowly when we had our weekly test. It is possible that he gets excited when hurried or under tension. Joel has a chemistry set in which he is especially interested. Recently he has brought to the classroom other science materials with which he spends his leisure time. In making use of these materials, Joel reads the directions aloud to the children and they make the necessary adjustments. Apparently he has difficulty in applying the ideas he reads aloud so fluently, chiefly because of his limited background. His primary difficulty is his lack of skill in reading for comprehension which may be due to a lack of mental content. Frustration and loss of confidence are becoming more apparent. Religious discrimination by one or two of Joel's associates and emotional conflicts having their origin in the home further threaten his sense of security. He tries extra hard to please everyone and he responds to appreciation of his efforts in a very satisfying manner."

In an interview with Joel's teacher it was learned that, according to data resulting from the administration of a reading test, Joel was reading as well as an individual six months in the fifth grade (5.6). Furthermore, it was learned that his teacher had made use of informal reading inventories and had determined his capacity level to be that of an eighth grade student. His instructional level was that of a pupil in the fourth grade, his frustration level was that of a fifth grade child, and his independent reading level was that of an individual in the third grade. This information provided by the teacher suggested that Joel was a boy of better than average mental ability who was not reading as well as his capacity level would indicate. In view of this inference on the part of the teacher, Joel was referred to the school psychologist for further study.

The clinician reported that Joel's IQ's as determined by the Wechsler Intelligence Scale for Children were 120, 108, and 116 on the verbal, performance, and full scales, respectively. Furthermore, it was reported that his grade score on a reading test was 5.6, that on an arithmetic test which measured only computational skills his grade score was 5.9, and that his grade placement on a spelling test was 4.9. These data substantiated the teacher's inference that Joel was a competent individual who apparently was not working to capacity, not only in reading but in the other subjects as well.

The school psychologist in discussing Joel's problem explained that in his opinion Joel was a mature boy physically, mentally, and emotionally who was beginning to lose confidence in himself because of a reading disability which could be corrected by regular instruction in the classroom. In explaining his point of view, he maintained that Joel for some unknown reason had not learned to read for main ideas and relevant details. This failure to develop reading skills essential to meaning had, in the opinion of the psychologist, resulted in emotional tension and a feeling of not belonging to the group in which Joel found himself. This situation, he explained, may have been intensified by pressures having their origin in the home, and especially those caused by the father.

Joel was a difficult boy to interview. He appeared either unwilling or unable to discuss freely his problems. His answers to questions were given carefully and deliberately. Frequently he made corrections in his statements obviously in an attempt to be accurate. In discussing his progress in reading he explained, "I have always liked to read aloud, and I think I have been good at it. Dad is an attorney and he certainly knows how to ask questions which I can't answer. He says I must read between the lines and get all the facts. I have tried to learn by heart all the words he has asked me to read, and I can't do it very well." This statement by Joel was one of the longest he made during the interview. Other information provided by him came only in response to direct questions. Some queries concerning his home environment were answered in the following words, "My parents think I am not as smart as they are. They do not care about the things I like. In school they think I am not doing as well as I should. I wish I could leave home, but I guess all boys feel that way when the going gets tough."

Several days later his teacher, in explaining her instructional plans for the group, pointed out, "We are going to spend more time in the fifth grade in formal reading. Incidental instruction as the children work on their own in social studies is apparently not sufficient. Our committee on reading at the later elementary level has plans for developing skills essential to meaning. We are preparing a syllabus which will emphasize reading for main ideas, relevant details, reading to follow directions, and to predict the outcome of stated events. In our study, we are concerned with the selection and adjustment of suitable materials to the individual requirements of our children. The whole problem of evaluating achievement in reading is being investigated. Some of our members are asking: Just what is reading and what do we want to measure? Our new developmental reading program is going to help all of us as we work with boys like Joel."

Several months later the teacher said, "Perhaps you will be interested in knowing what I have attempted to do with Joel and his group. During the last two months I have prepared and used exercises which I have hoped would aid the children in reading for main ideas. We have explained the purpose of a paragraph and have talked about topic sentences. We have shown that in constructing a paragraph the writer develops and enlarges upon the main idea in very much the same manner as a photographer would enlarge a 35 mm. film. I have also constructed exercises designed to furnish detail which would support the main idea expressed by the topic sentence in a paragraph. In my attempt to teach these skills, I have shown children not only how to reach paragraphs but how to write them as well."

In May of the same school year Joel reported progress in reading to the graduate student observing him. "I have learned to get the main ideas first and then to find as much detail as I need. I don't have to memorize," he said with more than his usual degree of confidence. "I have learned to ask questions and to look for answers. I have learned how ideas are put together so as to do the job the writer wants to get done."

Let us now review the significant factors in Joel's case.

1. Joel reads well orally but has difficulty in reproducing main ideas and related detail after reading silently.
2. In trying to conform to pressures applied by his father, Joel has attempted to memorize the facts which he has identified in his reading.
3. Joel is a boy of better than average intelligence who apparently is not working to capacity not only in reading but in the other school subjects as well.
4. Frustration and emotional conflicts having their origin in the home and school have been reported.
5. In providing instruction for Joel and other children having similar difficulties, his teacher has emphasized not only the identification of facts

and relevant ideas but their interpretation and evaluation as well. In other words, she has stressed an integration of reading skills rather than merely an accumulation.

6. Lack of adequate background and mental content in some subjects may be a significant factor in Joel's case.

In reading the biography of Joel, we see that the boy's chief problem has been his inability to read for meaning. We now turn our attention to some of the factors affecting meaning.

Factors Affecting Meaning

The ability to derive meaning from printed symbols is affected by maturity, mental content, interest, and states of anxiety resulting from frustration and emotional conflict. Furthermore, a lack of readiness is another factor adversely affecting the achievement of meaning. In the consideration of factors affecting meaning, it is well to emphasize the interrelation of maturity, mental content, and reading interests, for the individual must organize and give meaning to his own sense perceptions. In order to understand, he must contribute mental content which he himself has built up as a result of his experience. Deficiencies in mental content are frequently due to a lack of both mental and emotional maturity. Mental content is the result of experience but in order to profit from this experience there must be intellectual maturity.

Maturity

There is a positive relationship between mental maturity and achievement in reading. The Binet test of general intelligence and the Wechsler Intelligence Scale for Children can provide a fair estimate of reading expectancy. In predicting reading success, the mental age is probably more significant than the IQ. For adults one of the best measures of mental maturity is the Wechsler Adult Intelligence Scale. A study by Lazar [1] shows that the higher the intelligence level, the larger the percentage of children having library cards. In general, the girls at each mental level show a much larger percentage of library cards than the boys at the same level. Furthermore, this study shows that the actual number of books read by both boys and girls increases as the mental status of the children increases. One should not assume, however, that a high level of mental maturity is indicative of superior skill in reading, for reports by Witty and Kopel [2] show that some severely retarded readers are of average intel-

[1] May Lazar, "The Reading Interests of Bright, Average, and Dull Children," in *Research in the Three R's*, C. W. Hunnicutt and William J. Iverson (New York: Harper & Bros., 1958), pp. 119–125.

[2] Paul Witty and David Kopel, *Reading and the Educative Process* (Boston: Ginn and Co., 1939), p. 228.

ligence or better. Even at the college level it is not unusual to find students of superior intelligence who have reading difficulties.

A lack of emotional maturity can interfere with the acquiring of mental content, for some children avoid subjects and activities because they believe them to be difficult and without interest. Emotionally immature students at the later elementary and junior high school levels do not realize that in our changing world it is their responsibility to be interested in many subjects and in new and different ideas as expressed by leaders in our country and abroad. This attitude on the part of children and adults does not contribute to background, which is essential for the acquiring of meaning.

Mental Content

Mental content determines what the individual is to understand and what he is to feel. In other words, the cognitive and affective aspects of our reactions are determined by our previous experiences. Each individual organizes and gives meaning to his sense perceptions. For example, he may see four dots arranged as follows:

•   •

•   •

and perceive squareness. He may hear four short clicks sounded in rapid succession and perceive the letter *h* of the Morse Code. Again he may see four letters arranged as follows:

mean

and perceive one, or more than one, of several concepts. What one sees or hears is, of course, dependent upon his background and mental content. The individual has to contribute in order to secure meaning. If he has little to give, there indeed is little he can receive. In the act of reading, one learns to identify written symbols and to interpret their meaning. On every printed page there are many words arranged in the form of sentences and paragraphs. Ideas have been expressed by the writer which must be identified, interpreted, and, most important of all, evaluated. In these acts of thought mental content, an ever-changing element, imparts meaning which may vary greatly from that obtained by other readers. The affective or feeling aspects of our reactions are equally important, for how a person feels about a subject is determined by how he has previously felt. For example, a man who is a strong and enthusiastic Democrat may read in his newspaper that a Republican President is departing for a good-will tour to several nations. Because of this man's mental content and background, he may interpret the President's journey abroad as a gross waste of public funds, and furthermore, because of his mental content, he may react with resentment and disgust. The following is a thought-provoking stanza from Longfellow's "Psalm of Life":

> Let us, then, be up and doing,
>   With a heart for any fate;
> Still achieving, still pursuing,
>   Learn to labor and to wait.

These words may have been memorized and yet have little meaning to a boy in the fourth grade. Later, as the boy grows older, and as more and more mental content is built up, more and more meaning will be derived from these words. This added understanding is more than a by-product of intelligence and maturity; it is the resultant of experiences which have provided added meaning. It is obvious then that what we understand and how we feel is dependent upon our past experiences. Reading is a complex process which involves cognitive and affective reactions which are contingent upon mental content.

Interests

The quantitative and qualitative aspects of meaning which an individual gains from a story or a discussion of a science topic will be proportional to the degree of interest he already has in the subject. Interests vary with the sex and maturity of the child. Lazar [3] shows that both boys and girls like mystery, adventure, and historical stories. Girls, however, show a preference for fairy tales, novels, poetry, and stories of home and school. Boys are less interested in fairy tales, poetry, or stories of their immediate environment. On the other hand, girls have little interest in detective stories or in books dealing with science and invention. This study by Lazar also indicates a marked relationship between mental maturity and the types of books most frequently chosen. In general, children with high intelligence ratings preferred novels, science, and adventure while those with the lowest ratings were more apt to select fairy tales, nature, and animal stories.

States of Anxiety

Emotional conflicts, states of anxiety, and mounting tension can interfere with sustained effort and the attainment of meaning. The emotionally disturbed child who has endured unfortunate experiences at home or in the school may not be able to focus his attention sufficiently during the process of reading for meaning. Such children may show states of excitement and depression. Frequently they manifest antisocial behavior such as fighting, stealing, truancy, and other disciplinary problems. In these cases there may be a history of temper tantrums, persistent fears, tics, stammering, and stuttering. Some children under tension are shy and in-

[3] May Lazar, "The Reading Interests of Bright, Average, and Dull Children," in *Research in the Three R's*, C. W. Hunnicutt and William J. Iverson (New York: Harper & Bros., 1958), pp. 119–125.

troverted; others become easily tired and upset. Many emotionally disturbed children indulge in extreme daydreaming while others become hyperactive. These disturbed boys and girls, no matter how capable they may be, cannot be expected to maintain a high level of achievement in reading.

Lack of Readiness

Some pupils are unable to read effectively for meaning because they lack readiness for interpretation. Somewhere in their educational journey they have left behind or neglected basic skills which are necessary for their progress. Some children may manifest alphabet confusion and some inability to recognize words. Others may read words instead of ideas. Some may be unable to work out the meaning of words from contextual clues. Marked reversal tendencies may be found, and some children may have difficulty in recognizing significant word differences. Furthermore, some boys and girls may not want to put forth the effort necessary for effective reading. In all of these instances, the mechanics of reading are not adequate for the task ahead, *reading for meaning*.

Developing Skills Essential to Meaning

The effective reader should have a purpose for every reading activity. He should know what he wants and should proceed immediately to his goal. The teacher can by careful planning provide children with a purpose for reading and will find such general illustrative activities as the following helpful:

1. Aid pupils in setting up for themselves questions to be answered or problems to be solved so that their subsequent reading may be well motivated.
2. Make it possible for children to volunteer for oral reports on definite topics and subjects of special interest to them.
3. Show children how to translate into their own words information they have gained from reading and how to apply this information to their own problems.
4. Stimulate children to read for pleasure and satisfaction. Frequently this can be done through good oral reading to the group by the teacher.
5. Show children how to locate and select from many sources materials which are relevant to their problems, their interests, and their needs.
6. Encourage students to read printed directions carefully before beginning activities outlined in workbooks, procedures described on chalk or bulletin boards, and before beginning formal or informal tests.

7. Develop the habit of preparing for each activity in the classroom by giving clear and simple directions for that activity. When it is necessary, children can be expected to record these directions in their notebooks and to review them from time to time as their activities progress.

In the quest for meaning verbalism should be avoided. The immature reader, as exemplified by Joel, frequently repeats verbatim the words from a book without interpreting their meaning. For example, the following concept may be identified as a definition of personality and yet be inadequately understood.

Personality is the habitual mode of adjustment which an organism effects between its own egocentric drives and the factors in its environment.

This statement can be memorized and recited without much more than a glimmer of meaning. In order to interpret the sentence, one should have a background in general psychology and be familiar with the meaning of such terms as *habitual, organism, egocentric drives,* and *environment.* In this sentence the ideas expressed by the words, *egocentric drives,* may be difficult to understand, for they imply conflict within the ego, between the id and the superego or between impulse and inhibition, their equivalent. The expression, *the factors in its environment,* can be interpreted as satisfaction, security, and recognition which the human organism is seeking in his world. A fair interpretation of the sentence would then read: "Personality is a series of habits which an individual develops as he controls himself and acquires those things which he wants out of life." This interpretation illustrates the value of mental content which is required for an understanding of a comparatively simple sentence. Obviously, the conceptual aspects of reading are quite as important as the perceptual, and certainly, if thinking is to take place, the conceptual aspects must be emphasized. If this aspect of reading is to be developed by children and young students, well-planned instruction is a requirement. Some suggestions for the teacher follow.

Reading for the Main Idea

Young children can learn to listen for the important ideas in a story or when parents or teacher give directions for games and other activities. The habit of listening can be initiated in the home and later developed in the classroom. Some of the factors interfering with listening may also prevent effective reading for main ideas. For example, a limited vocabulary and the tendency to memorize words can limit any form of communication. The proneness to disregard a part of what is expressed and to accentuate preconceived ideas can only result in faulty interpretation. The immature and biased individual is apt to hear and find in print what he wants to hear and see, and he consequently fails to be objective in his understanding. All of these factors can contribute to an erroneous concept of the main idea.

Students like Joel can be taught to identify the main ideas first, and then later to clothe them in all the necessary detail. In becoming acquainted with any structure it is advisable for anyone first to perceive the whole and later to examine the essential parts. By means of questions children can be taught to read for significant ideas and to pass over, for a time, the intensive study of details which are not always pertinent. In fact, the individual who becomes unduly enmeshed in details may miss entirely the feeling and general impression that a writer is trying to portray. Consequently, it is advisable to show students how to read paragraphs, chapters, and textbooks first of all for the identification of the main ideas which have been expressed.

The Main Idea of a Paragraph

In any well-written material, a paragraph represents a unit of thought having one main idea. In some instances the first sentence expresses the central thought of the paragraph and the sentences which follow develop and enlarge upon this idea, making use of illustrations, examples, comparisons, and contrasting ideas. This may be illustrated by the following diagram.

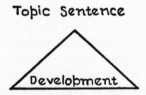

In other paragraphs, the writer may gradually develop a central line of thought and then summarize his contributions by a topic sentence calculated to express the gist of the whole paragraph.

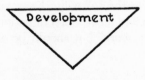

After some practice the mature reader will be able to spot the main idea of each paragraph and appreciate its relationship to those ideas previously expressed and to those concepts which follow in sequential paragraphs.

The Main Ideas of a Chapter

The main ideas of a chapter may be identified by carefully reading the introduction, the main headings, and the summary if these are provided. In the author's introduction to a chapter, he generally states what he intends to do and if he ends with a summary, he reviews briefly what he has accomplished. In well-written textbooks, large headings also facilitate the identification of main ideas. In non-textbook materials, headings are not provided. Consequently it may become necessary for the reader, if he is to identify the main ideas, to make his own headings. If the book is the property of the student, these headings can be written in the margin, or if the student wishes, in a notebook indicating page number and the paragraphs between which the headings are to be inserted. Surely, if a student is to read effectively any chapter, he must first identify the basic and fundamental ideas expressed by the author. The development of this skill was essential in the case of Joel.

The Main Ideas in Textbooks

In the introduction or preface to a textbook, the author generally states what he intends to accomplish and how the text differs from others in the field. The chapter headings as indicated in the table of contents point out the main ideas the author intends to develop in his treatment of the subject. The number of pages in each chapter suggests the relative importance to the writer of the ideas being developed. A study of the index shows in detail the author's concept of the subjects he believes to be essential to an adequate treatment of his problem. Even the glossary sets forth the concepts which are deemed necessary for a thorough understanding of the content of the text. It is obvious then that a systematic study of the introduction, table of contents, glossary, and index will provide the thoughtful reader with the main ideas expressed by the author in the development of his subject. The reader's task, however, has just begun, for he has merely *identified* these ideas and they are yet to be *interpreted* and later *evaluated*.

The teacher will find in the following list a variety of suggestions for helping students to find main ideas. Such directions to the students should not be regarded as "busy work" but should be an outgrowth of the students' own plans.

1. Copy from your book three sentences and restate each in your own words.
2. Read three paragraphs and assign to each a title.
3. Summarize a paragraph by stating the main idea in a single sentence.

4. Summarize the plot of a television program in two or three short sentences.
5. Read the table of contents of one of your textbooks and state in not more than three sentences the ideas the author has discussed.
6. Read the introduction to a chapter and state briefly what the author intends to do.
7. Convert a main heading in a chapter into a question, making certain that the paragraphs which follow this heading answer the question which you have asked.
8. Find a chapter with a summary and state what the author says he has accomplished in the chapter.
9. Find and read in your daily paper an interesting news story. Rewrite the heading so as to show more completely the content of the story.

These activities may be too difficult for immature readers; however, they do illustrate types of exercises which can be beneficial to growing readers.

Reading for Relevant Details

After an individual has discovered the main idea of a selection, he needs details to fill out the pattern and expand the idea. It is now the reader's responsibility to pick out those ideas that are essential to this expansion of thought and that support the contention of the writer. These minor concepts are related to each other and are relevant to the main idea. In the sciences and social studies such details are demanded by careful workers and critical students. Content material in these fields cannot and should not be read rapidly. The student can adjust his rate of reading to the nature and content of the material as he reads. Meaning should never be sacrificed for rate. In reading, the student is required to observe and evaluate details, to follow directions precisely, and to discriminate between relevant and irrelevant data. For some students this discrimination is difficult because of their deficiency in background and mental content. Frequently it is well to draw a diagram or picture of the conditions described and occasionally it may be necessary to consult other texts and do supplementary reading. Mature students usually find it advisable to take notes as they read.

Reading carefully for details is important when they contribute to a better understanding of the main principle or idea being developed. It is possible for children and adults to become lost in a maze of details and be unable to sense the direction toward which they point. Overemphasis can produce laborious readers who can recall much of the factual content but fail utterly to appreciate the relationship of the facts to the main idea. In attempting to avoid this misdirection of effort, teachers can help children identify facts which build up and provide support for a major concept. Relevant or helping facts can be accepted. Irrelevant or hindering facts can be rejected. The following activities can help children to listen and to read for relevant details:

1. Listen to a commercial on radio or television and pick out the reasons why the product is *said* to be valuable.
2. Listen to a short talk at school or on radio or television. Then write out the main idea expressed by the speaker and list the facts he gave to support it.
3. It is said that nutrition is essential to health. List the facts which will support this statement.
4. Select a paragraph of interest to you from one of your textbooks. Find the main idea and list the *important* facts the writer has given to support or make clear this main idea.
5. Convert a main heading in one of your textbooks into a question and then find in the paragraphs under this heading all of the *important* answers to this question.

Exercises similar to these may be devised so as to utilize the subject matter and materials available to children and of interest to them.

Reading to Follow Directions

Reading to follow directions is closely related to reading for details. The latter activity, however, is performed step by step in sequential order which may be *temporal, spatial,* and *causal.* Each sequence will be discussed separately.

In giving directions for making a cake, building a radio, performing an experiment, or solving a problem, the temporal sequence is important. Ideas have a time relationship if it is necessary to express one before another. First, one activity is performed, then the second, and later the third, and so on. For example, in making a cake the following sequence is maintained:

1. Grease generously and flour two nine-inch layer pans.
2. Cream together until fluffy two-thirds cup of soft shortening and one and three-fourths cups of sugar.
3. Sift together three cups of sifted flour, three and one-half teaspoons of baking powder and three-fourths teaspoon of salt.
4. Stir in alternately with one and one-third cups thin milk and two teaspoons of flavoring.

5. Fold in four egg whites stiffly beaten.
6. Bake until cake tests done.[4]

In reading material of this nature, cause-and-effect relationship can be clearly established if the reader has in mind the sequential order of events.

Objects and concepts have a spatial relationship if their relative position in space is essential for meaning. This relationship is important in descriptions and in directives showing how to reach a building on campus, park, or highway. The reader or listener must have in mind his present position and its spatial relationship to his destination. For example, anyone directing a student who is standing in front of the Health Center on the East Campus of Western Michigan University to the Waldo Library on the West Campus, must make clear the following pattern of spatial relationships:

1. Go down driveway to Oakland.
2. Turn right on Oakland.
3. Turn left at stop light on Michigan Avenue.
4. Turn left at VandeGeissen Road.
5. Turn left at Arcadia Avenue to library.

Time sequence may be implied in these directives but spatial relationships are of more importance and determine the pattern of organization.

Causal relationships exist only if one event or condition could not have taken place without the other. For example, a student's poor work in the classroom might be explained as follows:

1. Has pronounced visual defect.
2. Confuses *o, e,* and *c,* or *b, h,* and *n.*
3. Fails to recognize significant word differences.
4. Becomes confused and frustrated.
5. Develops dislike for reading.
6. Does poor academic work.

Causes always precede effects; consequently, there is a temporal as well as a causal sequence in this case. In other instances, there may be multiple and overlapping relationships.

From these illustrations of temporal, spatial, and causal relationships, the teacher will observe the importance of the sequence of ideas in the process of listening and reading for meaning. It is also apparent that sequence of concepts determines the *organization* of that which is spoken or written. In outlining and note-taking it is necessary for the young student to understand and appreciate the order of ideas being expressed as

---

[4] *Betty Crocker's Picture Cook Book* (New York: McGraw-Hill Book Co., and General Mills, Inc., Minneapolis, 1950), p. 148.

he listens or reads. These means of organizing information will be developed in Chapter 7.

The following activities would provide practice in determining the order and sequence of ideas being expressed. These activities should not be prescribed but are suggestive of similar ones which might grow out of the child's experiences in the classroom.

1. Locate in a science or social studies text examples of ideas expressed in temporal sequence.
2. Find examples of ideas expressed in causal sequence.
3. Write out the directions for proceeding from your home to your school.
4. Outline the steps for finding the length of line AC in the following right angle triangle.

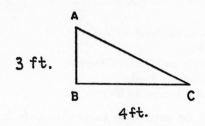

5. Show the sequence of steps in adding ¾ and ⅝.
6. Locate examples of ideas expressed in spatial sequence.
7. Follow a list of directions provided by your teacher.

Reading to Predict

Predictions are generally anticipated solutions to a problem which would require an indefinite amount of time for verification. In order to predict wisely, one must understand thoroughly what has gone before. He must know the past and be able to project his generalizations into the future. Consequently, reading to predict is probably one of the most important and surely one of the most difficult reading skills to attain.

As young students become able to predict outcomes, draw valid conclusions, and propose adequate solutions, they demonstrate real evidence of their ability to read for meaning. In the elementary grades children can be expected to explain what they think will happen next in a story. Later they can be asked to predict how a character will react in a new situation. Teachers can encourage children to read for facts and to interpret them in terms of their experiences. "Why" questions can be asked, and students can be expected to substantiate their inferences. Discussions by members of the group can aid in the development of critical attitudes and objective points of view. Teachers can explain how ideas are developed by both *inductive* and *deductive* thinking. In inductive thinking, facts are accepted and inferences are stated which are supported by these facts. In deductive thinking, major and minor premises are used to set forth certain conclusions. Each of these two processes of thinking can lead to valid predictions. In the sciences, inductive thinking fulfills the requirements of a most valuable tool which can be used to interpret data resulting from experimentation and to make logical assumptions. In Chapter 9 the steps in the scientific method are discussed and illustrated. In general, this search for new principles and their ultimate verification is for the more mature reader; young students in the elementary grades, however, should have the opportunity to deal with facts and to draw sound conclusions. Young children have questioning attitudes and this characteristic of growing readers should not be ignored by teachers and parents.

In our world where people are expected to participate in the activities of government, reading to predict outcomes needs to be developed, not only in preparation for adulthood but for more effective living on the part of the student himself. One of the best ways of getting children to think is to place them in an environment that demands thinking. Children need a place where they can express their ideas freely and without ridicule. Debate and discussion based upon well-substantiated facts should be encouraged. Teaching children to think is the chief function of the teacher, and this responsibility must be met in the public schools if our form of government is to survive.

The following activities are suggestive of others which the teacher can devise to provide her students with practice in reading and listening to predict the outcome of given events:

1. Read carefully in your local newspaper the report of a civic problem and predict what you think the outcome will be.
2. Read the first act of a three-act play and point out how you think the play will end.
3. Read a detective story until you have identified the crime which has been committed and the characters which have been involved. Work out your own solution to the mystery.
4. Your class in school may be about to elect new officers. After you have become acquainted with the problems and persons involved in the election, predict who you think will be elected.
5. Study carefully the weather map found in the daily paper and predict weather conditions which may prevail during the next twenty-four hours.

Reading to Appreciate Sensory Imagery

The reading of all imaginative writing is dependent upon the individual's ability to interpret words into images. The mature reader will see, hear, feel, smell, and taste as he reads. This ability to translate words into sensory imagery is particularly required in the reading of poetry, drama, and fiction. For example, these lines from Lowell's "Vision of Sir Launfal" [5] illustrate such a use of imagery.

> Down swept the chill wind from the mountain peak,
> From the snow five thousand summers old;
> On open wold and hilltop bleak
> It had gathered all the cold,
> And whirled it like sleet on the wanderer's cheek;
> It carried a shiver everywhere
> From the unleafed boughs and pastures bare.

In these words by Lowell there is visual, auditory, kinesthetic, and tactual imagery which is experienced with genuine pleasure by some persons. To other readers, these words are only words, words, words. They see no pictures, hear no sounds, and miss entirely the sting of the cold on the wanderer's cheek. It is not known why these differences exist; however, it is generally assumed that such factors as maturity, background, and mental content are significant. The imagery experienced by an individual while listening or reading depends in part upon his previous experience with words, their denotation and their connotation, and in part, upon the new word picture presented to him. For example, the words, "five thousand summers" actually denotes five thousand years. On the other hand, the connotation of these words may vary greatly from reader to reader. Furthermore, placing these words in the phrase "From the snow five thousand summers old" creates a new word picture with added enrichment of imagery.

It is assumed that children and adults can improve their understanding and appreciation of imagery. Reading in the content fields requires that children be able to visualize the situations making up a problem and the steps to be followed in conducting an experiment. In learning to drive a car, kinesthetic imagery is utilized. Teaching students to make use of imagery in listening and reading, however, is much more difficult. It is well to discuss and illustrate the different types of imagery and especially its use in literature. In the early grades the stories told to children or read by them evoke imagery which can be utilized by the teacher for group discussion. Children under adequate direction enjoy reporting the

---

[5] James Russell Lowell, "The Vision of Sir Launfal," Prelude to Part Second, lines 1–7.

pictures they "see" and the sounds they "hear." Short poems may be read aloud and pupils can be alerted for word pictures and for the *feeling* they experience. The teacher may point out that the way each child feels is determined by his environment and especially by his home, family, and way of living. She can show that the use of words, rhythm, allusions, symbols, and metaphors effectively contributes to each person's reaction. While children can be encouraged to feel differently, it is desirable for them to be able to identify the words or elements in the poem that contribute to their feeling. Children can be asked to assume the role of a character in history such as, for example, Washington, and report on what Washington might think and feel concerning his home at Mount Vernon. Such reports can be given orally or read aloud. In either instance, individuals in the group can be asked to identify imagery and to describe how it affects them. The teacher will understand that these activities may be the beginning of the child's appreciation of literature.

The Values of Oral Reading

In the elementary grades silent reading receives more time and attention than oral reading. There are two functions of the latter, however, which ought not to escape the consideration of the teacher. On the one hand, oral reading can be a means of expressing ideas and emotional qualities for the satisfaction of others, and it can also be used as an instrument of instruction. There are five possible types of oral reading, and it may be advisable to discuss each of these and its relationship to one or both of these functions.

The first type of oral reading frequently accompanies silent reading and is instructional in form. For example, as children are reading silently, the teacher may ask, "What did Debbie do when she saw her mother?" This question calls for selective thinking and gives purpose to the reading activities of the children. If answers are vague and indefinite, a member of the group may be asked to prove his point by reading aloud the exact words which in his opinion provide the correct response. This instructional device is commonly used in the primary grades; however, it can be employed profitably with older students.

The second type of oral reading involves the reading of new material orally without first reading it through silently. Sight materials are selected far below the frustration level of the child and generally two grade levels below his instructional level. An adept oral reader may read at sight content from his scout manual, directions for firing a toy projectile, or read an exciting story to his younger brother. This form of oral reading can be done fluently in a natural conversational tone so as to give satisfaction and pleasure to those who listen. Its instructional aspects are not generally stressed.

Reading in an audience situation is the third type of oral reading and involves both recreational and instructional elements. Previous preparation on the part of the reader is always stressed. Make-believe television telecasts can provide an excellent opportunity for reading before an audience. Panel discussions based upon research reading by several mature readers can be interesting, informative, and productive of active group participation. Another activity worthy of encouragement is the sharing of current news items and articles of interest by a good oral reader. Teacher and students can work cooperatively to set up criteria for effective oral reading. These may include such suggestions as the following:

1. Look up the meaning and pronunciation of unfamiliar words.
2. Use the voice to show and emphasize meaning.
3. Speak loudly enough so that all may hear and understand.
4. Maintain the mechanics essential to adequate communication, such as a comfortable position while reading, the satisfactory position of a book, and proper eye contacts with the audience.

The fourth type of oral reading stresses the mechanics of oral expression, such as the effective use of the voice, proper enunciation of words, adjustment of rate to emotional tone, action, and proper phrasing of sentences. This form of oral reading is used to express the dramatic and humorous elements in literature and is emphasized in speech courses. It is employed both as an instrument of instruction and as a means of expression.

Choral speaking is the fifth type of oral reading. It is an excellent way to give children an introduction to controlled expression and the feeling of poetry. For the first exercises in group speaking, simple poems which are suitable for choral rendition should be selected. Narrative and humorous verse and poems of spirited action are acceptable to children, especially boys. Some poems lend themselves to a pattern in which each child says a line or two. This is group speaking in its simplest form. As the children become more experienced, two group arrangements with alternating responses can be planned. In some poems a line can be read as a solo or a chorus. In others, grouping of high and low voices can be worked out so as to attain euphonious effects. The teacher may use her judgment in the interpretation of the poem and in casting the parts. Older children will be able to do their own planning and will enjoy assuming the responsibility generally associated with the more complicated and descriptive selections. Choral reading can serve as an instructional device and at the same time contribute to the satisfaction and pleasure of both children and adults.

Evaluation of Achievement

There are four approaches to the problem of evaluating performance in reading, and each may be regarded as a tool to accomplish a specific task. As a precautionary measure, it should be pointed out that evaluation is the result of an interpretative process and is not based entirely upon instruments of precision.

Objective Tests

Standardized tests for the appraisal of reading achievement are fairly satisfactory measures of some specific skills and abilities. These instruments can be used in determining the reading levels of children and, to some extent, in spotting the skills which they possess and those which they lack. Scores on reading tests are generally stated in terms of achievement ages, grade scores, or percentiles. In selecting measures of reading ability, it is well for the teacher to consider the educational significance of the test. In other words, the test should measure those aspects of reading which are of importance to the teacher. The value of any test is limited, for generally it is designed to evaluate only certain skills or aspects of reading.

The chief function of a reading test is to appraise the reading levels of children so that material may be adjusted to these levels. Consequently, measures of reading skills should be made early in the semester or school year. These tests should be easily administered and easily scored. Equivalent forms of the test should be available so that growth between the time of initial and final testing can be evaluated. The cost of the tests themselves should not be prohibitive, and in the selection of these instruments the matter of reliability and validity should be given careful consideration. Facts obtained from the use of tests should always be interpreted in terms of the history of the individual. In general, test scores are meaningless aside from the conditions under which they were obtained. For example, a new automobile may, under certain conditions, pass a given point at fifteen miles per hour. No one is justified, however, in assuming that an adequate appraisal of the potential speed of the car has been made. Lists of tests which have been found valuable by teachers of reading are provided in the section of Questions and References at the end of this chapter.

Informal Reading Inventories

Teachers of reading need practical devices which can be useful in evaluating reading performance. In demonstrating the uses of a systematic reading inventory in all grades through college, Betts [6] emphasizes

[6] Emmett A. Betts, *Foundations of Reading Instruction* (New York: American Book Co., 1957), chap. XXI.

the need for four basic types, or levels, of information: He considers first, the *independent reading level* of the student. This is the highest level at which the individual can read with full understanding and freedom from mechanical difficulties. The second, the *instructional level,* is the highest reading level at which systematic instruction can be initiated. The third, or *frustration level,* is the one at which the individual is thwarted or baffled by the language, vocabulary, sentence structure, and complexity of ideas. The fourth, the *capacity level,* is the highest level at which the student can comprehend what is read or spoken to him. In other words, this is the level for which he has adequate background, experience, and mental content.

Informal inventories to be used in determining these four levels may be constructed by the teacher from the Gray Standardized Oral Reading Paragraphs Test [7] or from selections from graded readers which are not being used for instructional purposes in the classroom. For example, the teachers may obtain copies of the Gray Standardized Oral Reading Paragraphs Test and prepare an informal inventory which can be used to evaluate reading performance in grades 1–8, inclusive. The paragraphs representing twelve levels can be cut out and pasted on 3″ x 5″ cards. Five questions can then be worked out for each level to appraise the reader's understanding of the materials read. Four questions can be constructed to determine the student's ability to identify factual content and a fifth question to measure the individual's ability to interpret and evaluate what is read. The following paragraph at the fifth level illustrates this procedure:

5

One of the most interesting birds which ever lived in my bird-room was a blue-jay named Jackie. He was full of business from morning till night, scarcely ever still. He had been stolen from a nest long before he could fly, and he had been reared in a house long before he had been given to me as a pet.

QUESTIONS

1. Who was Jackie?
2. Where did he live?
3. How did the bird act?
4. Where did Jackie come from?
5. Why do you think he was happy?

(Back of card)

[7] William S. Gray, *Gray Standardized Oral Reading Paragraphs Test* (New York: The Psychological Corporation, 1923).

The independent reading level can be determined by discovering the highest level at which the student can read without mechanical difficulties and can answer correctly the five questions. If the child is regarded as a poor reader, it may be advisable to start with a card several levels below his grade placement. Betts suggests that, in addition to the child's success in answering factual and inferential questions, the following criteria be used for determining the independent reading level:

1. Freedom from tension, finger pointing, and head movement.
2. Oral reading characterized by proper phrasing, accurate interpretation of punctuation, correct pronunciation of words, and use of a conversational tone.
3. Silent reading to answer questions characterized by absence of vocalization and a rate of comprehension higher than that provided by oral reading.

The *frustration level* can be determined next. For this purpose, the teacher should permit the individual being examined to read paragraphs of ever-increasing difficulty until errors increase so as to make aid by the examiner necessary. When this level of frustration has been reached, the student will be successful in answering correctly approximately 40 per cent of the questions based upon the content of the paragraph. According to Betts, the following points should be considered in estimating frustration level:

1. Inability to pronounce 10 per cent or more of the words.
2. Inability to anticipate meaning.
3. Emotional tension.
4. Attempts to withdraw from the reading situation by showing a reluctance to read.
5. Oral reading characterized by word-by-word reading, failure to interpret punctuation, repetition, omission or addition of words, reversals, vowel and consonant errors, and high-pitched voice.
6. Silent reading characterized by very slow rate, excessive finger pointing and lip movement, and inability to make use of contextual clues.

The *instructional level* will be located between the independent and the frustration levels. At this level the individual may be able to answer correctly 80 per cent of the questions. He should be able to pronounce 95 per cent of the words and should show evidence of ability to anticipate meaning. There should be freedom from finger pointing, head movement, and emotional tension in the reading situation. Oral reading should be rhythmic and carried on in a natural conversational tone. Silent reading should be characterized by adequate rate and ability to make use of the various methods of word attack.

The teacher can determine the *capacity level* by reading aloud the paragraphs above the frustration level and by asking questions in order to appraise the individual's understanding of the materials read to him. In all instances, the examining procedure should be continued until the student fails to answer successfully 20 per cent of the questions at the level under consideration.

Let us examine data resulting from the administration of an informal inventory to a student in the sixth grade.

Capacity Level	8.0
Frustration Level	6.0
Instructional Level	5.0
Independent Reading Level	4.0

These approximations of reading achievement suggest that although this sixth grade child can comprehend materials read to him at the eighth level, he becomes thwarted and baffled when he attempts to read materials at the sixth level or above. Furthermore, it is implied that reading instruction should be provided at the fifth level and that at the fourth level there is freedom from mechanical difficulties and a readiness for the selection of equivalent materials for free reading.

Informal inventories permit direct on-the-spot administration; however, they should not be regarded as complete or exact measures of reading achievement. Teachers have found that informal inventories are valuable means of appraising *tentatively* the performance level of their pupils, especially when more objective measures are not available. Valuable information can be secured by observing the student's responses to these inventories, for frequently *how* the individual reacts is more significant than his scores.

Making Use of Informal Inventories

When the teacher of reading meets for the first time her group of boys and girls, she is confronted with the problem of determining the reading levels of each child. In many instances the accumulative record provided by former teachers may provide this information. There will, however, be a need for the application of informal inventories in the case of children for whom these data are not available. Knowledge of the reading levels of the pupils is essential if materials are to be adjusted to the reading ability of each child. This is especially true if flexible grouping is utilized in facilitating instruction. Furthermore it is helpful in parent-teacher conferences if the teacher can explain clearly the child's independent reading level and his instructional level. An explanation of frustration and capacity levels would prove beneficial in many such conferences and would create the opinion that the teacher was fully aware of the child's achievement in reading.

Observation

The teacher of reading should systematically observe the students in her classroom in order to identify individuals who read words instead of ideas, who fail to enjoy reading activities, and who are unsuccessful in their academic work. Inability to identify and interpret new words should be investigated. Marked reversal tendencies, alphabet confusion, and low rate of reading may be significant. Evidences of physical handicaps, such as visual and auditory deficiencies, can be noted by the careful observer. The teacher can recognize and study students who lack persistence or ability to concentrate and those who demonstrate unwholesome attitudes toward reading. In making observations of children the teacher should always distinguish between facts and inferences, for she can be fairly sure of the former but never certain of the latter.

History

The history of a student from home through kindergarten and up to his present grade status provides a fairly satisfactory means of evaluating reading skills and their relationship to the student's adjustment. In dealing with reading problems of either the individual or of groups, the teacher should determine the relevance of known factors and not over-emphasize analytical testing and detailed history taking. She must have an interest in the child similar to that of a parent and at the same time the objective attitude of the laboratory technician. Anecdotal records maintained by the teacher can furnish valuable information concerning a child's background which may be essential to an interpretation of his achievement in reading.

An illustration of the significance of a segment in the life history of a child having difficulty in reading is provided in the case of Joel. The reader will recall that his teacher reported his progress in reading as spotty and inconsistent. Joel's history shows that he lacked skill in reading for meaning. The school psychologist expressed the opinion that this disability, which was causing frustration and a loss of confidence, was further intensified by causal factors in the home. The reader will recall that the clinician also expressed the opinion that Joel's difficulty in reading could be adjusted satisfactorily by the regular instruction in the classroom. This opinion was confirmed by the teacher, who reported success in carrying out a program for developing skills essential to meaning. The reader will remember Joel's statement that he "learned by heart" the words his father had asked him to read. Other factors making up this history are the psychometric data furnished by the school psychologist and Joel's statement concerning his home environment. This brief summary from the reading history of an elementary school pupil suggests that Joel's inability to read for meaning had been primarily due to inadequate instruction in the classroom and that resulting frustration was intensified by pressures applied by the father. These are the factors which are assumed to be relevant in this case and all others are probably of lesser weight. This brief history of Joel provides a moving picture of him over a period of time. Surely, it is of more value than a snapshot.

Providing for Individual Differences

In this chapter it has been emphasized that reading for meaning is an activity which should be stressed at all levels, from the elementary school to the university. In addition, the factors affecting meaning are equally operative at all levels. Furthermore, the practices and teaching techniques designed to facilitate interpretation are equally effective whether or not the teacher is dealing with boys and girls in the elementary grades or with students in the secondary school. The principles remain the same. The subject matter, however, must be determined by the reading and interest levels of the students. Four approaches to the problem of evaluating performance in reading have been pointed out, and it has been emphasized that each is a tool which may be selected to accomplish a specific task. We are now ready to consider the matter of individual differences.

Factors to Be Considered

Factors to be considered in providing for individual differences in the teaching of reading center around the child, his teacher, and the school administration. Each of these focal points will be discussed.

The child is the center of all instructional activities. What are his reading interests? What are his reading levels? What are his reading needs? Surely, the teacher must have answers to these questions. To arrive at these answers, consideration must be given to the social structure which has contributed to the child's background and mental content. Each child must be observed in his own world and be permitted to become acquainted with the wider world beyond his horizon. How far he can be urged to explore beyond his immediate environment is dependent upon his mental and emotional maturity and the singleness of his purpose. All these factors must be known to the teacher before any attempt is made to provide for the individual differences of her boys and girls. Teachers should be well prepared to study children, their growth and development. They should know how to select, administer, score, and interpret objective as well as informal measures of reading skills. They should understand the dynamics of child behavior and how to interview and integrate information from various sources. A pragmatic educational philosophy and a scientific attitude toward the problems of modern education are necessary requisites. Every teacher who is truly interested in the reading improvement of her children must become acquainted with children's reading materials and be able to find the right book for the right child at the right time. She must be able to modify her plans and adjust quickly to changing situations as they may develop. Well-grounded enthusiasm and persistent effort on the part of the teacher are essential to effective teaching. Children with the incapable teacher are frequently herded together without discrimination as to their interests, needs, and ability and certainly without guidance.

Administrators in the school system can facilitate the provision for individual differences. In fact, if this is neglected by school authorities the task of the teacher becomes almost an impossible one. Meeting individual differences is a point of view which can be shared by parents, school board members, school administrators, and teachers. It can be a policy accepted and implemented by those concerned with the instruction of children. Such an educational policy can lead to the provision of adequate equipment and suitable materials. Surely, movable chairs and tables, along with materials supplying a wide range of interest and reading levels, constitute the minimal essentials. Teachers can provide for individual differences if they are furnished the necessary tools. This is the responsibility of the school administration and the citizens of the community.

Various Plans for Working with Children

One of the most interesting approaches to the teaching of reading which has been introduced during recent years is the program at New Castle, Pennsylvania. The spokesman for the New Castle Reading Experiment is Glenn McCracken, whose many articles on the subject are listed in the Questions and References accompanying Chapter 4. The program is based on the assumption that a correlated visual image can serve as a medium for reading instruction at the primary level. From 1947 to 1949 the proponents of this method planned, experimented, tested, and prepared material. In September, 1949, the program was ready for use in the first grade. Filmstrips were prepared to accompany a basal reading series so that there was a frame of projected material for every lesson in the basic books. These filmstrips were used to introduce each day's lesson. In other words, in this program all initial reading instruction occurs at the projection screen. The basic textbooks are used only for extended reading practice and to test the quality and quantity of learning which has occurred. Evaluation studies of this approach suggest that children, regardless of mental ability, learn to read when textbook material is systematically correlated with and supplemented by filmstrips.

Most teachers, however, make use of basal readers and other reading materials as they engage in one or more of the following plans: (1) homogeneous grouping within the classroom on the basis of reading achievement; (2) regrouping into homogeneous sections for reading only; (3) grouping according to interests or needs; and (4) individualized reading programs.

Grouping on the Basis of Reading Achievement

The most prevalent plan of grouping is based on the reading achievement of the pupils. In the primary grades the teacher usually divides her students into three groups, whereas teachers in the upper grades usually limit the number of groups to two. This type of grouping has been attempted in the elementary schools of Ventura County, California.[8] Each teacher divided her class into three groups on the basis of reading levels. Standardized tests, informal reading inventories, and permanent record cards were employed to determine each child's placement in reading. Emphasis was placed on flexibility. Some children progressed faster than others and in order to keep pupils with similar abilities in the same group, teachers were required to modify their groupings several times each year.

Another plan, which has been followed in the elementary schools of International Falls, Minnesota, has been described by Morris.[9] Grade designations in the three primary grades were dropped. In their place, eight levels of attainment based primarily on pupil accomplishment in reading were substituted. Each pupil advanced from one level to the next whenever tests and teacher judgment indicated that he had satisfactorily completed the requirements of the present level. In each room pupils were grouped according to progress in reading so that there was not too wide a range of levels in any one room. Most pupils completed the work of the primary unit in three years. A few, however, took four or five years. Pupils who were unable to complete all the levels for a given year started the next year at the level above the last one completed successfully. In this way, according to Morris, progress was continuous and not marked by needless repetition of work already completed.

Harris[10] describes another form of homogeneous grouping which is being attempted in some of the elementary schools in New York City.

[8] Pauline Jeidy, "Improving the Program in Reading," *Elementary English* (January, 1949), 26:27–31.
[9] W. A. Morris, "Reducing Reading Problems Thru Organization," *Reading for Today's Children*, Thirty-Fourth Yearbook, The National Elementary Principal (September, 1955), 35:48–52.
[10] Albert J. Harris, "Grouping and Promotion in Relation to Progress in Reading," *Better Readers for Our Times* (1956), 1:69–73.

Each teacher receives two groups of pupils. Both groups are fairly homogeneous but there is a gap between the poorest reader in the upper group and the better reader in the lower group. Thus, a third grade teacher may have two groups, one reading at second grade level and the other at fourth grade level. One of the reasons for using this plan is to eliminate the labeling of some classes as "slow" by having both "good" and "poor" readers in the same classroom.

Another type of homogeneous grouping which, according to Robinson,[11] was used for a while in Toronto, is known as the "siphoned-off class." The very poorest readers are gathered into a special class taught by a skillful teacher who attempts to adjust materials and procedures to the needs of the children.

Regrouping into Sections for Reading Only

A number of schools have attempted to regroup children into homogeneous groups for reading instruction only. Some large schools set up homerooms on the basis of reading achievement. In such a plan, reading tests are administered to all the pupils in several grades. On the basis of test results pupils are divided into reading classes, all of which are scheduled for reading at the same time. For other subjects and for homeroom activities, heterogeneous or some other form of grouping may be employed. An example of this type of grouping has been described by Floyd.[12] An attempt was made in the schools of Joplin, Missouri, to develop a workable program for dealing with the wide range of reading abilities in grades four through six. Children were classified according to reading level into nine groups for basal instruction in reading and into five heterogeneous groups for recreational reading. Apparently this procedure is growing in popularity, and results which have been reported are quite satisfactory.

Another plan has been utilized by fourth grade teachers in Seattle, Washington.[13] Their procedure consisted in assigning pupils to heterogeneously grouped homerooms where all subjects except reading were taught. Each child was assigned to one of four reading rooms on the basis of his reading ability. Each day the children left the homeroom and went to the assigned reading room, where they spent one hour in concentrated reading study. At the end of this hour they returned to their respective homerooms for the rest of the day. In this way, each teacher worked with a group of pupils whose reading abilities were similar.

[11] Margaret A. Robinson, "Discussion of Grouping and Promotion in Relation to Progress in Reading," *Better Readers for Our Times* (1956), 1:73–74.
[12] Cecil Floyd, "Meeting Children's Reading Needs in the Middle Grades: A Preliminary Report," *The Elementary School Journal* (October, 1954), 55:99–103.
[13] Esther Skonnord Carlson and Joyce Northrup, "An Experiment in Grouping Pupils for Instruction in Reading," *Reading for Today's Children*, Thirty-Fourth Yearbook, The National Elementary Principal (September, 1955), 35:53–57.

Grouping According to Interests or Needs

Some teachers group boys and girls according to their interests. In this procedure the children select some aspect of a project or unit of study on which they wish to work. Committees are formed and the teacher helps each group to locate materials appropriate for the various reading levels within the group. The children then read and report on their topics.

Another procedure which is being utilized by some teachers is a modification of homogeneous grouping in which children are grouped on the basis of their reading needs rather than their reading achievement. Kathleen B. Hester [14] calls this plan "grouping by invitation." All students in a given class, regardless of their reading levels, work together for certain parts of the instructional period and at other times are divided according to their needs. In general, the whole class meets together for the presentation of the story. During this time attempts are made to develop background and interest. The next step in the procedure involves silent reading of the story for some particular purpose. After the students have read and discussed the story, a "skill for the day" is chosen which is dependent upon the students' needs. Children then may invite themselves into the group where intensive work is carried on. The final step consists of reassembling the whole group to evaluate the story.

Another procedure based on the reading needs of children has been described by Carter and McGinnis. [15] According to this flexible grouping plan, instructional aims, materials, and procedures are adjusted to the needs of children. Information for grouping is secured from reading test scores, reports of former teachers, informal observations made by the present teacher, and anecdotal records. Children are assigned to groups on the basis of specific reading objectives to be accomplished, interest, and availability of materials. Children work together in a group only as long as they share the same need.

Individualized Reading Programs

Individualized reading has been described by Lazar [16] as "a way of thinking about reading—an attitude toward the place of reading in the total curriculum, toward the materials and methods used, and toward the child's developmental needs." It is an approach to reading which is based on the needs of children. Instruction in reading is provided as each child reads material which he has selected because it is of interest to him. The

[14] Kathleen B. Hester, "Grouping By Invitation," *The Reading Teacher* (December 1957), 11:105–108.

[15] Homer L. J. Carter and Dorothy J. McGinnis, *Learning to Read* (New York: McGraw-Hill Book Co., 1953), chap. 9.

[16] May Lazar, "Individualized Reading: A Dynamic Approach," *The Reading Teacher* (December, 1957), 11:75–83.

teacher works chiefly with individuals but also with groups or with the whole class on difficulties observed during individual work periods. Although no two teachers work in exactly the same way, a teacher usually gives some directions to the class as a whole. Then time is provided for all children to read independently from self-selected material. Conferences with individual children are held. During this time the child may discuss the book he is reading with the teacher, or he may read a section orally to her, or he may work on the analysis of difficult words. The teacher keeps a record of the children's abilities, needs, and interests, and the children keep a simple record of their reading. Later the class meets as a group for the purpose of discussing the books which each child has read.

Individualized reading is based on the premise that skills are necessary to reading but must be introduced functionally. It is believed that each child should know what skills he needs and why he needs them. The program is also based on the assumption that each child should have an opportunity to proceed at his own pace and should not be compelled to compare his performance in reading with that of others. The difficulty level of the material is subordinated to successful and enjoyable reading. As Lazar [17] has so aptly stated, individualized reading is based on the belief that "reading is a way of life and not a skills gadget-collecting procedure."

In concluding this chapter it is well to emphasize that teaching students to read for meaning is the goal of every teacher and that the basic principles discussed here apply equally at all levels from the elementary grades through college.

Guided Activities

1. List the means available to teachers for becoming acquainted with the background and instructional needs of their students.
2. Organize a symposium to discuss various methods of grouping for reading.
3. Outline a plan for helping Joel develop skill in reading for the central thought in a paragraph.
4. Work out a plan for helping Joel select the facts which support the main idea of a paragraph.
5. Outline a plan for teaching children to read in order to follow directions.
6. Outline the procedure and select the materials you would use in teaching children to predict the outcome of a given situation.
7. Participate in a symposium in which the following topics are discussed:
    a. The teacher's responsibility in dealing with parents.
    b. Helping the student to achieve at his capacity level.
    c. Personality development and reading achievement.
    d. Advantages and disadvantages of teaching reading incidentally.
    e. Relationship of oral and silent reading.

[17] May Lazar, "Individualized Reading: A Program of Seeking, Self-Selection, and Pacing," *Reading In Action*, II, 1957, pp. 141–144.

8. Select a test of reading which you believe to be useful at the level you intend to teach. Justify your choice and show how you would use the results.
9. Interview an individual in the sixth grade and determine as far as possible the reading skills he possesses and those which may be lacking.
10. Using the suggestions made in this chapter and by Betts in Chapter XXI in *Foundations of Reading Instruction,* prepare an informal inventory which may be useful in evaluating the reading performance of children in grades one to eight.
11. Outline a plan for helping students build up mental content for a better understanding of their social studies textbook.

Questions and References

Questions	References
1. What library resources are available for schools?	1. Hildreth, Gertrude. *Teaching Reading,* Chap. 22. New York: Holt and Co., 1958.
2. How can comprehension skills be developed?	2. Dawson, Mildred A., and Henry A. Bamman. *Fundamentals of Basic Reading Instruction,* Chap. 10. New York: Longmans, Green and Co., 1959.
3. Why and how should oral reading be taught?	3. DeBoer, John J., and Martha Dallmann. *The Teaching of Reading,* Chaps. 10A, 10B. New York: Holt, Rinehart and Winston, 1960. Durrell, Donald D. *Improving Reading Instruction,* Chap. 8. New York: World Book Co., 1956.
4. What does research say in regard to systematic versus opportunistic methods in teaching reading?	4. Gates, Arthur I., assisted by Mildred I. Batchelder and Jean Betzner. "Systematic Versus Opportunistic Methods in Teaching Reading," in *Research in the Three R's,* C. W. Hunnicutt and William J. Iverson, pp. 94–102. New York: Harper & Bros., 1958.
5. How can children be taught to read silently?	5. Durrell. *Op. cit.,* Chap. 9.

Reading is essential to effective study.

An alert student is interested in her progress.

The student must read effectively in order to follow directions.

6. How can meaning be achieved and extended?

6. Hester, Kathleen B. *Teaching Every Child to Read,* Chap. 12. New York: Harper & Bros., 1955.

Yoakam, Gerald A. *Basal Reading Instruction,* Chap. 10. New York: McGraw-Hill Book Co., 1955.

7. How can teachers use effectively basic reading materials?

7. Hester. *Op. cit.,* Chap. 18.

8. Where can the teacher find practical exercises designed to aid the student in his quest for meaning?

8. Wood, Evelyn Nielsen, and Marjorie Wescott Barrows. *Reading Skills,* Chaps. 6, 9. New York: Henry Holt and Co., 1958.

9. Where can the teacher find measures of reading achievement, grade levels at which they may be applied, and names of publishers?

9. Dawson and Bamman. *Op. cit.,* Appendix B.

Strang, Ruth, and Dorothy K. Bracken. *Making Better Readers,* pp. 345–347. Boston: D. C. Heath and Co., 1957.

7

FINDING AND ORGANIZING INFORMATION

The reader's attention is now directed to the problem of teaching young students how to find and organize information and how to make it truly functional. The case of Elizabeth illustrates the value of such teaching.

Elizabeth Needs Help in Finding Information and Organizing Ideas

Elizabeth had asked for a conference with her teacher. "You see, Miss Walker, I have been drafted by our group in the eighth grade to debate on a subject for which I am poorly prepared. To make matters worse, I have to take the side I am sure my father opposes. Dad is a physician, and he objects to the whole idea of socialized medicine."

"What is the subject you are to discuss?" Miss Walker asked.

"It is," Elizabeth announced, "Resolved, that the principles of socialized medicine be accepted by the federal government of the United States."

"I can take the negative side of this question," Elizabeth continued, "and really do a good job. Do you think I could trade sides with one of the other speakers?"

Miss Walker thought for a moment and then said, "I believe, Elizabeth, that you can present some excellent arguments on the affirmative side of this question. A good debater should understand both sides of an issue in order to oppose the arguments of his opponent and build point by point his own case. You can present the affirmative side of this subject perhaps better than any other student in your group because you are already acquainted with the arguments they are prepared to advance."

"What will Dad think?" Elizabeth asked, still undecided.

"Your father is a scientist and he will be pleased to know that his daughter can look at a problem objectively and without bias and," Miss Walker continued, "he would be proud to learn that you were able to investigate this subject and construct by yourself strong arguments on the affirmative side of this question."

"Well, maybe you're right," replied Elizabeth somewhat doubtfully, "but just where shall I begin?"

"The answer to that question should not be too difficult for a capable girl like you," Miss Walker pointed out. "Your big problem," she continued, "is to find and organize your information. During the next three weeks the teachers of social studies and the teachers of English are cooperating in a plan to show our students how to make use of many sources of information in the library and how to organize the facts discovered so that they can be applied for several useful purposes."

"Does this mean," asked Elizabeth, "that we will learn in our English classes to do some of the assignments we are required to do in our social studies?"

"That is our plan," Miss Walker replied, "for knowledge does not always come from departmentalized sources. It is universal in its application and students should learn to use facts wherever they are needed. They also need to know where to find facts. All intelligent people can learn to make use of the card catalogue, *The Readers' Guide to Periodical Literature,* the encyclopedias, *The World Almanac,* and other standard reference works. Then, after suitable information has been found, students can be shown how to organize their facts by means of outlines and later express their ideas in short talks and written presentations."

"Really, that is just what I shall need in preparing for the debate," exclaimed Elizabeth with a high degree of assurance.

The reader is now acquainted with Elizabeth's problem and how, in general, her teacher intends to aid her and the other children as they gather and organize the information which is required for the completion of their projects. Let us now learn more of Elizabeth and her background.

Elizabeth is the only girl in a family of three children. She has two brothers, one older and one younger than herself. The older brother is a student in the university and is reported to have little except arguments in common with his "kid sister" of thirteen years. The younger brother is in kindergarten. Elizabeth's mother is devoted to her home and especially the welfare of her children. The father of the family is a physician who spends most of his time at his office and in the local hospital. He is the dominant member of the home and it is said that he is interested only in his work and in his family.

In discussing her home Elizabeth said, "I should be good in debating for I have been brought up on arguments. Bill, that's my older brother, and I are busy at it whenever we are together. Dad too stirs me up by proposing ideas which I discover later he has not accepted himself. We all like to discuss problems of one sort or another except Mother and my little brother. When Mother talks, we all listen, for she says what she means and means what she says. Our mother is strongminded and we appreciate her being so."

Records in the principal's office indicate that Elizabeth reads as well as an individual six months in the ninth grade (9.6). Her performance in spelling and arithmetic is that of a student two months in the ninth grade (9.2) and that of an individual four months in the tenth grade (10.4), respectively. Elizabeth's IQ as determined by the Wechsler Intelligence Scale for Children is verbal scale, 120, performance scale, 118, and full scale, 121. Her chronological age at the time of investigation was thirteen years and six months and her grade placement was that of a pupil four months in the eighth grade. Health and medical histories were satisfactory except for a marked visual difficulty which has been partially corrected by refraction. Fastened to Elizabeth's permanent record card was a codicil, evidently prepared by a consultant in guidance, which stated, "Elizabeth is well adjusted both socially and emotionally. However, she thoroughly enjoys an argument and at times she speaks frankly and without diplomacy."

"Miss Walker is helping me to get ideas across to others without antagonizing them," Elizabeth reported in one of her interviews a few weeks later. "I have learned that a really good debater tries to persuade people to think as the speaker thinks. Little can be accomplished by telling them off as I sometimes do. Facts count. A run-away-temper lessens the effectiveness of a debater."

"We have learned," she added, "to find sources in the card catalogue, in the *Readers' Guide,* and in other reference materials. Miss Walker has shown us how to skim for the facts we need to support our ideas. She has talked to us and expected us to take notes showing main ideas and the facts which support them. We have found that talking and writing are like building a house. Everything has to be planned for and put in its place. In our class we have learned about topic outlines and question outlines. It seems to me that question outlines are more natural and more usable than the former, for in our listening and reading we have been taught to ask questions and then listen or read for the answers."

A question concerning Elizabeth's preparation for the debate on socialized medicine brought out this reply: "Miss Walker has shown all the debaters how to prepare statements and list the supporting evidence for each. This information is filed on 3" x 5" cards and will be ready for use in the debate whenever these statements are needed. We are learning how speaking, writing, reading, and listening are alike and how they are different. Miss Walker shows us how to skim. This means we look for facts and ideas which can be useful to us. We have learned to read newspapers and magazines in this way. In doing such reading, we find fresh information which, as yet, has not found its way into books."

In review, the following salient factors in Elizabeth's case should be noted:

1. Elizabeth's primary problem is to find and organize facts so as to debate effectively the issues presented by socialized medicine.
2. In order to accomplish this objective, she must *discover, understand,* and *evaluate* new information.
3. Elizabeth likes to argue and in doing so she is apt to react emotionally to a specific issue and not consider carefully the total situation.
4. She is a girl of better than average intelligence who apparently scores well on tests of reading. It is obvious, however, that she has not learned to apply effectively what she has read.
5. Specifically, Elizabeth needs to locate sources, to skim for facts, to draw valid inferences, and to organize her information in the form of usable outlines.
6. Elizabeth's teacher has, through developmental teaching, shown her students how to integrate fundamental reading skills in the four acts of communication: speaking, writing, reading, and listening.

Some Means of Finding and Selecting Information

There are many tools which students can use in their search for information. They include the card catalogue, the *Readers' Guide to Periodical Literature,* such standard reference works as encyclopedias and *The World Almanac,* charts, and newspapers.

Teaching the Use of the Card Catalogue

One of the finest ways to help children learn how to use these materials is to acquaint them with the library. Some teachers find it expedient to take the children on a guided tour to provide them with first-hand experience in using the library's facilities. The teacher or librarian can explain that all nonfiction books are catalogued according to the Dewey Decimal System or the Library of Congress System and that these books are arranged on the shelves according to subjects. The Dewey Decimal System, for example, provides ten large subject groups. These groups and their corresponding call numbers are listed here:

000	General Works
100	Philosophy
200	Religion
300	Social Sciences
400	Languages
500	Science
600	Useful Arts
700	Fine Arts
800	Literature
900	History

Each book is given a call number which is usually printed inside the cover of the book and on the part of the book which shows when it is placed on the shelf. The call number helps the individual to locate the book in the library. Books of fiction are usually classified alphabetically by the author's last name.

The teacher can show how each book in the library has at least two cards which are filed in the card catalogue. She can demonstrate how all the cards in the drawers of the catalogue are arranged alphabetically by the author's name, by title, and sometimes by subject. The children can be given experience in locating cards corresponding to books in which they are interested. From each card they can learn a great deal about the book before they actually see it. For example, most cards show the title of the book, its author, the place where it was published, the publishing company, the date of publication, the number of pages in the book itself, and the number of illustrations, graphs, and plates. The students can be shown how to find the call number of the book from the card and how to use the call number in locating the book in the stacks. They should learn how to check a book out of the library and the importance of returning the book on the day that it is due.

The *Readers' Guide*

In addition to the use of the card catalogue, the teacher can acquaint her students with the value and use of the *Readers' Guide to Periodical Literature.* She can explain to them that the *Readers' Guide* is an invaluable aid in locating up-to-date information on a given subject through magazine articles. She will, if possible, give the children an opportunity to examine a file of the *Readers' Guide* and to note that current issues appear as pamphlets which are later combined when the material is assembled in book form. The teacher can demonstrate the method of classification of different types of material in the *Guide.* Magazine articles are grouped alphabetically by title under a subject or subjects and are also listed alphabetically under the author's name. Each entry provides complete information as to the title, the author's name, name of magazine, volume number, page number, and date. Stories are alphabetized by the first word of the title (except for the articles, *A, An,* and *The,* which are not considered first words) and also under the author's name. Poems are alphabetized under the author's name, but not by title. If the library maintains a Kardex file, the teacher can show the students how to determine from it whether the magazine they wish to consult is available in their library and where it is located in the stacks. The alert teacher can create situations during the school year which will stimulate the children to seek information from a wide variety of sources. If they are searching for current materials, the children will realize the value of the *Reader's Guide* and will undoubtedly develop considerable skill in its use.

Teaching the Use of Tables, Graphs, and Maps

As children progress through school, the need for developing skill in chart reading soon becomes apparent. In their social studies books, for example, it is essential that they be able to identify, interpret, and evaluate facts presented in the form of tables, graphs, and maps. Through direct instruction and demonstration, students can learn how to do this specialized kind of reading. They can understand that tables are valuable because they present statistical information in a compact way and that any graph can be presented in the form of a table, though a graph portrays data more vividly. The teacher can demonstrate various kinds of graphs; for example, the line graph, which shows a continuous curve and indicates that the facts are related; the bar graph, which is used when data are not continuous or related; and the pictograph and circle graphs, which are generally used when a comparison of the parts with each other and the whole is desired.

In reading a table or graph the children should be taught to read carefully the legend or title in order to find out what the author intends to show. Next they should determine what facts are shown vertically and what facts are shown horizontally. In the study of a table or graph the student should go from the general to the specific. Some teachers have found it advisable to have their students record all of the facts which they can observe from the chart. Then they show their students how to make inferences which are based upon these facts. When a table includes unusual data, students can be encouraged to answer such questions as: Why are these facts true? and What do they mean? They can be taught to find and read what the writer has said about the chart, to determine why he has used this tabular or graphical means of expression, and to compare their own inferences with those of the author. Teachers should emphasize the fact that tables and graphs are to be studied slowly, carefully, and critically.

Skill in map reading can be developed by explaining that maps are tools to be used in solving problems and that they have valuable assets which may be called "properties." The main properties of maps are shape, area, distance, and direction. Students should understand that map makers show these properties by using a technique known as "projection" and that, as a result, certain properties of maps may have to be sacrificed in order to show graphically certain other properties or relationships. In studying a map, students should first read the legend or title to determine its purpose and the geographical areas shown. They should know that generally as they face a map the east is to their right, the west is to their left, the north is at the top, and the south is at the bottom. They should realize that on most maps the horizontal lines are called parallels and the vertical lines which cross them are known as meridians. These lines are used in determining the latitude and the longitude of a certain point. Degrees of latitude are measured as either north or south of the equator and degrees of longitude are measured as either east or west of the prime meridian. Of course many small maps do not show these lines. Instead, intersecting lines or coordinates may be used which serve as "grids" to locate different objects. For example, a building may be located at the intersection of lines 6 and H.

Students should be taught how to study their maps in order to determine what facts are shown, that is, mountains, rivers, roads, rainfall, lakes, or political boundaries, and what symbols are used to indicate this information. They should be taught to observe carefully the scale which has been used in drawing the map. If the scale of the map is not the same in all parts, this should be noted and students should be cautioned never to compare maps with different scales. They should be encouraged to determine why a map was presented at a particular point in a text and how it helps the author to accomplish his purpose. To do this it will be necessary for them to read the text material. One of the most worthwhile activities in which students can participate is the listing of all facts and inferences which can be determined from the map. As a final step the students should compare their inferences with those of the author.

Reading the Newspaper

In the swift-moving world in which we live, it is essential that every thinking individual know how to read the newspaper effectively. The teaching of this important skill should not be neglected by the schools. Teachers at all grade levels can emphasize the need for being informed and can help their students to realize that the newspaper is one of the best means by which this can be accomplished. In fact, the newspaper is a record of each day in history. It is a contemporary textbook on the ways, acts, and ideas of contemporary man and the environmental factors which influence his life. Through the pages of the daily newspaper, young people can see the world as it is at local, state, national, and international levels. In the process they can obtain information much of which will not appear in standard textbooks until long after many of the students have completed their formal education.

Skill in newspaper reading can be developed. Students can be encouraged to read the time-saving summaries and indexes generally found on the first page and to scan the headlines to determine the news stories they wish to read. The teacher can explain that the essential facts in a newspaper story are usually tersely stated in the headline and in the "lead" or introduction to the story. She can demonstrate how the student, by skimming the leads, can determine immediately the *who, what, when, where, how,* and *why* of the story. She can show that the lead is followed by a "catch-all," in which minor details of the story are grouped together, and that the catch-all, in turn, is followed by the main body of the story, which is an elaboration of the facts presented in the lead. Students can be taught to read only as much of the catch-all and succeeding paragraphs as is necessary to satisfy them that the article has nothing more of importance to relate.

A newspaper is supposed to be an example of objective reporting, but editors and reporters often take facts and interpret them according to their own personal bias or according to the policy of their paper. Therefore, students must be taught to be critical and to evaluate what they read. They can answer such questions as: Is this statement reasonable and true? Who is the author? What is he attempting to do? Has he reported his facts accurately? Are his conclusions justified? Has he made use of "explosive" words? How have other papers interpreted this story?

Students like Elizabeth can be encouraged to read the editorial page of the newspaper. In an editorial the writer frequently states his, or his paper's, point of view on a controversial issue. In reading an editorial the student should realize that the writer is trying to persuade his readers to think as he does. An effective way to demonstrate this is to permit the students to read and discuss editorials dealing with the same issue published by different papers. They can be taught to be alert to the devices that writers use to influence their readers. They can learn to ask themselves such questions as: How has the writer slanted his statements? Does he appeal to reason or to emotion? Are all the important facts presented and are they accurate? Are his conclusions justified? Students should learn to do their own thinking and to draw their own conclusions.

There are many ways in which the newspaper can be used in the study of English, science, the social studies, and even arithmetic. For example, the English teacher can make use of the newspaper to introduce new words into the children's vocabularies. She can guide the students in gaining an understanding of what their local newspaper offers by helping them make an intensive analysis of it. She can encourage them to maintain a bulletin board of clippings from the paper for resource material in their study of science and the social studies. The newspaper can be used as a means of providing practical lessons in arithmetic by having the children compare advertised prices in planning for family shopping. High school teachers can center their instruction in social living around the reading of the daily paper by encouraging their students to discuss events currently taking place in the news, thereby developing a realistic idea of the world in which they will find themselves in adult life. At all grade levels the newspaper can be utilized to encourage interest, enliven study, and help students gain a more comprehensive conception of the world as it is today.

Skimming as a Means of Locating Information

Most students find that skimming helps them to make use of many sources of information. Skimming is the act of identifying specific information such as key words, statements of fact, and topic sentences. When the reader skims, he should know precisely what he wants and should be mentally set for its recognition. Students at all reading levels should be taught how to skim, for this skill is necessary for effective study. All content material contains some familiar ideas and much reading matter unrelated to the immediate problems of the student. Consequently, the individual should be able to survey such material rapidly and to select that which is relevant to the topic under consideration. Skimming is not thoughtless, inaccurate reading. Instead, the reader should acquire definite, precise ideas which are the answers to questions he has had in mind. Students may learn to skim by permitting their eyes to travel in spirals diagonally down the page as they look for certain words and ideas related to their purpose. Later they may identify concepts expressed in phrases, sentences, and paragraphs. They should observe topic sentences and transition sentences.

Frequently such signposts [1] as *first, hence, therefore,* and *however* suggest what is to be found. Words which can prepare the reader for other facts of the same nature are included in the following list:

further	furthermore	in addition
yet	finally	moreover
however	still	on the other hand
but	next	then
also	another	first, second, and third

Here are some signs from the reading trail which point to the fact that information is to be concluded or summarized:

| thus | hence | for this reason |
| in brief | incidentally | |

The following are words which indicate changes in time and space:

later	soon	finally
meanwhile	at last	before
beneath	there	following
above	preceding	

A smaller number of words may help to prepare the reader for specific illustrations or cases:

| especially | for example | in particular |

The student should be alert to identify significant information and recognize its relationship to his purpose. In skimming, one should not spend too much time with details, illustrations, comparisons, and examples un-

---

[1] Homer L. J. Carter, and Dorothy J. McGinnis, *Effective Reading for College Students* (New York: Dryden Press, 1957), pp. 191–192.

less it is necessary to do so. The more mental content the student has in regard to a subject the easier it will be to skim and select wisely the facts he wishes to utilize.

Students should be taught *when* to skim. If they are looking for information, names of persons or places, figures, and statistical data, skimming can be helpful. If they are looking over references in order to find information on a given topic, then alert skimming of the index, table of contents, and section headings of different chapters is an effective means of spotting the facts required. If the reader knows what he wants, then he is entitled to the economy of time which results from judicious skimming.

In chapter reading, skimming is essential in making a preliminary survey of the main ideas of the chapter. These may be identified in the introductory paragraphs, in the summary if there is one, and, of course, in the main chapter headings. In some books, essays, and reports, main headings and subheadings are lacking. It then becomes necessary for the reader to skim each paragraph and to find the central thought which is expressed in the topic sentence. These central ideas can then be adjusted into a developing pattern of thought which makes up a chapter heading. In this process of identifying and constructing main headings, skimming is an essential tool.

In all instances, the reader must know what he is looking for and where he is most apt to find it. In identifying ideas one must know *where* they may be found. They may be shown by a writer in a number of ways. The preface or introduction to a book generally shows the author's point of view and what he hopes to accomplish. Chapter titles state the content of the chapters and the table of contents shows the scope and an over-all picture of the information presented in the book. The introduction and summary of each chapter generally provide the main headings and subheadings. In the identification of outstanding concepts it is well to answer the following questions:

1. What kind of type is used in identifying the first, second, and third most important ideas expressed in the chapter?
2. What kind of type is used for the fourth most important ideas if these are expressed?
3. How many main points are there in the chapter?

Sometimes writers make use of systematic devices to facilitate the identification of ideas. Headings may be used not only to show main ideas but how they fit together in order to accomplish a given purpose. In the skimming of materials it is important to know how each writer organizes his facts. Most authors specialize in a particular way of arranging ideas which constitutes their pattern or style. This plan of organization, when perceived by the reader, will facilitate his comprehension. The young student should understand that it is safe to skim when looking for a particular fact or for general ideas, and that it is unwise to use this method when reading for mastery of detail or for appreciation.

Some Means of Organizing Information

Facts and information obtained through reading and listening should be organized in a systematic manner so as to be available and useful when needed. The classroom teacher can present and demonstrate procedures which the student can utilize as he tries to organize the ideas obtained from his reading or those presented in a lecture. The suggestions that follow may be helpful to the teacher.

Notetaking

In taking notes from a textbook the student can be taught to make a preview of the chapter as suggested in chapters 6 and 8. This procedure will help to determine the organization of the chapter and its main ideas. He should try to see the chapter as a whole and should not read for detail at this time. He can now examine the headings for the purpose of determining the relative importance of the ideas being expressed. If the author has not prepared headings and subheadings, the reader may find it necessary to prepare his own; most modern textbooks, however, provide these aids for the student.

With the main heading well in mind, the student can make a topic outline of the main points and the supporting ideas. In such an outline the most important concepts are usually indicated by Roman numerals and are placed at the left margin. The next most important points are preceded by capital letters and the next by Arabic numerals. The further the points

EXAMPLE OF CORRECT FORM OF OUTLINING

I.
   A.
   B.
II.
   A.
      1.
      2.
      3.

         a.
         b.
         c.
   B.
   C.
   D.

are to the right the less important they are in the total pattern of ideas. Ideas of equal importance or rank are placed under each other. Generally, an outline does not contain single subpoints, because each heading is normally supported by at least two points or statements. In all instances, the grammatical construction of the outline should be uniform. The pattern of a topic outline on the previous page may be helpful.

In order to outline effectively, the student must be able to identify the main ideas and supply the supporting evidence provided by the writer. Obviously, some of the minor details will be omitted from the outline. After it has been completed, however, it is advisable to compare the main heading with the major headings in the book. The chapter can then be read for more detail and, if necessary, modifications and additions can be made in the outline.

For most students, the ability to take notes as they listen is a desirable skill closely related to reading. The act of notetaking is almost certain to improve the listener's attentiveness to the ideas of the speaker. In following the words of the speaker, the students can first consider the subject of the address and then determine the main points developed in the discussion.

The question is the natural approach to both listening and reading. The student is apt to ask: What is the speaker's topic? What are his chief points? How does he support each of these main ideas? Consequently, the question-outline procedure is effective in recording and organizing the words of the speaker. In using this method the listener can follow the suggestions given for the topic outline but state the major headings in the form of questions. Sub-points are then listed as answers to these questions. In this question-and-answer outline, statements should be made in the form of complete sentences which are both brief and clear.

Another form of notetaking which functions well in many listening situations is called *précis* writing. In using this system the student writes only at spaced intervals of time. As the speaker begins his discussion, the notetaker listens for several minutes. He then writes two or three sentences which summarize what he has heard. This alternating process of listening and writing continues for the duration of the talk. After the presentation of the subject has been completed, the listener has a series of brief abstracts covering the discussion.

In the case of a well-prepared talk, a précis should always be written for the statement of the speaker's purpose or problem. This information is generally given early in the talk after a short introduction. After the listener has discovered the speaker's purpose or thesis, this concept can serve as a nucleus around which can be added all the essential ideas and details which the speaker presents. A précis should also be written for the speaker's conclusion, for at this point he generally reiterates his main ideas and suggests a plan for action. In all instances the alert précis writer listens carefully and pays special attention to generalizations.

The *fact-inference system* of notetaking is an effective procedure for organizing the facts and inferences in a lecture or talk. In using this technique the student can divide his paper into two columns, one can be labeled "Facts" and the other "Inferences." In the act of listening the student is chiefly concerned in identifying the facts presented and in differentiating them from the inferences. This task is not always an easy one but the effort and the training resulting from the effort are worth while. It is not the responsibility of the listener to determine what is important and what is unimportant. Instead, he is expected to listen for facts and for inferences as set forth by the speaker.

An illustration of this plan of organizing information presented by a speaker may be helpful to the reader. These facts and inferences recorded by a college student in a class in clinical audiology show some of the difficulties encountered in the organization of ideas. It is obvious that not all the facts presented in the left column support the inferences shown in

Facts	Inferences
1. Audiology refers to the study of hearing and hearing defects.	
2. The individual speaks in a relatively quiet voice.	
3. His speech discrimination is relatively unimpaired.	a. This individual shows some of the symptoms of a conductive type of hearing loss.
4. He tolerates loud sounds of an intensity sufficient to reach the threshold of discomfort of the normal ear.	
5. He shows about the same degree of loss for all frequencies.	
6. He complains of head noises.	
7. Another individual speaks with excessive loudness of voice.	
8. He experiences difficulty in understanding what is said to him.	
9. The loss is primarily in the higher frequencies.	b. This individual shows some of the symptoms of a perceptive type of hearing loss.
10. There is evidence of recruitment.	
11. Recruitment refers to a rapid increase in the sensation of loudness once the patient's threshold of hearing has been crossed.	
12. An audiometer is an instrument for measuring the efficiency of hearing.	

the column at the right. Surely facts 1, 11, and 12 are not used to substantiate inferences a and b. It is also apparent that mental content and experience is a requirement for the interpretation of the concepts set forth by the speaker. However, it may be that this procedure of spotting and organizing information provided by a speaker can be of marked value to the uninformed student of limited background, for he can set down the facts and inferences as they are presented and later make his own interpretation and evaluation.

Speaking and Writing

The speaker and the writer each build up a literary structure composed of ideas joined together into an organized framework and later equipped with all necessary detail so that the unified whole may serve a purpose. Both the speaker and the writer select materials with which they are already acquainted and arrange them to form a predetermined design. On the other hand, the listener and reader first focus their attention upon the structure as a whole and after recognizing its purpose, examine carefully the supporting details. They interpret and analyze what they hear and read in terms of their own experience and recreate a thought structure of their own. The activities both of building with words and of interpreting what has been built are active and constructive processes which express the purpose and skill of the doer. Each skill is an aspect of communication, and the mastery of the one can contribute to the mastery of the other.

Organizing Materials for a Short Talk

After a subject has been selected with which the student is fairly well acquainted and which will be of interest to his audience, he can be shown how to make use of the card catalogue and the *Readers' Guide* in selecting references to add to his general information or to deal with specific aspects of his subject. Notes based upon the substance of the materials he has read may be recorded in the form of a topic or question outline. Some students have found that it is advantageous to use the précis or the fact-inference technique, their choice, of course, depending upon the nature of the material and their degree of familiarity with it. After adequate information has been secured, the student can be shown what to include and what to omit in his talk. He can plan to bring his facts to a sharp focus in order to accomplish his purpose and to treat his topic adequately.

The student is now ready to prepare an outline of his talk, including an introduction, body, and conclusion. The introduction should stimulate interest and show why the listener should be attentive. Use can be made of a striking incident or other introductory material. Main ideas and all the supporting facts are centered in the body of the talk. In it are found the main attractions and all that the speaker intends to contribute to the subject at the time. In the conclusion, the speaker can restate briefly his main points and end his talk with a strong statement concerning the gist of his presentation. A simple, yet well-planned, speech outline is desirable for all talks given before a group. This outline aids in the adequate and precise development of ideas and is a far better speaking guide than a topic or question outline.

Organizing Materials for an Essay

All mature students should have frequent opportunities to select a subject for study, investigate available references, organize pertinent information, and express clearly their ideas in written form.

After the student has gathered his information, the problem should be stated definitely and specifically and should not be too general in nature. Information from all available sources should be summarized, especially those facts and inferences which have a direct bearing upon the immediate problem. The student can then be expected to elaborate upon the procedure he has followed in conducting his investigation of the subject. He can show exactly what has been done and can set forth the data resulting from his study, if possible in tables or in graphic form. When these facts have been shown, conclusions and inferences based upon the findings should be stated carefully and conservatively. If the inferences resulting from the investigation differ radically from those of other studies, the student should explain briefly why in his opinion this is the case. The young student can be taught to maintain at all times an open-minded and objective point of view. This is the responsibility of the teacher.

In this chapter speaking, writing, reading, and listening have been described as a reciprocal process, a point of view which contributes to a better understanding of each. Suggestions have been provided for helping the teacher to aid her students gather information from various sources and organize their ideas for expression as they speak and write. Furthermore, it has been suggested that formation of ideas through speaking and writing is reading in reverse and that mastery of one art of communication can facilitate the acquisition of the other.

Adjusting Rate of Reading

In all reading, the individual is chiefly concerned with meaning. If this can be secured at a rapid rate, an economy of time is achieved. If, on the other hand, the person cannot secure meaning when attempting to read rapidly, it is better to read slowly. The ability to adjust reading rate to the nature and purpose of materials is a characteristic of the good reader. Reading is a thinking process and the student should be in control of meaning at all times. It is unwise for him to attempt to read faster than he can think. It is easier for most students to read rapidly to identify facts than it is to interpret facts, and it is easier to read for an interpretation than it is to read for an evaluation. It is sometimes unwise to overvalue rate of reading. On the other hand, an increase in rate can be an advantage to the mature reader, for a rapid rate permits the student to identify facts quickly, thus permitting more time for interpretation and evaluation. It may be well to consider some suggestions for reading rapidly.

The student who knows in advance what he wants to get from the material to be read can increase his reading rate by aiming directly for his goal. If he is seeking facts, these can be identified, interpreted, and evaluated. Incidental information can probably be ignored unless there is an immediate need for it. If the student is reading for the story or main plot, his attention will be concentrated upon this goal, and other literary elements may be neglected until the chief factors in the plot are well established. A selection may be read several times with varying purposes on the part of the reader. On one occasion, the reader may be primarily concerned with people or places; at another time he may seek numerical quantities and statistical data; and again he may read for pleasure or recreation. Reading for a specific purpose can facilitate an increase in rate.

A knowledge of the writer's style and method of organizing his ideas can contribute to rapid reading. Introductory statements generally point out what the writer intends to do and sometimes he may indicate how he expects to accomplish his objectives. This information alerts the reader and tells him what he may expect to find. The summary, if one is provided, generally enumerates the main ideas and sets forth generalizations based upon the facts presented. Major and minor headings, if supplied by the writer, not only display prominently his main ideas but also show how these are supported. The location of topical sentences in the various paragraphs may also facilitate rapid reading. For example, some writers place their statement of the central thought early in the paragraph and conclude the development of their ideas with a sentence which summarizes the concepts expressed in the paragraph. Other writers may develop their ideas step by step and conclude with the topic sentence. In all instances, knowledge of the writer's way of arranging his ideas can be of assistance to the student who can afford to read rapidly.

The good reader who wishes to read rapidly can look for ideas and avoid emphasis of single words and even phrases. For instance, the reader may see b − − t − − n − t and be able, because of his mental content, to identify the word "butternut" even though he saw only four-ninths of the word. The student can be taught to move his eyes rapidly to see the words in advance of those he is actually interpreting and to refrain from looking back over the material he has scanned. Ideas like the illustration "b − − t − − n − t" are expressed in patterns which are quickly recognized by the experienced reader providing he has sufficient background and adequate skill. The good reader will see modifiers and connectives and will evaluate immediately their importance. He may make only three eye fixations in each line and he may show little or no regressive eye movement. Such reading skill can result only from well-planned training.

Extraneous activities such as finger pointing and especially lip movement can retard the rate of silent reading. If vocalization is employed as a crutch to aid pronunciation or if it is the result of faulty teaching methods, the rate of silent reading may be reduced to that of oral reading. Generally lip movement is a symptom of a reading difficulty and its cause may require investigation. Finger pointing may also be symptomatic and may suggest undue emphasis on word-attack skills and the possibility of visual difficulties.

In developing skills essential to rapid reading, the student can be encouraged to do some rapid reading each day as he learns to compete with himself. Interesting materials below the reader's frustration level should be selected. In the evaluation of the student's ability to read rapidly, meaning as well as rate must be considered. These skills, however, can be measured adequately only by valid and reliable tests of reading achievement. If change between the time of initial and final testing is to be evaluated, equivalent forms of the test must be administered.

Many students in junior and senior high school want to read faster. If these young people have adequate mental content, suitable vocabularies, and satisfactory reading skills, mechanical devices may be helpful in speeding up their unnecessarily slow habits of reading. Those who advocate the use of *acceleration* and *tachistoscopic* equipment stress the development of visual skills. Their immediate goals are shorter periods of fixation, longer spans of recognition, and reduction of regressive eye movement. The reader has an opportunity to focus his attention and to improve his concentration as he works with new and challenging equipment. Progress in reading can follow an improvement in concentration and increased coordination between the eyes and the central nervous system. The following devices to aid reading acceleration may be helpful:

1. *AVR Rateometer.* Audio-Visual Research, 531 South Plymouth Court, Chicago, Illinois.
2. *Controlled Reader.* Educational Developmental Laboratories, Inc., 9 Longford Street, Huntington, New York.
3. *Reading Pacer.* Keystone View Company, Meadville, Pennsylvania.
4. *Reading Rate Controller.* Stereo Optical Company, 3539 North Kenton Street, Chicago 41, Illinois.
5. *Shadowscope Reading Pacer.* Lafayette Instrument Company, Lafayette, Indiana.
6. *SRA Reading Accelerator.* Science Research Associates, Inc., Chicago, Illinois.

Tachistoscopic equipment is available in the following forms:

1. *Keystone Tachistoscope.* Keystone View Company, Meadville, Pennsylvania.
2. *PDL Perceptoscope.* Perceptual Development Laboratories, 115 North Meramec Avenue, St. Louis 5, Missouri.
3. *Projection Tachistoscope.* Stereo Optical Company, 3539 North Kenton Street, Chicago 41, Illinois.
4. *Renshaw Tachistoscopic Trainer.* Stereo Optical Company, 3539 North Kenton Street, Chicago 41, Illinois.
5. *SVE Tachistoscope.* Society for Visual Education, Chicago, Illinois.
6. *Tach-X.* Educational Developmental Laboratories, Inc., Huntington, New York.

Mechanical devices should be purchased and used with discretion, for they are not a substitute for a well-trained teacher or for a well-organized reading program. They are merely a means of developing certain perceptual skills which can facilitate reading, a thinking process.

There are times when it is advisable to read slowly. When the reader comes across a selection of beauty, he should stop and linger a while, for appreciation of an emotional quality cannot be deepened by superficial haste. Critical reading is generally done slowly sentence by sentence and in some instances word by word. In the appreciation of the writer's choice of words, diction, organization, form, and tone, speed can be wasteful and ineffective. Reading in science and mathematics demands a slow rate and close attention to detail. Eye movements may vary vertically as well as horizontally and the span of recognition may be shorter than in the reading of narrative or descriptive material. Eye fixations may be longer and regressive movements may be essential for meaning. Slower reading can result in an increase of understanding for those who, because of the nature of the material, must "inwardly digest" what they read. Consequently, it may be well to make some suggestions for reading slowly and deliberately.

If the young student or adult finds it to his advantage to read a unit of material at a slow rate, it is advisable to proceed from the whole to its parts. At the *first* reading, he can determine the general idea being expressed in the unit as a whole. After he has identified the main idea the writer has developed, he can then determine what parts make up the whole. In attempting to reaffirm his information, the reader then reverses his procedure and advances from the parts to the whole. This interpretative process really constitutes the second reading of the unit. The reader focuses his attention upon the contribution of each paragraph to the central idea of the unit. He examines carefully the concept supplied by each sentence in the paragraph and he is concerned with the denotation and connotation of the various words making up each sentence. During the third reading of the unit the reader can evaluate critically the writer's work. In achieving this objective the reader can determine whether or not he agrees with the writer and whether or not the author has accomplished his purpose. The experienced reader will not attempt to evaluate critically any subject of which he knows very little. Instead, he will study, investigate, and acquire additional information in order to build up background and mental content essential to valid judgments. In developing skills necessary for careful reading, the reader must have vocabularies in the various content fields commensurate with the skills required for critical reading.

Teaching Reading in the Subject-Matter Fields

Success in every subject from the work of the elementary grades through the university is dependent upon effective reading. In the content fields research is adding to and modifying subject matter to such an extent that unless students bring their knowledge up to date their understanding of a subject becomes inadequate and even obsolescent. Reading in every subject-matter field can be a part of the total developmental reading program. In suggesting means of helping students read content material, it is well to discuss some essential reading skills, means of developing background and mental content, selection and adjustment of materials, and some effective procedures requiring organization and integration of certain reading skills.

Some Essential Reading Skills

The student working in any subject-matter field should know how to add words to his vocabulary. He should be able to read a chapter effectively, and he should know how to read for detail preparatory to the solution of a problem. These skills can be developed specifically as they are applied in each field of concentration. Word study, chapter reading, and problem solving cannot be adequately taught in a vacuum as isolated reading attainments, for the nature of reading in one area may differ radically from that in another. Instead, specific instruction for the development of these skills should be given in different content areas at every grade level from the third to the sixteenth. It is the consensus of many leaders [2] in the field that these skills should be acquired by the student as the result of a well-planned developmental program in which the reading requirements of each subject-matter field are considered. It has been suggested that each teacher should be responsible for the teaching of these skills in his own classes. In brief, his problem is to demonstrate to his stu-

---

[2] Irma T. Halfter, and Frances M. Douglass, "Inadequate College Readers," *Journal of Developmental Reading*, 1:42–53.

dents how to study, a process closely associated with the teaching of reading.

Developing Background and Mental Content

Meaning resulting from reading in any content field requires background and mental content, which are built up by reading and experience. Not all students can be expected to read effectively materials in various subject-matter fields such as English, science, and the social studies unless they have adequate degrees of experience and background, for each individual perceives and interprets with what he has previously seen and understood. Obviously, amounts and qualities of mental content determine degrees and kinds of meaning. Consequently, it is the responsibility of the teacher to aid his students in building up concepts in the field of instruction. This may be done by class demonstrations and by the use of audio-visual materials. Well-planned and purposeful visitation of laboratories, social agencies, and manufacturing plants not only stimulate interest but, most important of all, provide background and experiences which contribute to an understanding of the material to be read and presented in class. Children can be encouraged to ask questions, report what they have observed, and to tell of their experiences, for in such a controlled discussion more and more mental content is made available.

Selecting and Adjusting Materials

Textbooks and reference materials provided by the school are frequently not adapted to the reading and interest levels of the student. It is possible, for example, that a pupil in the eighth grade will be required to read from eighth grade textbooks when his reading level is that of only a third-grade child. As this youth is promoted to senior high school, he soon discovers that he cannot possibly do the reading that is required of him. This problem, which is common in our schools today, is frustrating to the teacher and presents a challenge to thinking educators. In selecting and using materials in content courses, it is necessary for the instructor to understand that the reading levels within any class may cover a range of three to nine grades. This means that those individuals reading at the lower levels have difficulty in interpreting effectively the textbooks and references required by their teachers. Consequently, many students develop a mental set against the subject, the teacher, and especially the act of reading.

In attempting to alleviate this situation, the teacher and his colleagues should consider carefully the selection of textbooks and reference materials for their students. Vocabularies of technical and non-technical words should be noted and weighed. Some textbooks, even though the average level of reading difficulty is quite satisfactory, contain passages which are too difficult for individuals in the grade for which the book was written.

Studies [3] show that many science textbooks contain technical words that could be replaced by easier synonyms. Furthermore, the teacher should take into account the organization and clarity of the material, the style of writing, variety of illustrations, significance of guided activities, and provision for individual differences. Generally, a textbook with a glossary should be given preference over a similar book without one, providing that they are equal in other respects. Recently materials dealing with subject matter in many content fields, but written simply and directly, have become available.

A temporary grouping of students for the purpose of attaining certain objectives makes it possible to adjust reading materials to the needs and interest of the individuals in the class. Flexible groups may be established on the basis of interest or the purpose the children themselves wish to realize, the reading levels of materials at hand, and in accordance with changes in the individual needs of those participating in the groups. For example, a junior high school teacher of elementary science has thirty-six eighth grade students in her class whose reading levels range from the third to the eleventh grade. In adjusting textbooks and reference materials to the reading levels of her pupils she plans three temporary groups. Group A is composed of six students who are using their regular textbook and additional references in their investigation of how weather affects the industry of nations. These students are constructing question outlines and plan to present their findings to the class. Group B is made up of eighteen students whose reading achievements extend from the sixth to the tenth grade level. These boys and girls are using the five-step plan for reading two chapters in their textbook in elementary science. These chapters deal with the factors to be considered in a study of weather and the effects of weather upon mankind. The chief emphasis in this group is upon chapter reading because the teacher has discovered that these pupils become lost in a mass of detail and fail to recognize the main ideas as they read. In brief, the members of this group are learning to read as they do their regular work in elementary science. In Group C, the children are engaged in a study of words and technical terms which they have discovered in their reading of the first chapter in their science textbook on the subject of weather. The reading performance of these children in Group C ranges from the third to the fifth grade, inclusive. Their teacher is stressing vocabulary building as she explains and demonstrates terms and concepts presented in the chapters being read by the class as a whole. She has made use of contextual clues, structural analysis, and the use of the dictionary. Marked interest in this activity has been achieved by the construction and demonstration of such pieces of apparatus as the barometer, hygrometer, nephoscope, rain gauge, and anemometer. In the process of constructing

[3] George G. Mallinson and J. Bryce Lockwood, "Research on Problems in Reading Science," *Reading for Effective Living* (International Reading Association Conference Proceedings), 3:172–174.

these instruments, these students of lesser ability in reading have studied carefully the directions for assembling the different pieces of apparatus and have demonstrated a high degree of mechanical skill in their adjustment and application. These activities stimulate the desire to read and make reading a functional process directly related to the activities of the group.

After several days of intensive work each of the three groups is ready to report what has been accomplished. Each group member has had an opportunity to make a contribution to the subject being studied by the class and at the same time to improve some basic skills in reading. The young student has been encouraged to add words to his vocabulary and to use his text and supplementary materials as he has participated, to the extent of his ability, in the work of the class.

Effective Procedures to Be Emphasized

Reading and spelling vocabularies can be developed if the student is taught to select from his textbooks and class discussions words which he needs to understand and use. The various forms of *contextual clues,* if thoroughly developed by the teacher, can help the mature student to determine meaning which later can be verified by the *use of the dictionary.* A psychologically sound procedure, making sure of visual, auditory, kinesthetic, and tactual imagery, can be employed not only in a study of technical terms but also in a mastery of their correct spelling. In this process, the student should look at the beginning and ending words and observe phonograms within a word. *Structural* analysis can be helpful, for meaning can generally be determined from an understanding of prefixes, stems, and suffixes. The student can then say the word subvocally, making certain that he associates each syllable with its corresponding sound and that the proper sequence of syllables is maintained. He should be expected to spell the word subvocally, paying careful attention to each syllable. He should be expected to write the word and then compare the word written with the word that he has selected for study. This process should be repeated until the student can spell and write the word correctly. In all instances, the individual should be able to make use of the word in a complete sentence so that its full meaning is adequately expressed.

The teacher in all content fields can demonstrate the manner in which chapter reading can be done effectively in his field of specialization. A procedure widely used will be outlined in Chapter 8; however, it may be well to summarize briefly the five steps in the process. The student is shown how to make a preliminary survey of the chapter by first reading the introduction and the conclusion in order to identify the main ideas of the chapter. Generally, the writer in the introduction has declared his intention and in the summary indicated what he has accomplished in the chapter. Furthermore, a preview of the main headings of the chapter gives the reader some idea as to how the chapter is organized and an out-line of the chief points to be discussed. The student should then be shown how to convert these main headings into questions which are answered by the writer in the text. The student can then write each question on a 3″ x 5″ card. For example, the heading "Weather Defined" can be changed to read "What is weather?" The student can now be expected to read for the purpose of answering each question. These questions provide purpose and motive for reading. In discovering adequate answers, the reader can be taught not only to identify concepts but to understand them thoroughly in order that he may evaluate them and be able to arrange them in a proper sequence. Answers to the questions should be stated by the stu-dent in his own words and written on cards containing the questions. The student now is ready to try and test his knowledge of the chapter by re-viewing both questions and answers.

In developing skill in problem solving, especially in such subjects as mathematics, chemistry, and physics, the student can be taught to ask questions of his textbook and to read for detailed answers. For example, when confronted with a problem, he can ask: What is to be found? What facts are known? What other facts are needed that are not stated in the problem? What are the steps to go through for a solution? Can a drawing or illustration be made of the conditions included in the problem? What numerical quantities can be used in actually solving the problem? Is the solution reasonable? How can the solution be proved or demonstrated? This process of seeking the solution to any problem involves identification of concepts, their interpretation, and later their evaluation. In all instances the student should be encouraged to ask questions and work out his own answers, for this attitude is the essence of research and scientific investi-gation.

In retrospect, it can be pointed out that in teaching students to read effectively in the subject-matter fields, three basic reading skills are re-quired: vocabulary building, chapter reading, and mastery of detail in problem solving. Furthermore, it has been emphasized that adequate background and mental content can be developed, materials can be se-lected and adjusted to the reading levels of the students, and, most impor-tant of all, proficiency can be acquired in word study, chapter reading, and problem solving. These are the minimal requirements for effective reading in the content subjects. Underlying basic principles can be ap-plied at all levels.

Guided Activities

1. Outline a plan for helping Elizabeth with her problem of finding and or-ganizing information.
2. In one of your classes make use of the fact-inference procedure for record-ing the lecture.

3. Work out a plan for showing a group of sixth grade pupils how to use effectively the card catalogue.
4. Prepare to teach a class in science or social studies so as to provide instruction in both word study and chapter reading.
5. Outline a plan for the temporary grouping of children in order to accomplish a specific objective in reading.
6. Work out a plan for showing Elizabeth how to listen to the arguments of her opponents and to summarize their main points in the form of a précis.
7. Write out a plan for showing a group of junior high school students when and how to skim.
8. Plan to show a group of students how speaking, writing, listening, and reading are alike and how they differ.
9. Read a news item in a local paper and write out the inferences and the facts the writer employed to support them.
10. Locate in the *Readers' Guide to Periodical Literature* an article advocating, and one opposing, socialized medicine. List the main ideas and the supporting facts set forth in each.

Questions and References

Questions	References
1. How can reading be taught in the content fields?	1. Bond, Guy, and Miles A. Tinker. *Reading Difficulties, Their Diagnosis and Correction,* Chap. 15. New York: Appleton-Century-Crofts, 1957. Strang, Ruth, and Dorothy K. Bracken. *Making Better Readers,* Chap. 5. Boston: D. C. Heath and Co., 1957.
2. How can the student find and organize information?	2. Carter, Homer L. J., and Dorothy J. McGinnis. *Effective Reading for College Students,* Chap. 8. New York: Dryden Press, 1957.
3. How can the student learn to summarize and report data for a term paper?	3. Carter, Homer L. J., and Dorothy J. McGinnis. *Building A Successful College Career,* Chap. 11. Dubuque, Iowa: Wm. C. Brown Co., 1958.
4. How can the student prepare and give a short talk?	4. Carter and McGinnis. *Op. cit.,* Chap. 13.

Questions	References
5. How can the student learn to listen at school?	5. Nichols, Ralph G., and Leonard A. Stevens. *Are You Listening?* Chap. 16. New York: McGraw-Hill Book Co., 1957.
6. Where can one find suggestions on how to take notes while reading?	6. Judson, Horace, and Kenneth P. Baldridge. *The Techniques of Reading*, Chap. 13. New York: Harcourt, Brace and Co., 1954.
	Shaw, Phillip B. *Effective Reading and Learning*, pp. 313–326. New York: Thomas Y. Crowell Co., 1955.

8

EFFECTIVE USE OF BOOKS

One of the outstanding characteristics of modern life is the emphasis placed on audio-visual materials as a means of communication and entertainment. Movies, television, and radio play a prominent part in the lives of most individuals and will probably continue to do so in the years to come. Nevertheless, they are inadequate substitutes for books. Boys and girls and men and women still need to know how to identify, interpret, and evaluate ideas made available in written form. In order to do this, they need to develop skill in using books. This presents a real challenge to middle- and upper-grade instructors, for many children who read basic readers with accuracy and understanding have not developed an integration of skills essential to the effective use of textbooks. The kind of reading required in science, mathematics, and the social sciences differs significantly from the kind required for successful completion of a basic reader. Therefore, it is the responsibility of the teacher to show her students how to use the different parts of a book and how to integrate the many reading skills in the process of chapter reading. Furthermore, she must guide her students in developing the characteristics of the superior reader who can appreciate good literature.

To help prospective teachers understand the need for the integration of basic reading skills, the biography of Jim is introduced. This growing boy possesses many essential reading skills, but he does not know how to apply them in a work-study situation.

Jim Learns to Make Use of Books

Jim,[1] who is twelve years old, has just entered the seventh grade. His teachers report that he is a capable boy and substantiate this inference

---

[1] In attempting to illustrate clinical procedure, the case of Jim has been discussed in Helen M. Robinson (Comp. and Ed.), *Sequential Development of Reading Abilities*, Ch. 14: Problems of Students Retarded in Reading, "A Case Study of Jim," by Homer L. J. Carter, pp. 202–205. *Supplementary Educational Monographs*, The University of Chicago Press, 90, December 1960.

by quoting data from the Wechsler Intelligence Scale for Children. On this test he had a verbal IQ of 121 and a performance IQ of 117. The full scale IQ was 121. Jim is the oldest child in a family of four persons. In discussing his progress in school, Jim's mother said, "Jimmie has been an average reader and especially a good oral reader; however, he has not been able to make effective use of his textbooks. He apparently becomes lost in all of the detail. Jimmie entered kindergarten at the age of five years and has been promoted each year. His semester reports have been explained to us as excellent although their complexity has been baffling to both Jimmie's father and me. I am so glad that I have only two children and not a whole room full."

In discussing his school achievement, Jim said, "I have trouble in reading books in science and social studies. It is hard for me to see what is important and what is not important. The ideas in these books are confusing to me, and I get lost. I liked some of the books we had in the grades for they told us what to do. I like to read exciting stories and I spend a lot of my time reading. Dad says I read too much."

In an interview with Jim's teacher, it was learned that he could read stories at the sixth grade level with understanding and freedom from mechanical difficulties. But she pointed out that some materials at the seventh and eighth grade levels, especially in the social studies, became frustrating to Jim because of the complexity of ideas and because Jim apparently did not know the purpose for which he was reading. Jim's teacher further explained that he could comprehend well similar materials at the ninth and tenth grade levels if they were read to him. "In other words," she added, "Jim has the background and experience of an individual in the tenth grade."

Throughout his entire school history Jim has been interested in reading. A fifth grade teacher, however, explained that Jim was lazy and unwilling to complete his book reports on time. Retarded sex development and overweight have caused a physician to suggest the possibility of a glandular dysfunction as a contributing cause of Jim's lack of aggression. Some of his friends report that he is "too easygoing." They add, however, "Jim is a real guy and no square. We like him." All of his teachers have pointed out that "Jim is accepted by his friends because of his wholesome personality and interest in others."

Jim's progress in the first and second grades was quite normal. His first grade teacher made use of experience charts and helped the children in Jim's group to build up a reading vocabulary of nearly 150 words before introducing the basic text. Jim learned to recognize words and their meaning and to interpret short sentences and phrases. Later, in the second grade, he read silently to answer questions asked by the teacher. It is said that he learned to attack new words through picture clues, context clues, and

language-rhythm clues. At no time was he a "word reader." He easily
learned to follow printed and written directions in order to color, draw,
or play a game. It was in the second grade that Jim developed his interest
in books. In grades three and four Jim expanded his reading skills, for it
is said that he learned to identify words, phrases, and facts in printed materials. He learned to find the central idea in a short paragraph and answers to specific questions. Jim's mother states, "It was in the fourth grade
that Jimmie learned to read for pleasure." School records show that Jim
enjoyed reading to others for their satisfaction. It is said that his speaking
vocabulary was excellent and that he appreciated humor and dramatic
situations in books and children's magazines.

When Jim was in grades five and six, he developed skill in the use of
the dictionary. At this level he discovered problems through reading but
was unable to identify facts which were essential to their solution. His
teacher in the social studies reported that he was unable to locate in his
reading the main ideas and the facts which supported them. It is said that
outlining was extremely difficult for Jim. Records indicate that he was
reading as well as an individual two months in the seventh grade (7.2)
when the work of the sixth grade was completed.

After becoming acquainted with Jim, one is curious concerning the other
members of his family. Jim's parents are both college graduates. His father
is a successful businessman and his mother an excellent homemaker who
is chiefly interested in her family. Both parents are active in educational,
religious, and civic affairs. Jim has a sister of nine years who admires her
brother and tries to do all that he does. Jim says, "Kay, that's my sister,
bats a ball nearly as far as I can." In discussing their parents, both children agree that "Dad is the boss at our house and does most of the scold-
ing. Sometimes, though, he takes us fishing but generally he's too busy."
Jim, in a confidential mood, explained, "Dad tries so hard to get me interested in sports. Sometimes he tells me that Kay can catch a ball and even
box better than I can. I don't see why sports are so important." In discussing a vocational choice, Jim explained in detail that he wanted to be a
priest in the Episcopal Church. "I am in the choir and have served as an
acolyte. I like to read church history and help folks who are in trouble.
Mother says that I can become a good priest. I want to try." In a later conversation with Jim he said, "Mother helps me more than Dad and she does
not find so much wrong with me. I guess Dad likes Kay better than he
does me."

As a child, Jim developed normally. He was able to sit alone at six
months and was walking at fourteen months. At twelve months he spoke
several words and at two years he used simple sentences. It is reported
that Jim was a good baby except for outbursts of temper when hungry or
uncomfortable. Personal habits were normal and adjustment to others in

the home was decidedly above average. It is said the boy ate and slept well. "Jimmie could play contentedly in his pen for an hour or more. He did not need to be held or rocked," his mother reported.

Even as a young child Jim enjoyed drawing and later finger painting. It is said that he drew crosses, steeples, and churches. At the age of five he made a "painting" of an altar and was able to point out the reredos, frontal, and chalice. His mother said, "I have been very proud of Jimmie." As Jim grew older, he developed an interest in people, children of his own age and older individuals living in the neighborhood. Frequently he would bring home children who were separated from their parents. Stray dogs and cats were also befriended, much to the disgust of the neighbors and to the anxiety of his parents.

The school physician reports that Jim is a large, well-developed lad who is especially interested in people. Physical and mental health are reported to be excellent. There has been a history of much overweight with fat well distributed. For a time, the general impression was that of pluri-glandular insufficiency, but a lowered basal metabolism was not discovered. For nearly a year small amounts of thyroid were administered; however, at the age of twelve, weight was quite normal and medication was stopped. "James," the physician said, "is a normal, growing boy who has ideas of his own and the determination to put them into action."

The relevant factors in Jim's history may be summarized as follows:

1. Because of Jim's inability to make effective use of his textbooks, both the school and the parents have felt that it was necessary to furnish proof of his mental and emotional maturity.
2. Jim's history suggests that an individual may score well on a reading test and yet be unable to read effectively the books generally used in the classroom.
3. Frustration having its origin in both the home and school has been regarded as a concomitant factor in this case.
4. Jim, who is not interested in sports and psychomotor skills, pays special attention to objects and concepts having aesthetic values.
5. He is interested in people with problems and has decided, at least for the present, to enter the priesthood.
6. A history of being overweight and a general impression of pluriglandular insufficiency have suggested the possibility of a medical problem underlying Jim's reading difficulties.
7. It is reported that Jim is a determined boy and yet one who is well liked by his associates.
8. Jim's teacher reported that Jim was unable to discover main ideas and the facts which supported them. In substantiating this inference, it was said that outlining was extremely difficult for him.

The reader has now had an opportunity to become acquainted with Jim and his experiences in home and school. In many respects, he is like thousands of children who will enter the seventh grade in the fall. Teachers will ask, "What are the reading needs of this youth and how can they be met?" It is the purpose of this chapter to set forth some definite answers to the question.

Some Characteristics of the Good Reader

One of the goals of the conscientious teacher is to help her students become skillful in the art of reading. If Jim's teacher is to provide instruction which will lead to the development and integration of specific reading skills, she must possess considerable understanding of the characteristics of individuals who excel in reading. What are their habits? What skills do they possess?

The good reader is an effective thinker. He decides in advance what he wants to secure from his reading and then he goes after it. He always reads for a purpose and for meaning. Never does he overestimate the value of speed. He adjusts his rate of reading to the purpose and difficulty of the material and he knows when and how to read slowly as well as when and how to read rapidly. The good reader makes every attempt to increase his vocabulary and he constantly strives to improve his ability to concentrate upon reading activities. He can remember and make effective use of new ideas and concepts obtained from reading. The good reader never accepts at face value the ideas expressed by others. Instead, he is critical and questions the validity and the purpose of the writer's statements. In addition, he attempts to acquire an extensive background by reading a variety of materials. He appreciates the fact that by reading he can add to his knowledge, pleasure, and recreation.

Reading for the good reader is an integration of skills rather than an accumulation. Just as the human body is more than the sum of all its parts, so effective reading is more than a compilation of skills. These skills must be related to one another and operate as a whole. They may be separate in function but mutually dependent one upon the other. If Jim is to make effective use of textbooks and reference materials, it is essential that he have guidance in the integration of the reading skills discussed in this book. The growing reader should understand and appreciate how they function *together*. He needs to see reading as an organismic process, in which related skills, each dependent upon the other make their contribution.

Using the Different Parts of a Book

As a preliminary step in developing the characteristics and skills of the good reader, the classroom teacher can acquaint his pupils with the structure and function of the parts of a book. Much information, and in some instances all that may be required, can be obtained by thoughtfully studying the title page, the preface or introduction, the table of contents, the appendix, the index, and by skimming the body of the text. These parts making up the book can be understood and appreciated by the young student. In all instances reading can aid the individual in becoming independent and self-helpful.

The Title Page and the Copyright Page

On the title and copyright pages are given the names of the book and author, information about the author's position, the name of the publisher, and the place and date of publication. Often the editor's name, the name of the series, if the book is part of a series, and the edition of the book are given. These are important facts and students can be taught to make use of these pages as a means of judging the validity of the material presented in the text. The official title and position of the author provide data which suggest how well qualified he is to write on the subject. A book which has been recently copyrighted is likely to contain the results of the latest discoveries and investigations. A text in psychology published in 1930, for example, would hardly warrant scrutiny by modern psychologists unless they were interested in the historical aspects of a subject.

The Preface or Introduction

This important part of a book contains the author's declared purpose and intention. Frequently he expresses his point of view and shows how his work differs from that of others in the field. Furthermore, he may point out how the book can be used and in what ways it may be of value to the reader. The preface or introduction may also prepare the reader and set the stage for a detailed consideration of the subject discussed in the text.

The Table of Contents

In the front of every book is found the table of contents. A thoughtful skimming of this table helps the reader to determine the scope of the book. A brief outline of the text is thereby provided and a careful survey of this will often determine whether the book offers information of value and interest to the reader. The table of contents shows the page on which each chapter begins and the number of pages devoted to that topic. The mature reader can determine the relative importance of the different chapters by computing the number of pages devoted to them. A study of the organization and sequence of the chapters may also prove helpful in seeing the book as a whole and in determining how the various parts fit together.

Flexible grouping provides for individual differences in the teaching of science.

In order to do it yourself, the proper sequence of activities must be followed

In the social studies children read to identify and solve problems.

The Body of the Book

Under the direction of the teacher, students can examine the body of a number of books and can observe that in each case it is made up of sections, chapters, and paragraphs. They can learn the value of major and minor headings and, like Jim, can learn to make use of them in evaluating ideas. If the use of headings is properly understood, students in their search for data can skim the body of a book by attending to chapter headings and by reading in detail only when such headings indicate the presence of appropriate information. Again it should be pointed out that the good reader knows what he wants to find and that he reads with a definite purpose in mind. With this objective in view, chapter after chapter can be scanned and pertinent data spotted. If necessary, parts can be reread for important detail.

The Appendix

Valuable material is generally to be found in the appendix. This part of a book includes the bibliography, references, statistical tables, explanatory notes, illustrative material, and original data. Students can be taught to observe references to appendices and to investigate these sources of information. In many instances they are of inestimable value to the critical reader.

The Index

The index is an alphabetical list of topics and names occurring in the text with an indication of the page where each reference is to be found. It is a key to the book and provides the quickest and best means of locating a definite fact or specific information. Young students can be taught to select the most significant word in a topic in which they are interested and to look for that word in the index. Page numbers referring to the topic can be listed in order to avoid hunting through the index a second or third time to find additional page references. Frequently time can be saved by looking up words related to a topic on which additional information is desired. Demonstrations of this procedure on the part of the teacher and practice by the student can facilitate the development of this fundamental skill.

Some Steps in Chapter Reading

Many individuals, like Jim, have difficulty in reading a chapter effectively because they fail to see the chapter as a whole and the manner in which its parts fit together. Frequently they become lost in a mass of detail and miss the main ideas entirely. The effective reading of a chapter is dependent upon the integration of many reading skills separate in function but mutually dependent upon one another. In order to set forth this integrative process five steps will be discussed in detail.

1. Make a preview of the entire chapter in order to determine what the writer intends to accomplish and how he has organized his material.
2. Convert each major heading into a question which fits the content presented. Write each question on a 3" x 5" card.
3. Read to answer these questions, using minor headings as guides.
4. State in your own words answers to each question on 3" x 5" cards.
5. Test your knowledge of the subject by reviewing the questions and answers found on the cards.

How Can Students Be Taught to Preview a Chapter?

Many students, when they attempt to read a chapter, become so involved with minor topics and details that they lose sight of the major ideas. When they finish reading a chapter they discover that they have retained only a series of unrelated and specific minutiae with little understanding as to how these facts and details are related to one another. Frequently this difficulty is due to the fact that the reader, like Jim, did not perceive the chapter as a whole before he began to read for detail. "He did not see the forest because he was overly concerned with the intricate details of one small tree."

In order to help students to read effectively textbook material, the teacher can emphasize the importance of surveying the chapter as a whole in order to determine the fundamental and major ideas which have been expressed. There are four ways by which an individual can preview a chapter. These four approaches are not mutually exclusive but may be combined and modified when necessary. The *first* approach involves the reading of the introduction to the chapter in order to determine what the writer intends to accomplish. In addition to pointing out the problem to be discussed, the author may state in the introduction how he intends to treat the subject and may even briefly state the main points which he intends to discuss.

A *second* way of surveying a chapter is to read carefully the summary at the end of the chapter. In the summary most authors concisely state what they have attempted to accomplish and briefly present their conclusions. The summary is especially helpful in making a preliminary survey because it furnishes the reader with the fundamental and basic ideas of the chapter without details.

A *third* equally effective procedure involves the skimming of headings and subheadings. Major and minor headings furnish a framework or outline of the writer's ideas. In utilizing this method of previewing a chapter, it is well for the reader to determine the kind of type or printing which has been used to indicate the most important points. From this information he should answer such questions as the following: How many main topics are there? What are they? When these questions have been answered, the reader can skim the chapter in more detail by determining the kinds of type which have been used to indicate points of secondary and tertiary importance. Reading is thinking, and careful thought on the part of the reader at this stage may help him to understand the major ideas in the chapter, their relationship to one another, and the purpose of the minor details.

Of course, some books, essays, and reports do not make use of major and minor headings, and therefore it is not possible to use them in an attempt to determine what the chapter is about. Then a *fourth* approach must be utilized. The reader can scan each paragraph for the purpose of determining its central thought. Some students may require instruction and aid in doing this. Therefore, it may be advisable to explain and illustrate paragraphing. For example, students need to know that a paragraph serves as an aid to clearness of expression and that, if properly employed, it gives the reader much assistance in understanding what he reads. For example, suppose a brief essay on Lincoln discusses three topics: (1) events of Lincoln's life up to 1860, (2) his career as President, and (3) an estimate of his greatness. Since each topic is treated in a separate paragraph, the beginning and end of each topic becomes evident at once and thus the reader is enabled to determine without much effort the structure of the essay. The number of paragraphs in a composition, of course, does not always correspond with the number of main topics. The number of paragraphs is a relative matter, depending largely upon the extent to which the subject is developed. It is possible that in a very brief treatment of a subject, each main topic may be completed in a paragraph. But if the subject is developed at length, then each topic may require many paragraphs.

The central thought of a paragraph may be developed in several ways: for example, by the use of (1) definition, (2) illustration or example, (3) comparison or contrast, (4) generalization based upon particular facts and details, (5) repetition, (6) elimination, (7) relation of cause and effect, or (8) a combination of methods. An alert teacher can provide ample materials illustrating the various ways in which the central thought of a paragraph may be developed. Students must not be permitted to lose sight of the fact that in reading a paragraph they are primarily concerned with locating and understanding the central thought and that the eight methods of paragraph development which we have listed are all intended to clarify and expand the main idea for the reader.

In surveying a chapter by this fourth approach, the reader should realize that the central thought of a paragraph generally is expressed in a topic sentence and that the topic sentence is usually the first or last sentence in the paragraph. The reader can skim each paragraph in order to locate the topic sentence. Some students prefer to underline it, if the book is their own. Then after each topic sentence has been located, the reader can determine the relationship between topic sentences in a series of paragraphs. Undoubtedly he will find that several paragraphs discuss various aspects of the same subject. From this relationship of paragraphs the reader can prepare his own major headings and write them in the proper places in the margin of the book. Scanning of paragraphs and the development of major headings requires careful, mature thinking and a combination of integrated reading skills.

What Is the Purpose of Converting Each Major Heading into a Question?

It is suggested that the student be encouraged to convert each main heading into a question and to write each question at the top of a 3″ x 5″ card. For example, let us suppose that a chapter in a textbook on reading contains three major headings, namely:

Physical Factors Affect Reading
Psychological Factors Affect the Development of Reading Skills
Some Environmental Factors Affect Reading Skills

Let us assume that a reader, after previewing the chapter, decides that the three main questions which he will ask of the chapter are:

1. What are the physical factors affecting reading?
2. How do psychological factors affect the development of reading skills?
3. How do environmental factors affect reading skills?

Each of these questions should be written on a separate card, and these are the questions which the reader will attempt to answer as he reads the chapter in more detail.

The practice of asking questions while one reads has many advantages. It stimulates one to read for a purpose, and it helps the reader to concentrate upon the activity of identifying and discovering what the author has to say. The questions also direct the reader's attention to the answers to his questions and in this way prevent him from being lost in a perplexing labyrinth of subtopics, paragraphs, sentences, and words.

The preparation of useful questions is a difficult task. The reader cannot "tack on" a "what," "who," or "when" to a major heading and automatically have a suitable question. Instead he must consider the author's purpose, the relationship between various topics discussed in the chapter, and the general facts set forth in the discussion. It is obvious that the process of converting major headings into questions involves the integration of many thinking-reading skills and is an important key step in reading a chapter, for if poorly worded or misdirected questions are asked, the third step will be difficult indeed to carry out.

How Can Students Read to Answer Questions?

When students read to answer questions which they have prepared, they will be concerned with these three levels of reading:

1. Identification of facts
2. Interpretation of facts
3. Evaluation of facts

Identification of facts, which is the first level, is not too difficult to accomplish. It consists of determining answers to questions and of locating and identifying facts presented in the chapter. Many times minor headings are helpful in spotting answers to questions. For example, in our illustration four minor headings might follow the major one, "Physical Factors Affect Reading."

1. Visual Factors
2. Auditory Factors
3. Glandular Dysfunction
4. General Health

Obviously, there are four answers to the question "What are the physical factors affecting reading?" But the mere identification of these four factors is not enough. The reader must go on to the second and third levels of reading. He must interpret and evaluate the facts which he has identified. He must ask: How do these four physical factors affect reading? What effect do they have on reading skills? Of what value are these facts? The reader's skill in interpreting and evaluating that which he identifies is dependent upon his experience, background, and mental content. A good reader relates the new ideas gained from reading to the older ones in his experience. He brings to the printed page as much as he takes from it. There is nothing passive or mechanical in regard to this step in chapter reading. Reading with full understanding requires an active, aggressive, and creative attack upon the ideas presented in the chapter.

Why Should Answers to Questions Be Stated in the Reader's Words?

After the reader has discovered and interpreted answers to his questions, he can write these reactions on 3" x 5" cards. Use of these cards is suggested in order to prevent the student's misuse of detail. For example, in our illustration a student might prepare the following card.

What are the physical factors affecting reading?
  1. Visual defects related to eyestrain and a confusion of letters and words.
  2. Auditory factors. Some people omit endings, syllables, and some sounds because of difficulty.
  3. Glandular dysfunction. Results in immaturity and unwillingness to put forth effort.
  4. General health. Becomes apparent as general inability to sustain interest and effort.

Answers to questions should be stated, not in the words of the author, but in the reader's words. If the reader really understands the material which he has read, he should be able to state his answers simply, directly, and specifically. It should not be necessary for him to parrot the language of the book. The good reader should not be concerned with verbatim memorization of the textbook but should strive to understand, interpret, and evaluate the ideas of the writer.

What Procedure Should Be Followed in Testing One's Knowledge of a Subject?

The final step for the student is to test his understanding and ability to recall the major points in the chapter. This step is frequently neglected by many individuals because they fail to realize its importance. Garrett [2] has shown that when there are frequent periods of review, loss from forgetting is partially overcome and a larger amount of material is retained. The following procedures will aid the student in interpreting and assimilating facts obtained from the chapter:

1. Without looking at the answers on the 3" x 5" cards, attempt to answer each question.
2. Sort the cards into two piles: one for questions which can be answered easily and the other for those which cause difficulty.
3. Study the cards until you are able to recall answers to all questions.
4. Shuffle the cards and then attempt to answer the questions in the new order.
5. Reread or "skim" the original material in the textbook.
6. Keep the 3" x 5" cards for future reference and review the questions and answers frequently.

In these suggestions for making more effective use of books, an attempt has been made to integrate several basic reading skills in the process of reading a chapter. This is but the beginning, however, of a more significant task of developing appreciation and enjoyment of current and classical literature. If teachers can accomplish this end, they can help children to enter the world of reality with understanding and appreciation.

Nature of Appreciation

Teachers want their students to acquire a "taste" and "liking" for books. This comes about *indirectly* as children sample and dip into classic litera-

[2] Henry A. Garrett, *General Psychology* (New York: American Book Company, 1955), pp. 350–351.

ture. From a psychological viewpoint appreciation is an affective rather than a cognitive process. It is a realm of feeling in which one is satisfied. Appreciation and enjoyment are the resultant of interest, emotion, and an understanding of sense perceptions which have deeper significance than they appear to have at first. To appreciate, the reader must contribute from his own background. He must give in order to receive, and he must understand to estimate properly. All of this we must expect of our students if they are to value the good and identify the ineffective.

A Challenge to Teachers

The ultimate goal of the total reading program is to develop readers who enjoy books, who love to read, and who *do* read. The achievement of this goal presents a real challenge to the inventiveness of every teacher. She must, by her actions, attitudes, and originality, permeate the atmosphere of the classroom with an enthusiasm for reading. She must eagerly take advantage of every opportunity to develop and improve the reading tastes and interests of her pupils. This process requires alertness, imagination, and creativity and allows for little reliance on "cut-and-dried" procedures. The teacher must love to read and must by her every word and action convey her enthusiasm and appreciation for reading. Not only must she read and share what she has read with others, but she must encourage her students to read and to share ideas which they have obtained from reading.

To be more specific, the wise teacher provides ample opportunity for boys and girls to explore many types of literature such as biography, science, fiction, history, drama, and poetry. To do this effectively, it is essential that the teacher possess a broad and up-to-date knowledge of children's literature and an awareness of the interests of her pupils. As the class leader, she helps her students to become sensitive to the impressions and moods created by writers. She helps pupils to respond with esthetic appreciation to an author's skillful selection of words, phrases, and sentences. She realizes that personal living can be enriched and that social understanding can be developed through literature. She knows that literature has much to do with the formulation of personal values, and she firmly believes that, by reading, children can become acquainted with the rich heritage of their culture and that of others.

Some Procedures Which Can Be Useful in Developing Appreciation

The teaching of reading is both an art and a science. If the teacher is to be successful, she must have not only a goal but a plan for its attainment, for random responses are seldom effective. In general, appreciation is based upon interest, enjoyment, and an understanding of relationship to oneself. The practices discussed in the following pages form a basis which can contribute to the desired process, growing appreciation. It should be pointed out, however, that there can be no structured procedure which can work equally well with all teachers and lead directly to success on the part of the instructor.

Know the Interests and Aptitudes of Your Students

Books can be introduced to children in much the same way as an interesting and helpful speaker. Students can learn to approach books, stories, and poems as something to be understood and enjoyed and not as a source of facts and information to be studied and memorized. The literary selection to be introduced must become real, vivid, and stimulating to the student. He must catch the spirit as he reads or listens. This can only come about as a result of his mental maturity, mental content, and background. If these are lacking, he will fail to appreciate the literary gems placed before him. It is obvious, then, that not every student in a class is ready to appreciate, for example, the stories of Andersen, Stevenson, or Scott, and the poems of Longfellow, Tennyson, or Whittier. Furthermore, in junior high school classes and in all grades it is not unusual to find students who are reading far below their expected level and who are unable to achieve at the level of their associates. Other students, like Jim, may be good readers and yet lack skill, or an integration of skills, with the result that reading for appreciation becomes difficult and in some cases impossible. This blocking is frustrating to the student and destroys his ability to gain mental content through reading. Consequently, the teacher should give quickly whatever help she is able to provide. For example, she may be able to adjust materials to his interest and reading level. Again she may wish to group for a time students requiring specific instruction and special guidance. This flexible grouping, as suggested in Chapter 7, should be based upon the interests and aptitudes of the students as well as the objectives of the teacher.

Make a Positive Approach

The initial approach to any book, story, or poem must be comprehensive and never analytical. It is well for the student to identify the main ideas first and then clothe them with all the details suggested by the writer along with those which the reader has to contribute. Some students, like Jim, become so lost in a mass of detail that they fail to see the selection as a whole. Concern for elements such as choice of words, organization, or tone, can be reserved for the second and third reading or better still for the more mature and critical reader. The teacher can be mindful of the fact that nearly all literature for children is written to be enjoyed and not to be pulled apart for analytical study. Such details as plot, character, structure, and imagery are used to produce the total effect in a literary selection and when snipped out of context they lose their effectiveness. Disintegration has taken place and interest has been destroyed.

Stimulate Appreciation Through Participation

There is a need to emphasize sharing as an essential act in developing appreciation. When a book is reviewed, a story told, or a poem read, it is given a new quality. This new element is the appreciation of the reviewer, storyteller, and reader. Their personalities have found expression and satisfaction has ensued. Teachers can utilize oral reading in audience situations as a means of developing and deepening appreciation of books, stories, and poems. Make-believe television telecasts provide an excellent opportunity for reading or reciting before an audience. Choral reading by groups is most effective in developing interest and satisfaction in oral presentations. Informal panel discussions based upon research reading can prove to be interesting and productive of active group participation. The sharing of current news items and articles of interest by the good oral reader is an effective way of emphasizing the importance of contemporary events in the making of history. Participating in a discussion group is a means of clarifying thought and can be of value in the formation of opinion. The discussion of plots and characters observed on television not only alerts the student as to elements to be observed but aids him in evaluating adequacy of character development and portrayal. In participating in these activities the mature student will see for himself that the good reader and the good listener interpret the thoughts of the writer and speaker in terms of their own experiences, thereby enriching meanings and increasing appreciation.

The teacher can provide a classroom atmosphere that encourages independent reading. Every room can have a reading center, an attractive, inviting corner where children can read quietly. Books can be easily available, and effort can be made to display new collections and colorful book jackets as a means of stimulating interest. Bulletin boards can be used for special displays pertaining to recreational reading, articles of special interest, records of the children's reading, and interesting book reports which the children have voluntarily prepared. Librarians can be invited to visit the class for the purpose of discussing new books of particular interest. Exhibits and reading programs can be planned by the children. Book clubs can be formed. Club members can write to authors of children's books, plan a story hour for another classroom, and make posters for special book displays. Children can be encouraged to share in the oral interpretation of poems and in original poems which they have written. Definite periods can be set aside for recreational reading and for the sharing of stories with others. Teachers can create a receptive mood for the various types of literature which they read aloud to the class. They can read poetry in such a way that the children "feel" the rhythm and experience the beauty of the language. They can read prose in such a way that children will identify themselves closely with the characters, participate actively in the plot, and enthusiastically "catch" the esthetic quality of the selection. The ingenious teacher can and will create opportunities for her students to read for pleasure, and she will provide experiences designed to develop new reading interests and more discriminating reading tastes.

Select Interesting Materials

Materials of varying degrees of literary merit can be made available to children. If possible, students should have an opportunity to select for themselves what they wish to read. Through subtle guidance, selection can be made on the basis of reading interest, reading level, and effectiveness of material in achieving specific goals. In order to aid her students adequately in their selection of books and magazines, the teacher must become an authority on literature for children. In addition to the well-known classics, teachers of reading must be acquainted with the delightful children's stories published in recent years and they must be able to use contemporary literature in enriching the social studies and other activities of the classroom.

Interest is one of the criteria to be considered in the selection of reading materials. A knowledge of the interest trends of children in general can be helpful in choosing suitable books and magazines. Boys and girls who are beginning to read enjoy beautifully illustrated books which contain stories of children who are like themselves. They enjoy realistic books with swift action, elements of surprise, and humor. They appreciate stories in which animals talk. At seven or eight years of age children begin to be interested in fairy tales and adventure stories of real animals. In the middle grades children like to read the "tall tales" of Paul Bunyan and other literary figures. Sex differences in reading interests which are not very pronounced during the primary grades become quite apparent by the age of nine or ten. Boys like to read books about travel, famous people, modern inventions, and science while girls enjoy sentimental stories of home and school life. Both boys and girls like mysteries, adventure stories, and the comics. Intermediate and upper-grade students prefer the types of stories which have proved most satisfying to them in the past—adventure, travel, biography, mystery, or the classics.

The well-trained teacher realizes that the range of individual preferences in a group of children is tremendous and that in addition to knowing the general interests of boys and girls it is essential for her to know the particular interests of each child. The teacher can discover individual interests in several ways. One method is to observe the child's daily behavior. What does he talk about? What does he bring to school to share with others? From the many books in the classroom and library, which one does he choose? Another method of determining personal interests of children is to interview each child separately. The teacher can ask such questions as: What radio and television programs do you enjoy? In choosing a book to read, what do you look for? What do you want to be when you grow up? What do you like to do for fun? If the teacher wishes, a questionnaire can be used in place of the interview. Another procedure for investigating interests is to permit students to tell about the things they like to do. In this way not only does the teacher learn about each child's interests but other children may be stimulated to develop similar tastes. Talking with school librarians, home visits, and conferences with parents may also provide valuable information which can be used in finding the right book for the right child at the right time.

In order to enjoy and appreciate a good book, the child must be able to identify, interpret, and evaluate words, ideas, episodes, and the characteristics of personalities making up the plot. To a seventh grade child reading at the third grade level this activity is difficult and in most cases impossible. For this child, books and materials must be selected which he can read and enjoy. Today such books are available. For example, on almost any subject *The World Book Encyclopedia* [3] provides information which can be read and appreciated by students having reading levels ranging from the fourth to the sixteenth grade. Furthermore, *The American Adventure Series* [4] is made up of exciting and interesting stories which many adults enjoy but which are written with vocabulary, sentence structure, and general pattern of organization easily understood by individuals whose reading levels range from grades two to six, inclusive. It is the responsibility of the teacher to make use of reading difficulty formulas in the appraisal and selection of materials suitable for her students. At the end of this chapter references explaining the use of these instruments are provided.

In meeting the reading interests and achievement levels of her children, the teacher will find the following sources of materials helpful:

1. Carter, Homer L. J., and Dorothy J. McGinnis. *Learning to Read,* chap. 6. New York: McGraw-Hill Book Co., 1953.

    Materials for use in developmental and corrective reading have been classified into ten areas. Especially helpful is the section regarding materials reported to be of interest to retarded readers.

2. Kottmeyer, William. *Teacher's Guide for Remedial Reading,* pp. 189–201. St. Louis: Webster Publishing Co., 1959.

    A list of books which have been used with remedial problems for some time is provided. The books are grouped by levels of difficulty and interest.

[3] *The World Book Encyclopedia* may be purchased from Field Enterprises, Inc. Educational Division, Merchandise Mart Plaza, Chicago 54, Illinois.
[4] *The American Adventure Series* is published by Wheeler Publishing Co., Chicago, Illinois.

3. Strang, Ruth, Christine B. Gilbert, and Margaret C. Scoggin. *Gateways to Readable Books* (2nd ed.), New York: H. W. Wilson Co., 1952.

    More than 1100 books have been annotated and classified according to subject. An estimated grade level of difficulty of each book is indicated.

4. Witty, Paul. *Reading in Modern Education*, pp. 210–214, Appendix A and Appendix B. Boston: D. C. Heath and Co., 1949.

    Included in this worthwhile reference is a compilation of favorite books with their estimated grade level, a lengthy record of children's books, and a selected list of current news materials for children in the elementary grades and for high school students.

In the selection of literature for children, the function and effectiveness of the books should be considered. The teacher can appraise their impact upon the child's emotional growth and development, his attitude, and his appreciation. She can be more concerned with the child's ability to feel than his ability to know and to do. According to Russell,[5] the teaching of literature is directed toward such goals as the following:

1. The extension and enrichment of the child's experiences of the complex ways of man's living.
2. The opportunity to relive and re-experience the adventures and ideas of others.
3. Insight into one's own personality and problems.
4. Appreciation and understanding of the problems of others.
5. The development of love of country and democratic ideals.
6. The discovery of ethical values which are common to different creeds and which form the foundation of an effective personality in the modern world.
7. The providing of opportunities for fun and for escape.
8. The development of worthwhile tastes and permanent interests in good literature.

In making use of these objectives, no teacher will be foolhardy enough to announce these aims to her class and expect her children to accept them. Instead she will wisely use them in her selection of materials and in the evaluation of her teaching program. Surely no teacher will expect all her students to achieve all these goals. Neither can she assume that children enter the highway of literary appreciation at the level of the comic and finally attain the pinnacle of the classic.

  [5] David H. Russell, *Children Learn to Read* (Boston: Ginn and Co., 1949), pp. 282–285.

Make Use of Imagery

Teachers can utilize imagery in their presentation of reading selections. The enjoyment and delight derived from reading literature depends in part upon the reader's skill in seeing mental pictures. For example, many vivid types of imagery can be found in the sentence "The children were in the yard roasting marshmallows over the burning leaves and twigs." Many who read this sentence will "see" the children placing marshmallows on long slender sticks which Father has carefully whittled until they are clean and white. They will "see" the children holding marshmallows over the fire until the marshmallows turn a golden brown. They will "see" the child who, unlike the others, sets his marshmallow aflame and then blows it out. They will "see" him gingerly touch the charred, misshapen confection to determine if it is cool enough to eat, and they will "see" him pop it into his mouth and slowly smile with quiet satisfaction. They will "hear" the laughter and excited conversation of the children, the snap and crackle of the fire. They will "feel" the brisk fall wind with its touch of frost and promise of approaching winter. They will "smell" the smoky incense of the burning leaves. They will "taste" the warm, soft, sugary goodness of the toasted marshmallow. These pictures are vivid and enchanting and add to the joy of reading. To the child, however, who has never learned to use his imagination as he reads, the sentence will be just a number of words, and much of the pleasure and charm of reading will be lost. Fortunately, most children can be taught to translate words into pictures. The development of this skill can begin even before the child learns to read and can be facilitated by systematic instruction throughout his school career.

The astute teacher will take advantage of every opportunity that arises to help her students gain skill in reading with imagery. Before beginning to read a poem or story to the children she can ask them to listen with their eyes closed to find out what they see, smell, hear, taste, and feel during the reading. Each child can be given an opportunity to tell about the sensations which he experiences and these can be listed on the board. Children may be encouraged to draw pictures on paper to illustrate poems or stories read by the teacher or to dramatize certain exciting parts of a story. They can also be permitted to draw pictures illustrative of the stories which they read for recreation. The drawings and the stories can be shared with other children during discussion periods. The children can be encouraged to write a play, to plan and build scenery, and to present the play for their parents and friends.

These activities are only suggestive of the many procedures which the creative teacher can utilize to aid students in the use of imagery while reading. The "seeing eye," the "hearing ear," and the "feeling organism" can be stimulated and the imagination can be cultivated through creative work in dramatic form, in dance, or through contact with poetry, pictures, and music. From these experiences the individual may develop power to grasp and construct out of his own experience some creative form which will give him satisfaction.

Inspire Creative Writing

The speaker and the writer are concerned with the development of ideas while the reader and the listener are concerned with the interpretation of ideas. Both these processes are aspects of communication, and mastery of one can lead to mastery of the other. It is reasonable to assume that if a student can write an effective poem he will also possess the ability to read and appreciate other poems. In brief, creative writing becomes a means of increasing appreciation.

Children who have had interesting and exciting experiences want to tell others about them. With encouragement and guidance on the part of the teacher, written accounts of these experiences may be recorded. Such creative writing comes in occasional moments of inspiration and not as the result of an "assignment" or as a task to be completed and handed in on the morrow. Not every student in the class can be expected to do creative writing which would even compare favorably with accepted literary standards. However, each child's performance can be creative in that it is a new experience for him.

Working, thinking, discussing, and writing together in a group permit each individual to make his contribution; furthermore, he has an opportunity to see what is good and to understand why it is so. Teachers who have started stories and after creating an exciting episode turned them over to their students to complete have frequently found that their children have added to the plot and developed characters in such a manner as to contribute much of literary merit to the meager beginning. When children are beginning to take part in such productions, it may be well to tell their stories to the group, for frequently a dull tale can be brought to life by enthusiastic telling. As children work together in this manner, the more mature students will learn to appreciate some of the basic elements in effective writing. In all of this, one of the most important ingredients is enthusiasm on the part of the teacher.

Develop Standards for Judging

The ability to appreciate good books is gained by permitting the child to set up for himself, modify, and later re-establish his own standards of what is good. This is a dynamic and growing process which is continuous throughout the life of the individual. Young children enjoy stories and poems without knowing *why*. The characters in a story satisfy them, the choice of words delights them, and the humor pleases them. They appreciate the story without being aware of what contributed to their enjoyment. In their opinion the story is good. It is the responsibility of teachers first to make it possible for students to like good books and second to help them to know why they are enjoyable and satisfying. Both goals must be approached so as to stimulate growth to ever higher levels of literary appreciation.

Good speakers and writers make use of certain literary elements in order to produce a desired effect. Beautiful and musical speech is a quality of good writing. These attributes can be accomplished by choice of words and by making use of connotation as well as denotation. Diction, the manner of expressing ideas in words, can add to beauty and striking expression. Form has much to contribute to effective writing. It takes into consideration sentence length, arrangement, and rhythm. Tone, which makes use of metaphors, similes, and allusions, is the summation of intellectual and emotional effects of writing. It is produced by choice of words, diction, form, and organization. All of these literary elements contribute to an understanding of why books, poems, and stories have real merit and are worthy of appreciation. Several of these elements may be illustrated and discussed at length in some classes, while others may well wait for later periods of development.

Organization is a literary element which should be understood and applied throughout the elementary and secondary schools. Its use is dependent upon ability to evaluate ideas and appreciate their orderly sequence. Children can be made aware of what constitutes the beginning, body, and end of a chapter, story, or poem. They can see that the whole is made up of parts, each in its proper place, and each dependent upon the other. They can sense the economy and beauty of organization, which is more obvious to the uninformed than many of the other literary elements. Through unobtrusive guidance by the teacher, the worth of organization and orderly sequence can develop and expand with the student's ability to read. This is one standard which should be respected by all. Other standards can, and probably will, come later.

Standards of character portrayal can be developed in young students through a variety of dramatic forms, such as the puppet show, moving picture, television play, and spoken drama. Children appreciate the activities of people whom they can understand and the odds are more in favor of their understanding a Matt Dillon than a Hamlet. They can understand and identify the distinguishing traits of Evangeline and Tom Sawyer as well as those of personalities in real life. They are certain that the future of these characters will be but a projection of their past. The good will be good and the wicked will continue to be wicked until the day of their undoing. The understanding of the evolution of personality is for the more mature individual. As students grow and develop mental content, they will understand the delicate balance between impulse and inhibition and realize the importance of goals and the influence of environment. They will develop the concept of a man who is both good and evil. They will understand that traits and content of personality can change even though the general pattern remains more or less constant. Here again, standards of personality portrayal, like standards of organization, can develop and expand with the student's ability to read. Individuals learn to appreciate literary values as they learn to live.

In conclusion, it should be emphasized that a reader, in order to make effective use of books, must identify, interpret, and evaluate the ideas they contain. To accomplish this end, basic reading skills must be integrated and not merely accumulated like a collection of merit badges. The unitary activity is chapter reading, which can become useful both as a tool and as a means of appreciating classical literature.

Guided Activities

1. Talk with experienced teachers in junior and senior high school and ask them to estimate
   a. The range of reading ability within their classes.
   b. The per cent of students in their classes who are unable to read a chapter effectively.
   c. The per cent of students in their classes who are not achieving at their expected level because of deficiencies in reading.
2. Make a survey of several professional magazines devoted to the teaching of reading and summarize briefly the current thinking in regard to the following subjects:
   a. The improvement of reading in the subject matter fields.
   b. Teaching the appreciation of literature.
   c. The adjustment of reading materials to the interest and reading levels of students.
3. Participate in a panel discussion of the following questions:
   a. What facts substantiate the inference that Jim is an intelligent boy?
   b. Why do you think Jim is ready for chapter reading?
   c. Why would you expect Jim to have adequate vocabularies in different fields?
   d. Why do you think Jim has the background for the appreciation of good literature?
4. The teacher will be concerned with the reading skills Jim possesses and, of course, with those that he does not possess. Make a list of each as shown in his biography.
5. Jim's fifth grade teacher reported that in her opinion he was "lazy." Find, if possible, evidence of a physical basis underlying this characteristic.
6. Betts in *Foundations of Reading Instruction,* chapter 21, describes four reading levels. Identify these levels from the report of Jim's teacher.
7. Cite specifically the facts in Jim's biography which suggest that his background and mental content are commensurate with his mental maturity.

8. Apply the suggested procedure for reading a chapter to one of your college textbooks.
9. Interview a school librarian and determine the reading interests of children at the level at which you expect to teach.

Questions and References

Questions	References
1. What are some practical ways of discovering the specific reading needs of children?	1. Betts, Emmett A. *Foundations of Reading Instruction,* Chap. XXI. New York: American Book Co., 1957.
2. What suggestions and materials have been found helpful in reading textbooks with headings and textbooks without headings?	2. Carter, Homer L. J., and Dorothy J. McGinnis. *Effective Reading for College Students,* Chap. 4. New York: Dryden Press, 1957.
3. How can teachers become acquainted with literature for children?	3. McKee, Paul. *The Teaching of Reading in the Elementary School,* Chap. 17. Boston: Houghton Mifflin Co., 1948. Russell, David H. *Children Learn To Read,* pp. 440–444. Boston: Ginn and Co., 1961.
4. What experiences can children have in literature?	4. Jacobs, Leland B. "Children's Experiences in Literature," in Virgil E. Herrick and Leland B. Jacobs, *Children and the Language Arts,* Chap. 9. Englewood Cliffs, N. J.: Prentice-Hall, 1955.
5. What experiences can children have in dramatic interpretation?	5. Swickard, Sara R. "Children's Experiences in Dramatic Interpretation," in Virgil E. Herrick and Leland B. Jacobs, *Children and the Language Arts,* Chap. 15. Englewood Cliffs, N. J.: Prentice-Hall, 1955.

Questions	References
6. What are some ways of investigating and developing reading interests of children?	6. Dawson, Mildred A., and Henry A. Bamman. *Fundamentals of Basic Reading Instruction*, Chap. 8. New York: Longmans, Green and Co., 1959. Harris, Albert J. *How To Increase Reading Ability* (4th Edition), Chap. 17. New York: Longmans, Green and Co., 1961.
7. What are some advantages and disadvantages of comics?	7. Hildreth, Gertrude. *Teaching Reading*, pp. 524–529. New York: Holt and Co., 1958. Russell. *Op. cit.*, pp. 385–393.
8. How can one determine and predict readability?	8. Hunnicutt, C. W., and William J. Iverson. *Research in the Three R's*, pp. 176–213. New York: Harper & Bros., 1958.
9. Where can one find book lists and bibliographies of children's literature?	9. Russell. *Op cit.*, pp. 444–453.
10. What are some reading skills essential for successful work in junior and senior high school?	10. Strang, Ruth, and Dorothy K. Bracken. *Making Better Readers*, Chap. 3. Boston: D. C. Heath and Co., 1957.
11. How can one teach reading in the content fields?	11. *Ibid.*, Chap. 5.
12. What are the reading interests of young people?	12. Norvell, George W., *The Reading Interests of Young People*. Boston: D. C. Heath and Co., 1950.

13. How can readability of books be determined?

13. Farr, James N., and James J. Jenkins. "Tables for Use With the Flesch Readability Formulas," *Journal of Applied Psychology*, Vol. 33, No. 3, June, 1949, pp. 275–278.

Farr, James N., James J. Jenkins, and Donald G. Paterson. "Simplification of Flesch Reading Ease Formula," *Journal of Applied Psychology*, Vol. 35, No. 5, October, 1951, pp. 333–337.

Flesch, Rudolf. "A New Readability Yardstick," *Journal of Applied Psychology*, Vol. 32, No. 3, June, 1948, pp. 221–233.

Dale, Edgar, and Jeanne S. Chall. "A Formula for Predicting Readability," in C. W. Hunnicutt and William J. Iverson, *Research in the Three R's*, pp. 194–205. New York: Harper & Bros., 1958.

Lorge, Irving. "Predicting Readability," in C. W. Hunnicutt and William J. Iverson, *Research in the Three R's*, pp. 184–194. New York: Harper & Bros., 1958.

Spache, George. "A Readability Formula for Primary Reading Materials," in C. W. Hunnicutt and William J. Iverson, *Research in the Three R's*, pp. 177–179. New York: Harper & Bros., 1958.

9

DEVELOPING THINKING SKILLS

Man, if he is to be successful in our world, must adjust to new situations imposed upon him by a changing environment. It is not possible for him through experience and education to store up enough facts and information to meet sufficiently every contingency. Man, if he is to survive, must think. This means that he must read not only to identify ideas but to interpret and evaluate ideas. These processes require a critical appraisal of concepts and should be a part of instruction at all levels, from the primary grades through college. Young children can be taught to differentiate between facts and opinions and between reality and fantasy. Surely, the development of ability to think and to read critically is the chief function of the classroom teacher. If the teacher is alert, she will be aware of the problems of her students, and if she is well prepared for her work, she will utilize the opportunity to help them to solve their problems and at the same time to improve their thinking skills.

In this chapter the reader's attention is directed to the brief history of Kathryn, an intelligent high school student of sixteen years, who, when confronted with one of the major problems of life, is able to put aside her emotional bias and to think and read critically.

Kathryn Faces Some Problems

Kathryn is in her senior year of high school. She is the middle child in a family of nine. Even though there have been financial difficulties, the father has insisted that the mother remain at home with the children. Each member of Kathryn's family has been taught to assume responsibility for certain household duties. In discussing Kathryn's background the mother said, "Kathryn's responsibilities in the home have always been promptly and neatly completed. She is a very dependable young lady."

School began for Kathryn at the age of five years, six months. Her teachers reported: "Kathryn's social adjustment was excellent, probably because she had already had the companionship of many children, including that of her own sisters and brothers. Kathryn received average grades in her school subjects. She loved to read and seemed to look forward to our reading classes." She frequently took library books home and, according to the mother, "read aloud to her younger brothers and sisters. Kathryn is very much like her oldest sister. Neither of them was ever found sitting with nothing to do. They always had a book or a magazine in their hands." Apparently Kathryn enjoyed junior high school. According to school history, she had an A record in all her academic courses. She participated in school activities and was described by her teachers as a well-liked and popular student.

Kathryn describes her high school experiences as "most interesting and rewarding." She is enrolled in the college preparatory curriculum and plans to major in elementary education when she attends college. Kathryn said, "Since I've been in high school, I've led a busy life. I spend a lot of time studying for my classes, and I'm in many extracurricular activities. I am general manager for the Student Council. This has been good experience for me because it has helped me to become aware of the many problems in my school. Frequently I have had to explain teachers to students and students to teachers."

Kathryn's English instructor stated, "Kathryn is an interested student who is very attentive and eager to learn. She always has her assignments prepared and is ready to recite. She is in the upper fourth of the class and her grade average is B+. She is well liked by her classmates, and to show their esteem they elected her as the recipient of the Good Citizenship Award provided annually by the Daughters of the American Revolution. She was very proud and honored."

The school counselor reported: "In this school we keep complete records of the progress of each of our students. Kathryn's folder indicates that she was five years and six months old when she entered kindergarten at the Elmwood School. She adjusted well to the group and by the end of the year showed a readiness for reading activities. She was promoted to the first grade. The school psychologist, as a matter of routine, administered the Revised Stanford-Binet Scale to Kathryn when she was six years and six months old. Her mental age, as measured by this test, was eight years and four months. The IQ was 128. Kathryn's progress in school was normal. Her marks were satisfactory, and she was promoted each year. The comments of her elementary teachers are somewhat similar. All of them indicate that Kathryn is a conscientious student who applies herself to her studies. She is cooperative and shows initiative. Although she is not aggressive, she is a leader and is well liked by her classmates.

"When Kathryn entered Central High School, the Wechsler Intelligence Scale was administered. She was fifteen years and eight months old at the time and in the tenth grade. On this test she had a verbal IQ of 131 and a performance IQ of 125. The full scale IQ was 131. On the Iowa Silent

Reading Test, which was given to all the seniors, Kathryn's percentile was 96."

One day during the spring semester of her senior year in high school, Kathryn approached the school counselor and said, "Mrs. Johnson, I have a problem and I thought that you might help me with it."

"I'll be glad to help you if I can. Let's sit down and talk about it," replied Mrs. Johnson.

Kathryn continued, "I hope that what I am going to tell you will not sound trivial. I realize that I'm still a senior in high school and that marriage shouldn't be a problem to me just yet, but it is."

"You mean that you are thinking of marriage?"

"Well, yes. Maybe I ought to start at the beginning. As you may know, during my first three years in high school I dated several fellows. Then last fall I met Tom. The more we saw of each other, the more we realized that we were in love, so we stopped dating others and began to 'go steady.' Recently we've been talking about the future. You see, I'm in love with Tom and he loves me, and we want to be married."

Mrs. Johnson said, "In what way is marriage presenting a problem?"

"Our big problem is *when* to be married. Tom wants to become a dentist and so he knows that he must go to college. I want to become a teacher and so I too want to go to college. Our problem is this: Should we marry this summer and plan to go through college together or should we wait and marry after Tom finishes his training? Maybe we shouldn't follow either of these plans. Maybe we should marry now, and I should get a job and help Tom through college."

Kathryn continued, "Tom and I have more or less ruled out the plan of my working while he goes through college. We both realize that I would never be satisfied if I don't further my education, but the problem remains: Should we marry before or after college? Can you help me to do some clear thinking? I don't want to make mistakes."

Mrs. Johnson explained to Kathryn that she would be willing to help and asked the girl to explain in more detail some of the factors in the situation. Kathryn said, "Oh, I'm so glad that you are willing to help me. I've talked this over with my parents, but they say the solution is up to Tom and me. What I really need right now, Mrs. Johnson, is someone like you who can tell me what to do."

Mrs. Johnson replied, "I'm very willing to help you solve this problem, Kathryn, but the final decision must be yours and Tom's. Perhaps by discussing your problem with someone who can view it objectively, you will be able to work out your own solution more easily."

"Well, I suppose you can't tell me what to do. It would be easier for me if you could. I realize that it is my problem and that it's unfair of me to expect that either you or my parents can solve it for me. But I do need help. I need to talk to someone. It seems to me that I can think better if

I talk." There was a pause in the conversation. Then Kathryn continued, "Maybe I should begin by telling you more. As I said, I have talked it over with my parents. They are concerned with my happiness. They won't object if Tom and I decide that we should marry before entering college, but both our parents have made it clear that we cannot expect to receive financial aid from them. Tom and I feel that money will not be a factor, at least not a very big one. Tom has a scholarship for next year, and I've applied for one at the same university. I'm reasonably sure that I shall receive it. Our scholarships will take care of our tuition. We both plan to work this summer and save our money. Then next year we can get part-time jobs on campus to supplement our incomes."

Mrs. Johnson, in reflecting on the situation, said, "Then you feel that you will earn enough money during the summer and with part-time jobs on campus so that finances will not be a problem."

"Well, we might run into financial difficulties," Kathryn responded, "but I doubt it. Of course, we would be on a very tight budget. We wouldn't have much money for fun, but we probably wouldn't have much time for fun either."

Before Mrs. Johnson could comment on this statement, Kathryn continued, "This really bothers me. I've looked forward to college for a long time. I've wanted to live in a dormitory with other girls and to have a chance to meet new people. I suppose if I were married, I would become acquainted with people through classes, and Tom and I could attend social activities together, but frankly I'm concerned about missing out on college life."

"Do I understand," Mrs. Johnson inquired, "that missing out on dormitory living and extracurricular activities is one of the reasons why you think you should postpone marriage until after college?"

"It bothers me, yes. But this is not the greatest objection to our marrying before college. I don't quite know how to say this, but I think the main reason why I hesitate to marry Tom immediately is because, because, well . . . What would we do if we had children? I want a degree. I want to graduate from college. I wouldn't want to have a baby until I was through school."

"You believe that if you and Tom are married that there is a strong possibility that you might not be able to finish college," Mrs. Johnson said.

"Yes, very definitely. I'm wondering if we wouldn't be much happier if we waited until after college to be married. By that time Tom would be settled in his office, and I would have had two years of teaching behind me with some money saved for the future. It seems to me that we could begin our marriage with fewer problems if we waited. And besides we would still be together because we would both be attending the same college."

Mrs. Johnson commented, "You seem to be giving many reasons why you and Tom should wait until after college to marry."

"I know, but we are in love, very much in love, and we want to be together all of the time. We want to be married now. Several of our friends plan to marry this summer. We would like to marry too, but we don't want to make a mistake. It is obvious, isn't it? I want to marry Tom now and yet I don't want to marry him now. I guess I need to do more thinking before I can come to any conclusion. Can you help me to think critically about this problem? Are there any books that I can read which will provide more information?"

Mrs. Johnson replied, "You have already begun to think critically, Kathryn, and I'm willing to help you at any time you wish."

"Thank you, Mrs. Johnson. I feel more secure already. Could I come to see you again next Monday at this time?"

"Yes, Kathryn, I'll plan to see you then. In the meantime you may be interested in reading these books.[1] They may help you to answer some of your questions."

The chief relevant factors in Kathryn's history may be briefly summarized as follows:

1. Kathryn is a mentally and emotionally mature senior who, having grown up in a family of nine, is well acquainted with the problems of family living.
2. Evidences of excellent social adjustment have been presented.
3. Kathryn, like many high school girls, is concerned with the problems of marriage.
4. Because of her emotional and mental maturity, she is desirous of entering the university and in completing the requirements for a degree preparatory to teaching.
5. Kathryn, in spite of her emotional bias, has demonstrated her ability to think and read critically.
6. The reported interview between Kathryn and her counselor illustrates a non-directive technique which facilitated critical thinking.
7. The teacher, being aware of Kathryn's problem and the problems of other young students, is in a position to give guidance in critical thinking and reading.

Kathryn wanted help. She is a normal, intelligent young woman who lives in a world of many impulses and many corresponding inhibitions. She wants a husband, home, and family and yet she wants a university

[1] Clifford R. Adams, *Looking Ahead to Marriage* (Chicago, Illinois: Science Research Associates, Inc., 1949); Oliver M. Butterfield, *Planning for Marriage* (Princeton, New Jersey: D. Van Nostrand Co., 1956); Morris Fishbein and Ernest W. Burgess (eds.), *Successful Marriage* (Garden City, New York: Garden City Books, 1947).

degree, friends, and social advantages. How and when can she attain all these objectives? These goals must be adjusted in time, place, and circumstances. Her problems must be identified, understood, and evaluated before actual solutions can be worked out.

Let us examine the process by which all these aims can be accomplished. That process is thinking. Reading and thinking are closely related. In the process of reading, the individual takes to the printed page his mental content, his information, his wishes, and his problems. Reading is a two-way mental activity which involves carrying ideas to and from the printed page. A pool of information and emotional qualities is built up to which both reader and author contribute and from this common source the reader has the opportunity to generalize affirmatively, negatively, or hypothetically. In other words, he can accept, reject, or agree conditionally concerning the worth of the ideas being considered. Better still, the reader may be stimulated to further inquiry, further thinking, and further investigation. He may not only accept or reject the thinking of others but he may measure his own ideas in terms of their accuracy and degree of social conformity.

In all reading situations there is an organizing activity which is suggestive of thinking, and as a result of this activity, new concepts and ideas are born. For example, Kathryn, as she attempts to think, will add the information she possesses to that of the three authors recommended to her by Mrs. Johnson, and from the sum total of all the contributions she will be able to identify, interpret, and evaluate in accordance with her purpose the various concepts under consideration. This is reading and this is thinking. As a result of this activity, she will be on her way to the solution of her problem and to changes in her behavior. This is the final proof of good reading and good thinking.

In some complex situations the organizing activity makes use of components not actually present to the senses. Thinking is a form of behavior in which at least some of the elements dealt with are not physically present but are represented by symbols or signs. Some of these common symbols will be utilized as we proceed in our discussion of thinking. Let us now turn to a consideration of these factors.

What Is Thinking?

Thinking is an act of using words, sounds, pictures, numbers, and other symbols or signs to secure new meanings and to achieve new purposes. It is the act of manipulating symbols representing concepts and objects which are not present to the senses. For example, in dealing with the equation $\frac{3}{4} + \frac{1}{2} = 1\frac{1}{4}$, the symbol $\frac{3}{4}$ suggests that a unit is divided into four parts and that three of the parts are being considered. Likewise, the symbol $\frac{1}{2}$ suggests that a unit is divided into two parts and that one part is being considered. Furthermore, the equation suggests that the symbols are to be added and this appears difficult because fourths and halves are not similar. It is known, however, that ½ is equal to ¼ and that it is possible to add ¼ and ¾ and secure the sum ¼ or 1¼. In making this manipulation, one deals with symbols which represent objects and ideas as one would deal with the things they represent. These symbols can be placed, turned, and adjusted in the organizing process in much the same manner as one would put together the parts of a jigsaw puzzle. This process is thinking, and it can be done at various levels.

There are two extremes in thinking: autistic and creative experimentation. Autistic thinking, which is self-centered and tinged with emotion, satisfies the individual's desires, often with disregard for realities. It is manifest in daydreaming and frequently becomes a substitute for real achievement. It is observed that Kathryn has faced her problem realistically and that she has not indulged herself in wishful thinking. Creative experimentation, the other extreme, is a difficult process requiring special training and a desire to make a contribution to knowledge and the welfare of mankind. The levels or degrees of thinking between the two extremes of autistic thinking and creative experimentation may be briefly stated in the following order: reverie, decisive thinking, trial-and-error procedures, casual search for insight, rational learning, problem solving, and scientific analysis.

Some Benefits of Thinking

Thinking is a requisite for adjustment in our changing world. Life is the solution of one problem after another, and one's success or failure depends upon the number of correct responses. Each individual must find satisfactory answers to his problems of time, ability, money, and health by reading, learning, and *thinking*. This is essential if he is to attain satisfaction, security, and recognition. Some values of thinking have been suggested by Ruch [2] and these will be briefly discussed.

Thinking Prepares for Action

If one is to write a good book, build an adequate home, have a successful garden, or go on a restful trip abroad, careful plans must be made, and planning requires thinking. By taking thought, one can save time and money and even avert loss and disaster. Careful and thoughtful planning can contribute to success if the plans are based upon facts and useful information. It is obvious that Kathryn and her fiancé are well aware of this and that they are ready for facts and new meanings.

[2] Floyd L. Ruch, *Psychology and Life,* Third Edition (Chicago: Scott, Foresman and Co., 1948), pp. 387–389.

Thinking Can Produce New Meanings

The thinker can take concepts and ideas from one field and apply them in others. Facts can be separated from several areas and assembled into a new pattern and applied in a new manner. Procedures developed in mathematics can be utilized in all branches of learning. Compounds developed by the chemist can be put to good use in medicine, agriculture, papermaking, and in many other vocational areas. In order to manipulate concepts, however, they must be identified, interpreted, and evaluated. Ideas are the building materials of a new structure. Reading, at its highest level, is one of the ways in which these materials can be found, understood, evaluated, and applied. Reading is essential to creative thinking and new meanings.

Thinking May Produce Belief

Concepts which have been identified, understood, and evaluated in terms of experimentation can withstand the light of investigation. They can be maintained with confidence and accepted as a matter of belief. This rational acceptance of a point of view becomes a foundation and starting point for further study and investigation. Hunches can lead to proof and belief and on and on to ultimate truth. Belief based upon sound experience is necessary for effective living in our time. Reading as a thinking process can result in rational belief.

Thinking Affords Enjoyment

Thinking can provide pleasure and satisfaction. The individual whose mind is well stocked with ideas is not apt to be bored even in a humdrum and confused world. Thinking as problem solving can be interesting, and certainly it offers a challenge to real achievement. In order to construct a building, for example, there must be materials and in the process of thinking there must be facts and mental content resulting from experience. The manipulation of ideas resulting from purposeful living and from extensive reading can provide pleasure and real enjoyment.

Essential Processes in Creative Thinking

In creative thinking four mental processes are essential. These are a part of the total learning act in the solution of problems and are quite universal in their application. These four basic processes will be discussed in order.

Developing an Awareness of and an Interest in a Problem

The keen, alert, and mentally mature individual is aware of inconsistencies in his environment. He experiences needs for himself, his associates, and for society. There may be, for example, a need for a larger home, a more economical method of refrigeration, a more satisfactory means of lowering blood pressure, or a new text dealing with the psychology of personality. Any one of these needs suggests a problem and in some cases a whole system of interrelated problems. In each instance, if creative thinking is to take place, there must be an awareness of the problem and an active interest in its solution. Furthermore, if one is fully aware of a problem, he should be able to state it clearly, accurately, and concretely. It will be observed that Kathryn with the aid of her teacher has been able to do this precisely and effectively.

Developing a Number of Postulates, Hunches, or Possible Solutions

With the problem clearly in mind and with an insatiable desire to solve it, one must gather information, facts, and concepts with which to work. These materials expressed as symbols can then be turned, adjusted, and organized into a pattern which, if a successful solution is to be accomplished, must meet the requirements of the problem. In solving most problems, many hunches or possible solutions are tried, found wanting, and are immediately rejected. In this act of building patterns and discarding some of them, facts and more facts are required. These can be provided by extensive reading and careful research.

Discovering Facts Which Substantiate the Hunch and Explaining Their Contribution to the Solution of the Problem

Hunches or possible solutions to a problem come easily to mind. Facts, however, must be found which specifically show that the hunch is reasonable and immediately related to the situation. Furthermore, the explanation must be pertinent and rational. Even when pertinent facts are found and their relationship to the problem is clear, one essential element is still missing; that element is proof.

Predicting the Final Outcome and Securing Positive Verification

After a possible solution has been worked out, that is, after facts have been discovered and their relationship to the problem has been explained, the next step is *prediction*. Prediction must then be subjected to *verification* and final proof or disproof. In the field of medicine, for example, drugs are available which theoretically may be useful for the reduction of blood pressure in hypertension. It has been predicted that they will be found successful in clinical treatment; however, this fact has not been definitely established. Prediction has not yet led to verification.

Materials with Which We Think

In the process of thinking and reading it is possible for an individual to see, hear, feel, and experience that which is not in his immediate environment. It is even possible for him to think creatively and to solve problems with respect to objects and substances in times and places far removed from his person. In order to accomplish his purpose he uses symbols, which chiefly assume the form of imagery, word symbols, concepts, and implicit bodily movements.

Use of Imagery

Each sense modality is capable of producing imagery. Those more applicable in the activity of reading are visual, auditory, kinesthetic, and tactual in nature. The use of imagery is an essential factor in mental life. It is utilized in speaking, writing, reading, listening, and in all the aspects of our behavior. Through the recall of images in the various sense modalities one is able to enjoy past experiences which at the present time are far removed from our senses. One may relive an exciting trip through the mountains, hear again the babbling brook, and feel the tug of a trout on the line. The splash of the surging water and the pleased expression on the face of a companion, along with the tangy taste and fragrant smell of a pipe are but a few of the images associated with a fishing expedition in the mountains. All such images are pleasant and are useful aids in thinking. Some people, however, have not gone trout fishing. They can share these experiences through the art of effective reading.

Symbols and the Thinking Process

Symbols are a part of our daily living. We experience them in the classroom, in church, on the street, and in our homes. Words, songs, badges, flags, and even money are symbols which replace, stand for, and are substitutes for institutions, experiences, objects, and causes. Thinking, which is an inner activity, is dependent upon the use of symbols, imagery, and concepts. In determining, for example, the circumference of a circle these tools of thinking are essential. The terms "diameter," "pi," and "circumference" must be reintegrated in the process. The symbols provide a valuable means of manipulating and organizing ideas in order to accomplish a desired purpose. Symbols *can* become the language of thought. The term "sine" can mean the function of an angle, or it can mean nothing, depending upon the mental content of the observer. Word symbols may be memorized and used correctly and yet be empty of meaning. In the thinking process there must be reintegration of meaning, and meanings, like gems, are frequently more appreciated in new settings.

Use of Concepts in Thinking

As a result of our background, experience, and education, generalizations gradually develop. These generalizations, when they become formalized, may be spoken of as concepts. These may continue to grow or they may become static depending upon certain physical and psychological factors inherent in the individual. A child, for example, thinks of watches and all clocks as "tick tocks" even though his behavior may indicate that he senses a distinction between them. As the child grows older and as he profits from his experiences, he forsakes his primitive generalizations and develops new and more adequate concepts of the different time-keeping devices. In other words, he learns to group these devices according to certain important properties which are not recognized at first, but which are common to all measures of time. In this learning activity, he acquires skill in identifying and interpreting many abstract concepts such as clockwise, as represented by a pocket watch, wristwatch, alarm clock, hall clock, or chronometer.

Implicit Body Movement and Thinking

There is experimental evidence [3] which indicates that thinking is accompanied by muscular contractions. These minute reactions which occur during thought are called implicit or inner speech. For example, as one recites a poem or thinks of an act performed with a hammer, muscular contractions occur which can be detected and measured by a sensitive electrical apparatus. It has been observed that when some individuals read with interest or listen attentively their lips frequently move. This suggests that vocalization is taking place, a practice most teachers wisely discourage. Some individuals, however, "talk to themselves" when engrossed in thinking and this vocalization may provide aid in the process. Even though inner speech is associated with thinking, it is not certain whether it is a cause or an effect of thinking. Certainly, it is as reasonable to assume that the thought causes the implicit movement as it is to assume that the implicit movement causes the thought. Obviously, this connection between inner speech and thinking is related to reading. It is essentially applicable to vocalization, rate of reading, and the appreciation of the emotional qualities of literature.

Teaching Reading as a Thinking Process

Thinking is a creative act and can be productive of new ideas, concepts, and points of view. As previously indicated, symbols expressing ideas may be taken from two or more contexts and then manipulated so as to form symbols representing new concepts. This reintegrative process requires background, concentration, and time. The act of thinking should be deliberate with no emphasis upon speed. If reading is to be taught as a thinking process, the student must possess some essential reading skills. His vocabularies should be adequate and he should be able both to skim and to read for detail. Furthermore, the mature student should be able to

[3] Floyd L. Ruch, *Psychology and Life*, Fifth Edition (Chicago: Scott, Foresman and Co., 1958), pp. 355–356.

read a chapter effectively and well. In addition to these skills, it is necessary that he learn to read to solve problems and to think critically.

Emphasizing the Process of Thinking

In content fields such as the social studies, some teachers stress the importance of facts and more facts. Numerous questions are asked of the students until every fact stated by the writer has been extracted. Thought-provoking "why" questions are neglected, and the student is left with the idea that the whole field of knowledge is an aggregation of independent and unrelated facts. Even as a builder is concerned with more than a pile of bricks, so the thinker is conscious of more than a compilation of isolated ideas. The understanding of relationships is fundamental if creative production is to be achieved. In the interpretation of facts the relationship of cause and effect should be understood. In the process of identifying facts the *what, where, when,* and *who* factors are easy to determine. It is the *why* and *how* elements of any situation that become difficult to establish. When these questions are asked, the interpretative activity begins if the student has developed a sufficient degree of readiness. As a result of this activity, cause-and-effect relationships are recognized generally with a degree of satisfaction. The value of "why" and "how" questions cannot be overemphasized. Surely they stimulate the process of thinking more than questions which merely aid in the identification of isolated facts. The reported interview between Kathryn and her teacher illustrates not only a non-directive approach in interviewing but an effective use of questioning as well.

This stress on thinking can serve as a motivating factor in any instructional procedure. For example, in an elementary science class it was the purpose of the teacher to show causal factors affecting rainfall.[4] The students were asked to determine from the rainfall maps in their texts the annual amount of precipitation on the western slopes of the Rocky Mountains. In the state of Oregon the annual precipitation on the western slopes was found to be over 100 inches. The students were then asked to find the annual rainfall on the eastern slopes of the mountains and this was found to be less than ten inches. So far two facts had been identified by the class. Now in order to have these facts interpreted and really understood it was necessary for the teacher to ask: *Why* is there such a marked difference in annual rainfall between two areas so close together? In guiding the students in their thinking the teacher kept referring them to the various parts of their text, such as the index, table of contents, maps, charts, and illustrations. They were encouraged to ask questions and read for answers. It was necessary to develop the meaning and application of

---

[4] Homer L. J. Carter, "Reading, A Contributing and Concomitant Factor in the Study of Science," *School Science and Mathematics,* October, 1954, pp. 567–570.

such terms as high and low pressure areas, air mass, altitude, condensation, convection, dew points, evaporation, Fahrenheit, front, isobars, isotherms, barometric pressure, water vapor, relative humidity, temperature, and velocity. In attempting to understand why there was such a marked difference between the western and the eastern slopes of the mountains in the amount of annual rainfall, the students discovered that they must have the answers to each of the questions in the following list:

1. Why are the prevailing winds from the west?
2. Why do winds blow?
3. Why are the prevailing winds moisture-laden?
4. Why do ocean currents exist?
5. Why does condensation take place?

In the thinking and problem-solving activity which finally resulted in the answering of the major questions, facts were gathered and used in establishing inferences. Causes and effects were understood. The students were encouraged to substantiate their inferences by careful reading of their texts and supplementary references. A critical evaluation of all inferences was stressed, and it was obvious to even a casual observer that these students had an opportunity to learn as they learned to read.

Solving Problems

Reading as an interpretative process is a requirement for problem-solving in mathematics and science. Textbooks in arithmetic and mathematics employ a language expressing quantity, relationship, and processes. The student must understand this language if he is to make accurate computations and solve problems. He must identify and understand such terms as π, sine, $3x^2$, and $\sqrt{1225}$, for they suggest relationships and operations which are more complex than numbers. These expressions can, however, be used like nouns and pronouns and with symbols which modify their meaning and application. For example, sine of angle BAC in the following figure may be expressed: Sine $\angle BAC = \dfrac{BC}{AC}$.

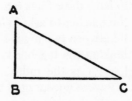

This relationship must be understood and thoroughly appreciated if this concept is to be applied in the solution of a trigonometric problem. Read-

Reading to learn often precedes actual experience
in classes of art and handicraft.

Individuals can have many happy experiences with books.

ing of these and similar materials requires a slow rate and careful attention to details. Eye movements may vary vertically as well as horizontally
and the span of recognition may be shorter than is required in the reading of textbooks and narrative materials. Duration of eye fixation may
be longer, and regressive movements may be essential for effective comprehension. A rapid rate of reading can be wasteful and even disas-
trous.

In developing skill in problem-solving, especially in such subjects as
mathematics, chemistry, and physics, the teacher of reading should explain and demonstrate the importance of an analytical reading of the
problems before a solution is attempted. The following suggestions should
be systematically followed by the student:

1. Determine what is to be found.
2. Determine what facts are known.
3. Discover what other facts are needed that are not included in the
   problem.
4. Visualize the steps essential for a solution. The best way to see the
   steps is to rewrite the problem, omitting all numbers, so as to get the
   meaning. The numbers are not important so far as the steps of the interpretation are concerned. Another set of numbers would do just as
   well. Read the problem as one would a story—for its meaning.
5. Make a picture of the problem or summarize the procedure you would
   follow in solving the problem.
6. Show the actual work, the figures you have used.
7. Prove your answer. Is it reasonable?

If the student can develop the habit of applying these procedures in the
interpretation and solution of his problems in mathematics and the sciences, he is almost certain to become an independent and accurate reader
who can do creative and productive thinking. Surely, in our time, there
is need for this fundamental skill.

Developing Creative Thinking

Creative thinking is productive of new solutions to a problem or of new
modes of artistic expression. It brings into existence a product new to the
individual but not necessarily new to others. Creative thinking may be
carried on by an individual or by several persons working together. The
case history of Mildred is an illustration of this process.

Mildred is a freshman in the university who has failed in succession
three examinations in biology despite the fact that she has spent more
than thirty hours each week in study. Obviously, her *problem* is: Why did

she fail these examinations? During a discussion of her problem with a staff member of the Psycho-Educational Clinic on the campus, the *hunch* was developed that because Mildred was doing only work of C grade in her other courses there was a possibility that she lacked the mental maturity generally required of successful university students. Consequently, the Wechsler Adult Intelligence Scale was administered. From the resulting data a *discovery* was made that Mildred was a young woman of superior mental ability and that a lack of mental maturity was not an adequate *explanation* of her failure. It was apparent, then, that this hunch must be rejected. In additional interviews with Mildred, another *hunch* became a possibility. It was postulated that Mildred had a serious reading disability, for she reported that in doing chapter reading she was lost in a mass of detail and that notetaking and outlining were difficult for her. After a reading test had been administered to Mildred, a discovery was made which indicated that she was reading at the third percentile for freshmen and only as well as a person six months in the seventh grade (7.6). Furthermore, this *discovery* showed that Mildred could identify ideas but that she had difficulty in understanding and evaluating them. These discoveries led to the *explanation* of her disabilities in reading, notetaking, outlining, and consequently her failures in biology. As a result of these findings, a *prediction* was made that if Mildred could improve her ability to identify, interpret, and evaluate ideas in the process of reading and listening, she would do satisfactory work in biology. After fifteen weeks of study in the reading laboratory, this prediction led to *verification* and ultimate proof, for during this period her percentile in reading changed from 3 to 32 and her grade equivalent from 7.6 to 12.7. Good grades in biology and an increase in point-hour-ratio further substantiated the *prediction*.

The four essential processes utilized in solving Mildred's problem were described earlier in this chapter and are quite universal in their application. In her case the utilization of these procedures has been productive of an adequate solution which is creative in nature. The alert classroom teacher can apply and demonstrate these processes again and again so that his students can become familiar with their use. These procedures in thinking can be used by Kathryn as she works out a solution to her problem. Students can be given the opportunity to make a list of their problems, stating them as impersonally as possible. Later, they can select one problem and attempt its solution by using the procedures outlined in this chapter.

1. State the problem as briefly as possible.
2. State the "hunch." What was its source? If it came from reading materials, give the exact reference.

3. What was the discovery and explanation? What is the source of your information? Give references and explain in detail.
4. What is your prediction? How and when can this be verified?

The student should realize that in thinking through his problem he may have to reject several "hunches" before he obtains a satisfactory solution. In developing hunches and insight as to possible solutions, the thinking student will require suitable reading materials which are adjusted to his reading level and interest. The criteria for effective use should be readability, interest, and the effectiveness of the references in achieving specific goals. Every teacher who is truly concerned with creative thinking on the part of his students must become an authority on reading materials. In the case of Kathryn it was observed that her teacher suggested references having a direct bearing upon marriage and related problems. The school librarian can be especially helpful with respect to reluctant readers in finding for them books which are pertinent to the problem under consideration by the class.

The creative aspects of reading appeal to the more mature and able students. They are eager to anticipate outcomes and to use reading as a means of problem-solving. This is especially true when the teacher shows a high degree of interest and enthusiasm. These capable readers, for example, may make use of information gathered from historical materials in preparing plays or in writing stories for young children. A dramatic event in a news item may become the theme of a poem. A vivid description by a favorite writer may be portrayed effectively in black and white or colors. Creative thinking finds expression in various forms, all of which improve with encouragement and guidance.

The development of productive thinking can, and probably should, begin early in the life of the intelligent child. Little boys and girls, unless completely discouraged by their elders, are prolific interrogators who specialize in "why" and "how" questions. This quest for knowledge and the accompanying desire to communicate should be encouraged through the elementary grades, high school, and college. By means of creative thinking facts are organized into new and functional patterns.

Questions, a Requisite for Thinking

The primary purpose of the question asked by the teacher in the classroom is to provoke thought. Its use as a means of testing for facts has been overdone. However, as a means of selecting and organizing facts it can be useful. In general, the best questions are those whose answers are not found in a textbook but which lead to identification, interpretation, and evaluation of ideas; in other words, to creative thinking. Students should be required, through questions by the teacher, to prove the inferences and generalizations they have made. This challenge can be stimulating to thought, for proving a statement means giving evidence and citing authority. This requires thinking. In order to arrive at valid conclusions, students must compare one pattern of facts with another and show likenesses and differences. The following are examples of questions which accomplish this purpose of comparison:

1. How does the school described in "Snowbound" compare with the one portrayed in "The Legend of Sleepy Hollow"?
2. What are the essential differences between adjectives and adverbs?
3. In the presidential campaign of 1960 what points of view did Democrats and Republicans have in common?
4. Why has the Senate become a much more powerful body than the House of Representatives?

Obviously, these questions are more provocative of thinking than those asked solely for the purpose of sampling a knowledge of facts. Questions which can be answered by "yes" or "no" do not require thinking at a high level. In fact, the more an individual knows about a subject the less he is likely to answer a question concerning it with an unqualified "yes" or "no." Questions should deal with problems worthy of consideration and should be broad enough to involve the various steps of the thinking process. They should be devised to bring out an important aspect of a subject and to stimulate thought. This kind of questioning constitutes the highest function of the teacher.

Students, if they are to think effectively, should learn to ask questions and read for answers. This practice motivates reading and, as previously pointed out, the good reader always reads for a purpose. As a means of bringing thinking to a sharper focus the student may ask:

1. What are the main facts in this presentation?
2. What inferences has the writer drawn?
3. What other illustration could he have given?
4. What words and technical terms must I thoroughly understand to appreciate the writer's point of view?
5. How is the problem presented by the writer related to me and my goals?
6. How has the author organized his materials?
7. What is the author's purpose and has he accomplished his objective?

These questions are but examples of the many which the mature reader can ask of the writer. If this practice can become a habit, the student will not only learn to identify ideas, but to interpret, evaluate, and apply them in terms of his own needs and background.

Learning to Read and Think Critically

No mature and intelligent person believes or accepts all that he reads. The critical reader not only determines *what* has been expressed in words but *why* the writer has written what he has written. Critical reading implies reading between the lines to find the concealed implications and motives of the writer.

Students at all levels should be taught how to read with a critical attitude. Today children and adults read books, magazines, and newspapers which contain stories and statements which are biased, exaggerated, untrue, or unimportant. The young adult should be taught to evaluate their worth and determine the writer's motive or bias. The student should determine whether statements are based on facts, opinions, suppositions, or the hunches of the writer. In all of his reading the mature student should be able to spot cunningly devised generalities, faulty reasoning, and clichés constructed to trap the thoughtless, naive reader. Propaganda, good and bad, is constantly expressed in the written word. It is utilized by political, religious, and labor groups to persuade others to think and act in accordance with their wishes and desires. Advertisers overwork fine-sounding words and neglect the real facts. The critical reader can learn to sift the grain from the chaff and let an appeal to reason, rather than emotion, govern his behavior. He learns what to accept, what to reject, and what to investigate further. He values that which is good and casts aside that which is cheap, shoddy, and of little worth.

Some Suggestions for Critical Reading

Criticism is the act of judging well. In order to appraise adequately there must first be identification of concepts and then understanding of them. Here are some specific suggestions to young students for critical reading. Read first to identify the ideas expressed by the writer. Determine the writer's purpose in preparing the chapter, writing the essay, or producing any written material. Generally the introduction to a chapter indicates what the writer intends to accomplish and the limitations he places upon himself. The summary of the chapter, if one is available, points out what the writer believes he has accomplished. With these statements well in mind, the reader is ready to interpret the ideas expressed in the article by making use of the five-step plan suggested in Chapter 8. Once the reader understands the contribution of the writer, he is ready to judge its merit.

In showing students how to evaluate a unit of writing, the teacher can illustrate the importance of the following questions:

1. To what extent did the author do what he said he was going to do?
2. What materials selected by the writer does the reader find to be inappropriate and irrelevant?
3. How can the organization of these materials be improved?
4. Wherein has the writer been illogical?
5. Wherein has he been uninformed?
6. What is the author's special contribution to the subject?
7. What does he suggest or infer that he has not stated directly?
8. Show where the writer has been subjective in his presentation.
9. How has he shown his slant and bias?
10. What propaganda techniques has he used?

In answering these questions the student should be encouraged to read for different purposes. He should skim as he looks for main ideas and as he reads to find answers to *his* questions. Some materials will need to be read again and again as he seeks his varying objectives. His rate of reading should fluctuate according to the nature and difficulty of the materials. Analytical deliberation, not speed, is his goal.

Children and even adults should not be encouraged to evaluate and pass judgment upon subjects of which they know very little. The skilled architect may create a beautiful structure which an ignorant person would criticize. In order to judge well, there must be knowledge and understanding. The critical reader must have adequate standards in order to sense the good as well as the faulty. These standards can only be built up by studying, learning, acquiring, experiencing, and adjusting in order to establish background and mental content essential to valid judgments.

Teaching Students to Read Critically

In our world great masses of written materials are made available to those who read. Some of these products of the printing press are worthy of careful reading and may be classified as good literature. On the other hand, some of the printed material presented to modern readers is cheap, shallow, and trashy.

If high school students are to be given an opportunity to develop a taste for good literature, they should learn to know some masterpieces. For example, a high school English teacher might use Lincoln's Gettysburg Address to demonstrate the value of critical reading. Members of the class should have marked copies of the Gettysburg Address and should have access to reference materials such as the card catalogue and the *Readers' Guide to Periodical Literature*.

LINCOLN'S GETTYSBURG ADDRESS
(Each sentence has been numbered)

(1) Fourscore and seven years ago our fathers brought forth on this continent a new nation, conceived in liberty, and dedicated to the proposition that all men are created equal. (2) Now we are engaged in a great civil war, testing whether that nation, or any nation so conceived and so dedicated, can long endure. (3) We are met on a great battlefield of that war. (4) We have come to dedicate a portion of that field as a final resting place for those who here gave their lives that that nation might live. (5) It is altogether fitting and proper that we should do this.

(6) But in a larger sense we cannot dedicate, we cannot consecrate, we cannot hallow, this ground. (7) The brave men, living and dead, who struggled here have consecrated it far above our poor power to add or detract. (8) The world will little note nor long remember what we say here, but it can never forget what they did here. (9) It is for us, the living, rather, to be dedicated here to the unfinished work which they who fought here have thus far so nobly advanced. (10) It is rather for us to be here dedicated to the great task remaining before us; that from these honored dead we take increased devotion to that cause for which they gave the last full measure of devotion; that we here highly resolve that these dead shall not have died in vain; that this nation, under God, shall have a new birth of freedom; and that government of the people, by the people, for the people shall not perish from the earth.

The procedures which the teacher might employ with these materials may be briefly summarized as follows:

1. Outline for the class the historical events which led up to the giving of the Gettysburg Address by Lincoln on November 19, 1863. The teacher should remember that the Civil War was still in progress.
2. Describe briefly the address given on the same program by the Honorable Edward Everett which was over two hours in duration.
3. Describe Lincoln's preparation for his presentation, showing his indecision as to which of five copies he would use.
4. Describe Lincoln's presentation and its effect on his audience, and on him, as he sensed his "failure."
5. Determine why this address is one of the greatest in all our history. Remember it contains only ten sentences and 267 words. Point out some of the factors to be considered, such as:
   a. *Choice of words,* with stress on both denotation and connotation.
   b. *Diction,* the manner of expressing ideas.
   c. *Organization,* to show the relation of ideas and the way they fit together. The figure at the top of page 206 may help.

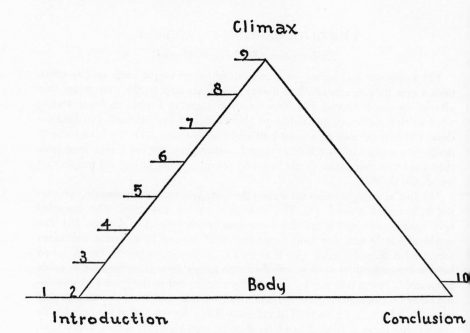

Time: less than three minutes
Length: ten sentences

    d. *Form*, to show physical and mechanical characteristics such as sentence and paragraph construction as well as length of sentences and paragraphs.

    e. *Tone*, the summation of intellectual and emotional effects of writing.

6. In developing the criteria suggested, and in stimulating interest, ask questions such as the following:

    a. In sentence (1) why not use the words "eighty-seven" instead of "fourscore and seven"?

    b. Should this address have been written in two paragraphs or in one?

    c. What is accomplished by the short sentences?

    d. What is the effect of the last sentence, the longest?

    e. In sentences (9) and (10) what is the effect produced by the word "rather"?

    f. In sentence (7) why is the word "poor" used? Did Lincoln include this word in his original address?

    g. What emotional qualities do you find?

7. Guide the students in answering these and other questions by constant reference to historical sources, with frequent use of such helps as index, table of contents, and glossary.

Some Difficulties to Be Avoided in Thinking Clearly

There are many hazards to be avoided in order to think clearly and judge well. Four such risks related to problem-solving should be pointed out.

Preconceived Ideas and Emotional Bias

Some individuals fail to think clearly and judge well because of their preconceived ideas and emotional bias. People experiencing these handicaps find it easy to select those facts which prove their contention and to neglect as useless those facts which fail to substantiate their inferences. In the case of Kathryn the desire to marry is reinforced by a strong emotional drive. It will be observed, however, that Kathryn has interpreted this desire in terms of her ultimate goal, a college education, and her preparation for self-support. The biased student finds what he wants to find as he reads and seeks information concerning his problem. Belief is frequently determined by the desire to believe, irrespective of the evidence for or against the truth of the assertion. For example, such preconceived ideas as that Jewish and Scottish people are penurious and that Indians are savages are not only naive but ridiculous.

Mistaking Relationship for Cause

Events appearing simultaneously are frequently thought to be related as to cause. This hasty conclusion may lack both truth and validity. A student, for example, may come from a poor environment and at the same time have a limited vocabulary in science without any relationship existing between the two sets of conditions. To make valid conclusions, one should be certain that there are no other factors operating at the same time which may have been immediate or contributing causes.

Confusion of Facts and Inferences

Failure to differentiate between facts and inferences is a hazard to clear thinking. To say that Kathryn's percentile rank on a reading test is 96 is a fact. To say, however, that Kathryn is a good reader is to set forth an inference which probably is, and yet may not be, true. The validity of inferences depends upon the training and experience of the person who makes them. The individual who thinks clearly and who reads critically does not accept tailor-made inferences at their face value; instead, he seeks the facts upon which they are based. He abhors any confusion of facts and inferences.

Hasty Conclusions

Some individuals are "conclusion jumpers." They impulsively accept the first solution of a problem which is presented to them. Some teachers assume immediately that one or more of the retarded readers in their class are mentally incapable and consequently these children are permitted to "sit" without adequate instruction. The die is cast and no further investigation of the problem is made. A satisfactory solution must take into consideration the whole pattern of the situation and its application to reality. More and more facts must be obtained, and when a valid conclusion has been reached, it should be held only tentatively or until all reasonable doubt has been removed.

Some Mechanisms Used to Trap the Naive and Careless Reader

Most individuals can identify and reject the bellowing propaganda of heated politicians and inane salesmen on television and radio. These are all too obvious. Many of us, however, fail to recognize the more clever and subtle devices employed by many writers to confuse and trap the immature and careless reader. Some of these obstacles will be pointed out.

Suppression and Distortion of Truth

The critical reader treats with suspicion the writer who suppresses the undesirable and distorts the desirable. In order to be objective, the whole truth should be told. Frequently, some individuals who express their ideas in writing accentuate the positive aspects of their position and conceal the negative, even though the importance of the latter far outweighs the former. This scheme is effectively used by politicians, salesmen, and exhorters who wish to advance their cause by not telling the whole truth, the whole story, and all the facts. Another device practiced with similar purpose is to take out from context a phrase, sentence, or paragraph which, when considered by itself, can be interpreted in a way opposed to the author's original meaning. Such extractions, snipped out of context, can then be used to distort the true meaning and intent of the writer. It is apparent that such quotations should always be examined with caution by the critical reader and that an attempt be made to identify mechanisms designed to suppress and distort any of the facts involved in the presentation.

False Analogy

The analogy is used by writers to simplify and in some instances to dramatize a complex idea. In many instances, however, the relationship is more apparent than real. For example, the argument that the prices of cars must be lowered because "all that goes up must come down" is false chiefly because there is no relation between the law of gravity and the prices of automobiles. On the other hand, a teacher of reading in explaining the need of adjusting rate to the nature and difficulty of materials may simplify her instruction by saying that students should "learn to shift gears" as they read. In this case, she implies that there is a similarity between driving a car under varying conditions and reading different materials with changing purposes. In every instance, the critical reader must think his way through the hazards of the analogy, whether it be true, false, or both true and false.

Begging the Question

Some speakers and writers expect that their statements will be accepted as truth because they say that the statements are true. In these cases the truth of the assertion is demanded in advance of proof. In fact, there is no expectation on the part of the writer that substantiation will be required. The premise and the conclusion are identical for no reason except upon the insistence of the writer. Those who indulge in generalities and name-calling make repeated use of this common form of faulty logic. The critical reader will identify this treatment of a subject and promptly reject it.

The Danger of Oversimplification

The simple statement that water is good can lead to misinterpretation and error, for obviously in some situations it is not true. Few statements indeed are true without question and reasonable doubt. A statement, to be precisely accurate, must contain some reservations and qualifying restrictions. Those who write and instruct encounter the hazard of oversimplification in their attempt to state their ideas in understandable and simple terms. Few concepts are either all true or all false. Even truth is held by some to vary in kind and degree. In the educational world, liberal educators frequently speak of those who disagree with them as traditionalists who are only interested in the mastery of subject matter and highly structured procedures. On the other hand, more conservative educators accuse their more liberal colleagues of being chiefly interested in socialization and the development of personality. This characterization is really not so simple, for the critical reader appreciates the fact that both liberals and conservatives in the field of education vary in all their ideology both quantitatively and qualitatively. The critical reader will analyze carefully the words of any writer who specializes in stereotypes, in which things are all good or all bad. Our world is not that simple.

Use of Inadequate and Faulty Evidence

Speakers and writers often introduce inadequate and faulty information as evidence. Some writers put aside their responsibility to prove their point and attempt to prejudice their readers against their opponent. They attack the man and refuse to discuss the real issue. Arguments are neglected and feelings emphasized. Words charged with emotion are repeatedly employed to bias the reader. Expressions such as "communist," "capitalist," "warmonger," "imperialist," "progressive," and "traditionalist" are used to arouse the prejudice of the reader for or against an opponent. Reference to mother, home, the common man, and Biblical characters are not without significance. Casual identification with well-known person- alities is generally made for effect and is not always relevant to the sub- ject being discussed. Frequently, a writer will quote opinions of well- known individuals who have written outside of their field of specialization. For example, an outstanding authority in the field of nuclear physics can write only as an amateur in the field of education. Obviously, his opinions concerning developmental reading should be substantiated by well-chosen evidence. Contemporary writers invoke the prestige of laboratory scien- tists, physicians, and other well-known persons and suggest that these "authorities" agree with them. This may or may not be true. The careful reader must investigate the competence of these individuals to pass judg- ment upon the issues being discussed.

Some Suggestions for Teachers of Reading

You have now come to the conclusion of this book. Therefore, it may be well for us to summarize and re-emphasize the fundamental concepts expressed throughout the nine chapters. We shall do this as briefly as possible.

1. Pay attention to the individual student.
2. Emphasize interpretation of his performance rather than merely an evaluation of his achievement.
3. Secure adequate materials and adjust to the interest and reading level of the student.
4. Select and modify instructional procedures so as to accomplish specific objectives.
5. Guide the student step by step, demonstrating the human interest of the parent for his child and at the same time the objective attitude of the laboratory technician.
6. Avoid frustration and emotional set against reading.
7. Emphasize the wholeness and continuity of the instructional process in reading.

Learning to teach is a process without end. As research continues, new facts and new generalizations are set forth. The alert teacher must identify, interpret, and evaluate that which is new, and in doing this she will need the stimulation found in educational organizations devoted to the teaching of reading. Professional journals in the fields of psychology and education can contribute facts and points of view which no teacher can afford to neglect. Day-by-day learning is the method of acquiring knowledge, skill, and proficiency. Professional competence is the attainment of that goal. Progress is the teacher's business.

Guided Activities

1. What evidence can you find in the biography of Kathryn to substantiate the inference that she is an excellent reader?
2. In your opinion, is Kathryn ready for critical reading? Substantiate your point of view.
3. Work out a plan which you believe you could use in helping Kathryn solve her problem. Why would a non-directive approach be the more satisfactory?
4. What evidence, if any, is there of faulty thinking on the part of Kathryn?
5. Visit grades 2, 4, and 6 and list the "why" and "how" questions asked by the different teachers or the children in the different classrooms. Which teacher is the most successful in stimulating critical thinking? Why?
6. Work out a plan at any grade level you may choose for showing children how to read and think critically. Consider carefully the matter of aims, materials, and procedures.
7. Work out a plan for explaining to a group of boys and girls the values of (1) "who," "what," "where," and "when" questions, (2) "how" questions, (3) "why" questions and their relationship to the thinking process.
8. Find examples in newspapers and magazines of mechanisms used to trap the naive and careless reader.
9. Select one of your personal problems and work out a solution using the four processes described in this chapter. What hazards to clear thinking have you encountered?
10. List and discuss with the members of your class the advantages and disadvantages of group participation in problem-solving.

Questions and References

Questions	References
1. In doing critical reading, what are some basic factors to be considered?	1. Altick, Richard D. *Preface to Critical Reading* (Revised Edition). New York: Holt and Co., 1951.
2. What are some clever criticisms of the social and educational problems of our time?	2. Benjamin, Harold. *The Saber-Tooth Curriculum.* New York: McGraw-Hill Book Co., 1939.

Questions	References
3. How does a psychologist deal with the problem of thinking?	3. Ruch, Floyd L. *Psychology and Life* (Fifth Edition), Chap. 13. Chicago: Scott, Foresman and Co., 1958.
4. What can the teacher of the intermediate grades do to encourage critical thinking in relation to reading?	4. Burton, William H. *Reading in Child Development*, pp. 324–328, 373–378. Indianapolis: Bobbs-Merrill Co., 1956. Durrell, Donald D. *Improving Reading Instruction*, pp. 305–307. Yonkers-on-Hudson, N. Y.: World Book Co., 1956. McKim, Margaret G. *Guiding Growth in Reading*, Chap. 12. New York: Macmillan Co., 1955.
5. How can reading in the social studies be improved?	5. Strang, Ruth, Constance M. McCullough, and Arthur E. Traxler. *Problems in the Improvement of Reading*, Chap. 10. New York: McGraw-Hill Book Co., 1955.
6. How can critical reading be utilized in mathematics and science?	6. *Ibid.*, Chap. 9.
7. Is reading thinking?	7. Yoakam, Gerald A. *Basal Reading Instruction*, pp. 13–16. New York: McGraw-Hill Book Co., 1955.

GLOSSARY

This nontechnical glossary, made up of terms generally associated with the teaching of reading, is provided for the purpose of making unfamiliar expressions intelligible to the student. In many cases the definition given is not the only possible one, but is the one most frequently encountered in this text.

Ability: actual power to perform any act; a resultant of environment and capacity.

Ability grouping: the practice of subdividing a group of pupils into smaller groups of relatively equal ability, either in some one subject or in general ability. This practice is not to be confused with flexible grouping.

Abnormality: a state or quality deviating from the normal or average; condition markedly or strangely irregular.

Accommodation: the act of adjusting the lens of the eye to keep a sharply focused image on the retina.

Accuracy of comprehension: the exactness with which a person understands what he reads.

Achievement age (A.A.): the level of ability of a student, especially in school work, measured in terms of the average for a given age group.

Achievement test: a device for measuring the level of ability or performance actually reached in a given field.

Adjustment: the establishment of a satisfactory relationship.

Affective process: an activity characterized by emotion or feeling.

Age norm: a standard in respect to some quality or characteristic (including especially ability as measured by some standard test), based on the average of a large, unselected group of children of a given age.

Analogy: a form of inference in which it is reasoned that if two or more things agree with one another in one or more respects, they will probably agree in yet other respects.

Anecdotal record: a record of facts which can be used in establishing inferences.

Antonym: a word so opposed in meaning to another word that it negates or nullifies every one of its implications.

Appendix: matter added to a book but not essential to its completeness; for example, a bibliography, notes, or tabular matter.

Aptitude: readiness in learning; natural capacity or ability.

Attention: a set, attitude, or adjustment of the organism which makes it better able to respond to a given stimulus.

Auditory defect: an imperfection of hearing.

Auditory discrimination: ability to discriminate between sounds of different characteristic frequencies.

Auditory imagery: a mental reconstruction of sensory experiences obtained by hearing.

Auditory memory: memory for what is heard. The term is used chiefly in connection with tests of memory span.

Autistic thinking: absorption in fantasy to the exclusion of interest in reality.

Automatic promotion: promotion from grade to grade irrespective of academic attainment. Sometimes called social promotion.

Background: the sum of one's experience, training, and education.

Basic reader: a special textbook designed to develop basic reading abilities and skills.

Basic words: sometimes called tool words, which make up over 50 per cent of the content of intermediate textbooks in reading, geography, and history.

Blend: in phonics, the sound resulting from the combination of two or three consonants within a word without loss of identity of the sounds of the separate letters. For example: *bl* in *blue* is a blend.

Capacity: the power of receiving, containing, or absorbing.

Capacity level: the highest reading level at which the individual can comprehend material read to him.

Catch-all: a term used to describe the detailed part of a newspaper article which generally follows the "lead."

Causal relationship: a subject or ideas arranged in the order of effect or consequences.

Central thought: main idea.

Choral reading: reading in a group or chorus. Sometimes called "choric speaking" or "group speaking."

Chronological age (C.A.): calendar age or age since birth.

Cognitive process: an activity whereby the individual becomes aware or obtains knowledge of an object.

Compensation: action which is intended to make amends for some lack or loss of personal characteristics or status.

Comprehension: in reading, the understanding of meanings obtained through the medium of printed symbols.

Concentrated repetition: an act repeated at one sitting; a short period of study. This term is opposed to *distributed repetition.*

Concentration: exclusive and persistent attention to a limited object or aspect of an object.

Conclusion jumper: an impulsive individual who arrives at a conclusion or opinion without sufficient evidence.

Configuration: the pattern, general form, or shape of a word.

Configuration clue: over-all form of a word which aids in its recognition.

Confusion in dominance: a term sometimes used to describe confusion resulting from cross dominance. *See Cross dominance.*

Connotation: the significance suggested by a word apart from its explicit and recognized meaning; the overtones of meaning.

Consonant: a speech sound formed by the obstruction of the breath stream as it passes through the mouth. Each of these letters is a consonant: *b, c, d, f, g, h, j, k, l, m, n, p, q, r, s, t, v, w, x, y, z.*

Context clue: in reading, a means of identifying a new word through the words and ideas adjacent to it.

Corrective reading: instruction in reading in which an attempt is made to correct bad habits and deficiencies in this skill.

Critical reading: the interpreting and thoughtful evaluation of reading materials.

Cross dominance: control that is right-handed and left-eyed or left-handed and right-eyed.

Cultural level: the stage of enlightenment and refinement of taste acquired through intellectual and esthetic training.

Cursive writing: the longhand or script writing commonly used above the primary grades.

Data (plural of *datum*): a group of facts on which an inference is based.

Decisive thinking: thinking that is concerned with successful arriving at decisions.

Deduction: the mode of reasoning in which a logical conclusion is drawn. Given premises; also, the conclusion so reached.

Deductive reasoning: a form of thinking which proceeds from the general to the particular, i.e., from premises to the logical inference from them.

Defense mechanism: a means of protecting the ego; any mode of behavior or belief adopted by a person to avoid awareness of that which is unpleasant or anxiety-arousing.

Deficiency: state or quality of being deficient or lacking in some quality necessary for completeness.

Denotation: the meaning or definition of a term, such as may be found in a dictionary or glossary. *Cf. Connotation.*

Derivation: (1) that from which a thing is derived; (2) the development of a word from its more original or radical elements.

Development: changes in an organism from its origin to its death, but more particularly the progressive changes from origin to maturity.

Developmental age: the combination of all indices of development to indicate a person's relative status.

Developmental reading: reading instruction given to children in accordance with their individual maturity levels.

Dextral: right-handed and right-eyed.

Diction: (1) choice of words to express ideas; (2) manner of speaking or singing, especially in public; enunciation.

Digraph: two letters representing one sound, such as *ea* or *ai.*

Diphthong: the sounds of two vowels so closely blended together that they give the impression of one sound, such as *oi* and *ow.*

Directed reading activity: a reading activity carried on under the direction of a teacher for the purpose of instruction.

Dissociation: a condition in which mental processes lose their usual modifying influence upon one another.

Dominance: control of the actions of another. *Ocular dominance:* preferential use of one eye so that objects are usually fixated by that eye only, the other eye remaining a little off from exact fixation. *Manual dominance:* preferential use of one hand.

Drive: in psychology, a persistent or recurrent urge.

Educational age (E.A.): a pupil's average accomplishment in school subjects, stated in terms of the average accomplishment of those of similar chronological age.

Educational guidance: assisting pupils to select the best program of studies in the light of their capacities, interests, plans, and general circumstances. Remedial instruction is occasionally included.

Educational measurement: methods of determining school attainments by means of standardized tests or other types of examinations.

Egocentric drive: concern with oneself; urge to satisfy self.

Egocentrism: behavior characterized by concern with oneself; preoccupation with one's own concerns.

Emotion: an intensified feeling; any of the feelings of joy, sorrow, guilt, fear, hate, love, etc.

Emotional bias: prejudice resulting from feeling.

Emotional blocking: inhibition of thinking or of other forms of adjustive response due to excessive emotions, usually of the fear group.

Emotional conflict: an unpleasant emotion resulting from a discrepancy between two opposing goals or between a goal and actual attainment.

Emotional maturity: the extent to which an individual is able to control impulses and emotions consistent with his stage of development.

Emotional stability: consistent and dependable emotional reactions.

Experience chart or *record:* individual-, group-, or grade-dictated composition.

Eye fixation: see Fixation.

Eye movement: a change in position of the eyeball.

Eye pause: brief moment during which the eyeball is at rest. Only during such a moment is it possible to make visual discriminations. Point of fixation.

Factual material: reading matter which primarily contains facts.

Fantasy: a daydream.

Fixation: holding the eyeballs in position for vision to function in reading a part of a line as the eyes travel across the page.

Fixation pause: the length of time required for the eyes to fixate on a given part of a line in reading.

Flexible grouping: practice of grouping individuals temporarily in order to accomplish a specific purpose.

Free reading: independent reading for information or pleasure.

Frustration: a sense of emotional or mental unease, the result of one's inability to satisfy a need or desire because of environmental or self-imposed obstacles.

Gazetteer: a geographical dictionary.

General vocabulary: words used in everyday conversation and correspondence.

Generalization: an inference or number of inferences based upon a collection or observation of facts.

Glossary: a list of basic, technical, dialectal, and difficult terms in a subject or field, with definitions.

Grade expectancy: the school grade in which a student may be expected to work efficiently in terms of his intelligence and chronological age.

Grade placement: the grade in which the student is actually placed.

Grade score: average achievement in terms of grade level. For example, a grade score of 3.2 means the performance level of an individual two months in the third grade.

Guiding question: question used by the teacher to lead a beginner through the thought of a unit. In the initial stages of learning to read, the guiding question may focus the attention on the reading of a single sentence. As the pupil grows in reading power, the guiding questions will focus attention on paragraphs, pages, and story or chapter units.

Head movement: extraneous movement of the head while reading.

Homogeneous grouping: grouping according to capacity or ability. This should not be confused with flexible grouping.

Homonym: a word having the same pronunciation as another word, but differing from it in origin, meaning, and often, in spelling; for example, *week, weak.*

Hypothesis: a tentative theory or assumption.

Identification: the act of associating oneself closely with a person or group.

Idiom: a form of expression peculiar to a people, a district, a community, or a class.

Image: a mental reconstruction of sensory experiences. Three levels: after images (A.I.), eidetic images (E.I.), and memory images (M.I.).

Imagery: collective mental images, which may be visual, auditory, kinesthetic, gustatory, olfactory, pain, thermal, or tactual.

Incidental teaching: instruction which is concerned with by-products as well as the accomplishment of an immediate goal.

Independent reading: reading done without assistance from an instructor.

Independent reading level: the highest reading level at which the individual can read with full understanding and freedom from mechanical difficulties.

Index: a table, list, or file, usually arranged alphabetically, for facilitating reference to topics, names, and objects.

Induction: act or process of reasoning from a part to a whole, from particulars to generals.

Inductive reasoning: a form of thinking which proceeds by *induction.*

Inference: a logical conclusion from given data or premises.

Informal reading: reading differentiated from that provided by a basic text; independent reading for information or pleasure.

Informal test: a test which is prepared and given informally, as contrasted with one which has been standardized by statistical procedures.

Inhibition: a mental condition in which a person finds it difficult to begin or continue a course of action. Inhibition sometimes amounts to suppression or repression.

Instructional level: the highest reading level at which systematic instruction can be initiated.

Intelligence: ability to exercise the higher mental functions.

Intelligence quotient (I.Q.): mental age in years and fractions of years divided by chronological age; i.e., by the number of years and fractions of years one has lived.

Intelligence test: a device for measuring the intelligence of individuals.

Irrational material: illogical and unreasonable interpretation of facts or subject matter.

Irrelevant material: facts or information unrelated to the subject under discussion.

Kinesthesis: the sensation of movement or strain in muscles, tendons, joints; the muscle sense.

Kinesthetic imagery: muscle imagery.

Kinetic reversals: confusion of directional sequence, such as *left* for *felt.*

Language-rhythm clue: a word which suggests a relationship or an opposite, such as *one, two, three; up, down; high, low.*

Lateral imbalance: a tendency of one or both eyes to deviate inward or outward from their normal position.

Lead: a short summary serving as an introduction to a news story or article.

Lesson plan: a brief statement of aims, materials, and procedures to be considered during an instructional period.

Lip movement: extraneous movement of the lips in reading, spelling, or listening.

Listening vocabulary: the number of words understood when heard.

Location clue: a suggestion as to geographical placement.

Main heading: a brief statement of the chief topic or subject in a chapter or other composition.

Major premise: in a syllogism, the proposition which contains the general truth from which the particular inference is deduced.

Maladjustment: state in which a person falls short of being able to do what is expected of him by others or by himself.

Manuscript writing: "printing" or lettering by a freehand process in which the letters are not connected as in common longhand or script writing. Recommended for use in the primary grades by both teachers and pupils.

Maturation: development consistent with mental or chronological age.

Mechanics of reading: habits developed in connection with reading but apart from the reading process itself, such as following lines of print from left to right across the page, from top to bottom of a page, and from one page to another.

Mental ability: an untechnical term meaning intelligence or mental maturity.

Mental age: level of development in intelligence expressed in terms of the age at which the average child attains that level.

Mental content: the result of experience.

Mental deficiency: state of having less than normal intelligence.

Mental maturity: mental capacity.

Mental measurement: quantitative determination of a person's abilities and tendencies.

Mental set: an attitude.

Mental test: measurement in which interest centers on the differences between different individuals' responses.

Metaphor: a figure of speech in which a word or phrase literally denoting one kind of object or idea is used in place of another in order to suggest a likeness or analogy between them.

Minor premise: in a syllogism, the proposition which introduces the minor term. It is the second proposition.

Mirror writing: writing words or numbers backward. The term was derived from the fact that such writing can be read when held before a mirror, which reverses the order of the letters or numbers.

Modality: a group of sensory qualities having certain rather ill-defined similarities; e.g., all visual qualities belong to the visual mode, all sounds to the auditory.

Motile: motor-minded.

Motivation: the act of arousing or stimulating an inward urge to action in order to achieve a goal.

Multiple-track plan: homogeneous grouping of children on the basis of intelligence.

Narrative material: reading matter which tells a story.

Negativism: marked resistance; the tendency to do the opposite of what one is requested to do.

Neurosis: mental disorder generally of milder character than a psychosis. "Nervousness" and "nervous breakdown" usually mean neurosis. *See Psychosis.*

Non-directive: an adjective descriptive of a form of counseling or therapy in which the interviewee assumes full responsibility for solving his own problem. This approach is advocated by Carl Rogers.

Norm: a numerical score representing the average or median achievement of a given group.

Objective test: a test which can be scored with a minimum of dependence upon individual interpretation of the answers.

Ophthalmologist: a physician specializing in defects of vision and diseases of the eye.

Otologist: a physician specializing in hearing defects and diseases of the ear.

Overcompensation: an extreme form of compensation.

Paragraph analysis: the process of finding the main idea of a paragraph together with its details perceived in their right relation to the main idea.

Pathological: pertaining to disease.

Percentile: a point in a distribution of scores so selected that a certain percentage of cases are above it and a certain percentage of cases are below it.

Perception: mental awareness and integration of sensations.

Phoneme: a group, or family, of related sounds.

Phonetic alphabet: a combination of letters and symbols representing speech sounds.
Phonetic analysis: the analysis of a word into its phonetic elements for pronunciation purposes; commonly used as a synonym for *phonics.*
Phonetic approach: a procedure for studying words by associating appropriate sounds with printed forms.
Phonetics: the science of the sounds of letters as used in speech.
Phonics: the science of the sounds of letters as applied to the pronunciation of words in reading.
Phonogram: a letter or group of letters forming a sound that can be articulated.
Pictograph: a record or story consisting of pictorial symbols.
Picture clue: an element in a picture which provides meaning.
Picture dictionary: a dictionary of commonly used words with corresponding pictures illustrating each word.
Précis: a brief summary.
Preconceived idea: a predetermined point of view unmodified by the introduction of new and relevant concepts; a prejudice.
Preface: an introduction to a book in which the writer often declares his intentions.
Prefix: one or more syllables added at the beginning of a stem word to change or modify its meaning.
Premise: a proposition stated or assumed as leading to a conclusion; either of the first two propositions of a syllogism.
Preview: the act of making a preliminary survey of a chapter, book, or other written composition.
Projection: the act of placing blame or failure on another person or thing.
Projective technique: a procedure for studying an individual by observing his responses to a situation that does not elicit a particular response.
Psychometrist: a person trained to give psychological tests.
Psychosis: a relatively severe mental disease; i.e., one in which there is loss of, or disorder in, mental processes.

Rapport: unconstrained, intimate, and friendly relationship between two persons.
Rationalization: an attempt to give a socially acceptable motive instead of the real one.
Readers' Guide to Periodical Literature: an index to magazine articles and periodical literature.
Readiness: a physical, mental, and emotional preparedness for a given learning activity.
Reading: a process of securing meaning from symbols; a physical, mental, and emotional activity consisting in identifying, interpreting, and evaluating messages conveyed through the medium of printed symbols.
Reading deficiency: lack of adequate skills in reading.
Reading laboratory: a reading clinic or workroom in which corrective and remedial work in reading is carried on.
Reading level: the stage of development which a person has reached in reading skill.
Reading maladjustment: inability to adjust to the use of the reading process.
Reading vocabulary: words that can be identified and understood in context or in isolation from the printed page.
Regressive eye movement: turning the eyes to the left to retrace a part of a line while reading from left to right across a line of print.
Reinforcement: the act of making appropriate responses "pay off." A psychological concept used by Skinner and others.
Reliability: extent to which a measurement is uninfluenced by variable factors.
Remedial reading: clinical procedures in which particular effort is made to discover the exact cause or causes of deficiency and means of removing or mitigating

these causal factors, coupled with instruction designed to remove special reading deficiencies.

Repression: the rejection and shutting out of the awareness of a reaction pattern (thought, feeling, impulse, memory) in order to avoid distress.

Reversal tendency: the tendency of an individual to reverse letters or words while reading.

Scanning: the act of examining point by point. Generally the term is used to describe rapid reading for a specific purpose.

Schwa: the soft, unstressed vowel sound heard only in unaccented syllables; for example, the second *a* in *canvas,* the *e* in *problem,* the *i* in *engine,* the *o* in *gallop* and the final *u* in *August.*

Score: credit or value given to a specific response to a test item; sum of the credits obtained on all the items of a single test.

Self-concept: an individual's awareness of his existence; his conception of who and what he is.

Sensation: impression received by the sense organs.

Sibilant sound: a hissing speech sound. The sibilants in English are *s, z, sh, zh,* and *ch.*

Sibling: one of two or more offspring born at different times from the same parent.

Sight approach: the method of teaching children to read by recognizing word wholes by sight, as contrasted with the phonetic method by which words are analyzed into sound parts.

Sight vocabulary: words that are memorized or recognized as wholes.

Somatic: having to do with the body. The "opposite" of psychogenic.

Span of attention: the number of objects which can be unified in a single act or "moment" of apprehension.

Spatial relationship: relationship which is dependent upon place or location for meaning or significance.

Speaking vocabulary: words that are used and understood in conversation.

Speed of comprehension: the speed at which one can read and still understand the import of what is read.

Spotting: see Scanning.

Standardized test: a scientifically constructed measure possessing both reliability and validity.

Stem: a word form from which words have been developed by the addition of prefixes, suffixes, and inflectional endings.

Structural analysis: the process of studying an unknown word for the purpose of identifying the root or base.

Substitution: an attempt to replace one goal with another.

Subtopic: a subheading in an outline.

Suffix: one or more syllables added at the end of a word to change its meaning.

Suppression: the psychological blocking of vision in one eye; the involuntary exclusion of anything from awareness.

Syllabication: the division of words into syllables, usually for purposes of pronunciation.

Syllogism: a logical scheme or analysis of a formal argument, consisting of the major premise, the minor premise, and the conclusion.

Sympathism: an attempt to secure aid in the solution of a problem and to avoid the responsibility for failure.

Synaptic transmission: the act of conducting a nervous impulse across a synapse, the point at which a nervous impulse passes from one neuron to another.

Syndrome: collection of symptoms which characterize a particular disorder or disease.

Synonym: one of two or more words of the same language having the same or nearly the same essential meaning; for example, *little, small.*

Tachistoscope: an instrument for providing a brief exposure of visual material, used in memory and attention experiments and as a means of increasing perceptual span in reading.

Tactile, tactual: having to do with touch.

Tactual imagery: the mental reconstruction of sensory experiences secured by touch.

Technical vocabulary: words used in specialized fields such as chemistry, engineering, medicine, and agriculture.

Temporal relationship: subjects or ideas arranged in a sequence in which time is an essential factor.

Therapy: treatment intended to cure or alleviate a disordered condition.

Tone: the summation of intellectual and emotional effects of writing.

Tool subject: a school subject considered valuable because of its service to other subjects or to practical pursuits rather than for itself. Reading, writing, arithmetic, and English are considered tool subjects.

Topic outline: a plan for the organization of ideas in the form of topics expressed as nouns.

Topical relationship: subjects or ideas which fit together to make up a unified whole.

Topic sentence: the sentence in a paragraph which provides the subject to be discussed and developed.

Trial and error procedure: finding a correct solution by trying out a variety of means and eliminating those that prove to be unsatisfactory.

V.A.K.T: a visual, auditory, kinesthetic, tactual method of word study described in Chapter 5.

Validity: state of being valid or trustworthy.

Verbalism: an empty form of words.

Visual acuity: keenness of vision.

Visual defect: an imperfection of vision.

Visual discrimination: in reading, the ability to differentiate between word forms.

Visual imagery: a mental reconstruction of sensory experiences secured by means of vision.

Vocabulary test: a sample list of words selected from a complete general dictionary presented for definition. The score is an index of the testee's total vocabulary.

Vocalization: movement of lips, tongue, or vocal apparatus of the throat during silent reading.

Volition: a state of decision or choice, the end condition of voluntary activity.

Vowel: an unobstructed letter sound made with open throat, mouth, teeth, and lips. The vowels are: *a, e, i, o, u,* and sometimes *w* and *y.*

Whole-word method: word analysis without the physical separation of the word into its phonetic or structural elements.

Word analysis: The division of an unfamiliar word into known elements for the purpose of identification.

W.P.M.: the average rate in words per minute at which a person reads a section of printed material.

Writing vocabulary: words used and understood in ordinary writing.

INDEX